CYNEFIN, WALES AND THE WORLD

Today's Geography for Future Generations

First edition: 2024
Reprinted: 2025
© publication: Gwasg Carreg Gwalch

All rights reserved.

No part of this publication may be reproduced, stored in a retrieval system, or transmitted in any form or by any means, electronic, electrostatic, magnetic tape, mechanical, photocopying, recording, or otherwise, without prior permission of the publishers, Gwasg Carreg Gwalch, 12 Iard yr Orsaf, Llanrwst, Conwy, Wales LL26 0EH.

ISBN: 978-1-84527-931-8

A Welsh Government subsidy towards the production of this resource is gratefully recognised.

Piloted by teachers in:
Ysgol Uwchradd Glantaf; Ysgol Uwchradd Botwnnog;
Ysgol Gynradd San Siôr, Llandudno; Ysgol Gymraeg Aberystwyth

Text editor: Marian Beech Hughes
Photograph and image researcher: Iestyn Hughes
Front and back cover illustrations: Elin Manon
Cover design: Dylunio GraffEG
Volume design: Dylunio GraffEG

Published by Gwasg Carreg Gwalch,
12 Iard yr Orsaf, Llanrwst, Conwy, Wales LL26 0EH.
Tel: 01492 642031
email: llyfrau@carreg-gwalch.cymru
Website: www.carreg-gwalch.cymru

Printed and published in Wales

CYNEFIN, WALES AND THE WORLD

Today's Geography for Future Generations

Editorial and Advisory Panel:
Dafydd Watcyn Williams
Toni Schiavone, Bethan James, Irfon Jones, Huw Prys Jones

Director: Myrddin ap Dafydd

Thank you to the following lecturers at Welsh universities for their guidance and assistance with specific sections:
Dei Huws (Geology, Bangor)
Rhys Jones and Hywel Griffiths (Geography, Aberystwyth)
Penri James (Agriculture, Aberystwyth)

This volume is dedicated to the memory of

Gareth O. Jones *(Gareth Geog)*

Newcastle Emlyn and Carmarthen

Geographer and Educator

and to the memory of Bethan James, historian and educator, who provided valuable guidance in producing this book.

A brief note

No volume like this has appeared before in the whole history of education in Wales. For the first time, we can examine the Earth by starting at our feet. From page to page, it is remarkable that most of the main elements of geographical studies are to be found in our own cynefin, on the land and in the rocks of Wales. By examining what we experience in our own country, we can interpret and understand what can be seen and what is happening in other countries of the world. This is a book to browse through. There are sections focusing on some of the main topics. It is not intended as a syllabus to work through from start to finish. Different schools and different classes will be able to design work units from these sections as they see fit. Such flexibility is a key element in the Welsh Curriculum. Presented are facts and patterns, along with graphics and visual material, and there is freedom to adapt them, so they are relevant to the school's local area.

Highlighted words

Highlighted words signify that fuller explanations of those words are provided in the glossary at the end of the book. There are Welsh translations of the highlighted words as well.

Contents

What is the cynefin of Wales?   8
Country, Cynefin, Home, Land, Diversity, Identity, Governance, State, United

What has created Wales's relief?
Geology and tectonic processes	32
Glaciation	46
Rivers	56
The coast	68
Weather and climate	82

Where do the people of Wales live?
Population	92
Migration	106
Language and culture	110

How is the economy of Wales changing?
Connections	116
Work	130
Farming	144
Forests	156
Shopping	170
Tourism	182
Energy	192

How to protect Wales's environment?
Pollution	204
Conservation	216
Climate change	228
Glossary	239
Acknowledgements	253

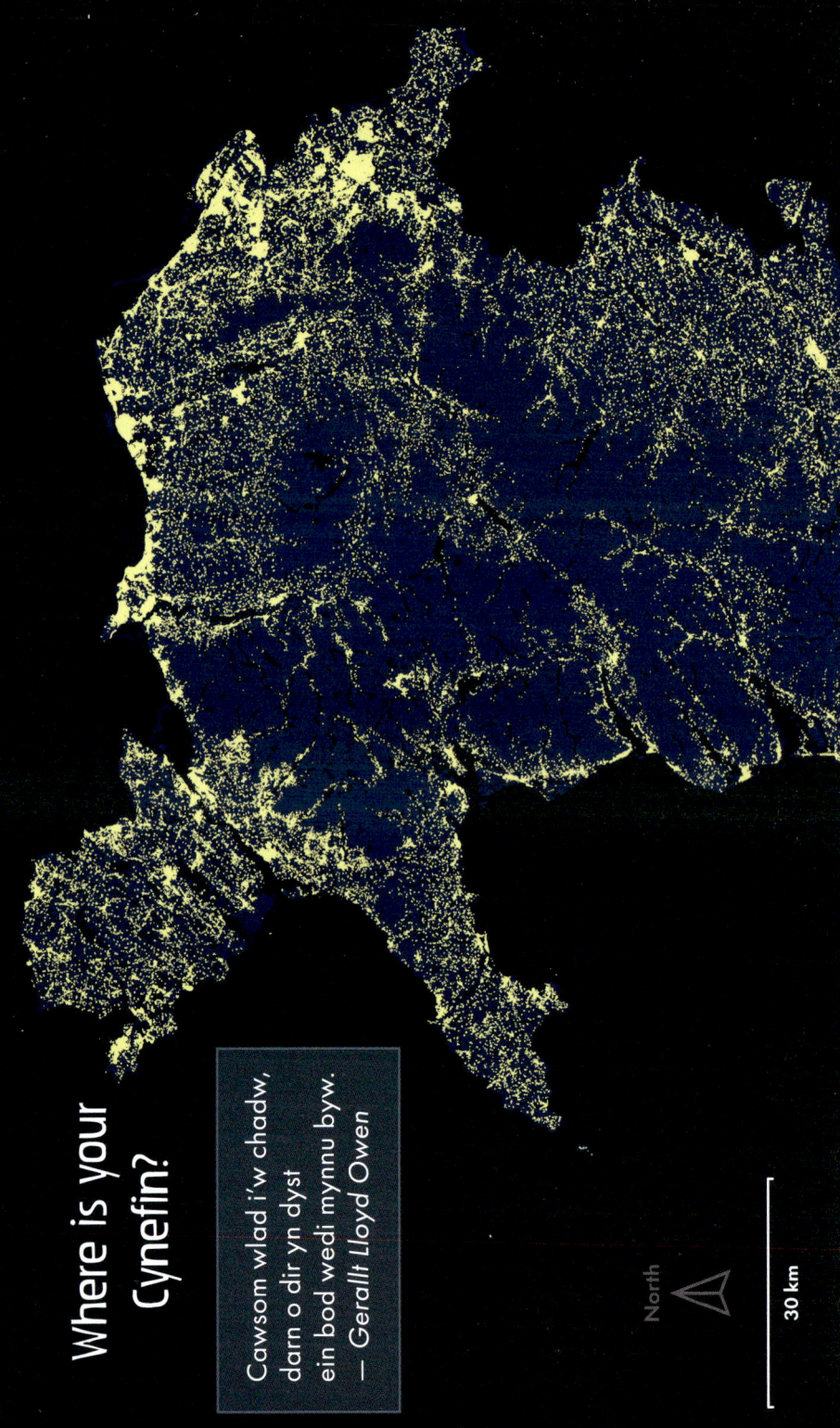

Where is your Cynefin?

Cawsom wlad i'w chadw,
darn o dir yn dyst
ein bod wedi mynnu byw.
— Gerallt Lloyd Owen

North

30 km

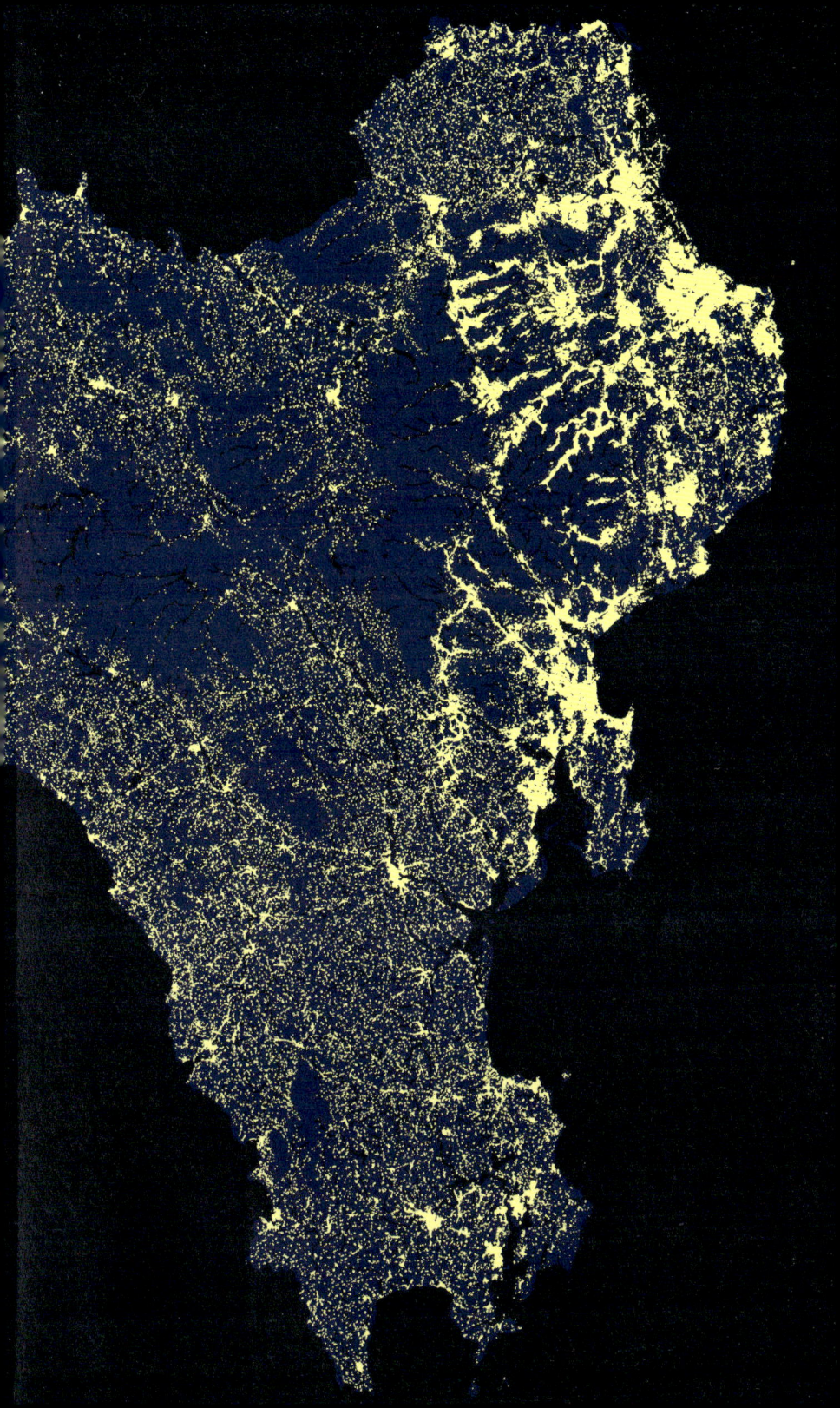

What is the cynefin of Wales?

This is a book for children and young people, teachers and parents to help them research and understand:

- **the physical Earth** – land and rocks, rivers, coasts, and the climate
- **human society** – how and where people live and the differences between countries and between rural and urban areas
- **the natural environment** – the entire diversity of the natural world and the need to protect and conserve it.

Geographers study the connections between the natural world and humans, as well as the influence of humans on the natural world.

Cynefin, Wales and the whole wide world

Offa's Dyke – the former Welsh border; old borders can be found in each cynefin

The landscape of Cardiff Bay in the capital of Wales that attracts many visitors

Uluru (formerly 'Ayers Rock'), the sacred landform of Australian Aboriginals, where ceremonies have been held for 10,000 years

... and people on a riverbank at a religious meeting in India

Wales 2023 – a few facts

- **Area**: 20,779km^2
- **Population**: 3,107,500 (2021 Census)
- **Status as a country**: Parliament in Wales and part of the state of the United Kingdom
- **Capital and largest city:** Cardiff
- **Official languages**: Welsh and English
- **Welsh speakers**: 538,000 (17.8%) of usual residents aged three or over in Wales (2021 Census)
- **National flag**: The Red Dragon
- **National day**: St David's Day (1 March)
- **Landscape**: mountainous, with the highest summit (Yr Wyddfa) rising to a height of 1,085m
- **Longest rivers**: flowing within Welsh borders: the river Tywi (120km); flowing from Wales into England: the river Severn (354km)
- **Longitude and latitude**: 52°04', 3°41'

Welsh language names and historical names of Wales

Today, the people of Wales are making more use of original and historical names rather than using English names. This is also happening in the indigenous languages of Australia and among the Māori in New Zealand, and in many other cultures around the world.

- **Cymru** – the Football Association of Wales wants to use this name for the national teams in future international tournaments
- **Eryri and Yr Wyddfa** – Eryri National Park announced in 2022 that these are the correct names, rather than Snowdonia and Snowdon

Llyn Glaslyn and the summit of Yr Wyddfa

- **Bannau Brycheiniog** (formerly the Brecon Beacons) — in 2023, this national park also joined the campaign, making this its only official name

Keyword: Country

Some words are important in describing each country and nation:

language	piece of land	identity
history	borders	traditions
songs	cynefin	religion.

The next few pages discuss some of these terms. They are important as we come to understand and protect where we live. But why do we live here in Wales? At one time, no one lived here. Then, people started migrating to Wales.

Who were the first migrants to Wales?

- People have migrated to Wales over thousands of years.
- Remains have been found of Neolithic Age people (Neanderthals), who lived 230,000 years ago.
- About 12,000 years ago, Bronze Age migrants came here from Europe at the end of the last Ice Age.
- The Celts then arrived about 2,500 years ago. The Welsh language originated from the Celtic language.

Who else has come to Wales?

- The Romans, about 50 until 383.
- Saxons, around 580, began to establish in the east.
- Normans, around 1090, began erecting castles on low ground.
- Religious refugees (French Protestants), late Middle Ages.
- Workers of the Industrial Revolution, including people from Ireland, Africa, Asia.
- More recent migrants: people from Russia, the Basque country, Poland, the West Indies, Ukraine.

Remains of early humans were found in Pontnewydd Cave, Denbighshire

Dinas Emrys: 'dinas' is the Welsh word for 'city'. Many 'dinas' on Welsh maps refer to the Celtic meaning of the word, a hilltop defence

Where are the borders of Wales today?

- to the north and west: the Irish Sea
- to the east: England
- to the south-west: the Celtic Sea
- to the south: the Bristol Channel.

How do you spot a land border?

Think about travelling by car from Wales to England or from England to Wales. How do you know that you have crossed the border from one country to another? One method of knowing what country you are in is to study the road signs: English signs – England; bilingual signs – Wales.

The Irish Sea, to the north and west of Wales

Road signs in Wales did not contain the Welsh language before 1975

A look at another country – FINLAND

A country that respects three languages

Swedish speakers live in some parts of Finland. Only 6% of the country's total population speaks Swedish. But if more than 8% of them live in a particular area, that area is then considered completely bilingual – Swedish/Finnish.

In northern Finland, there is a different language again, called the Sami language. It is the native language of the Sami people, who are called 'Lapians' by some. But that is a disrespectful name, which mocks their traditional costumes. The Sami are a nomadic people. They have been living for thousands of years in an area now divided between Norway, Sweden, Finland and Russia. One people across four countries.

The Sami language is respected by the Finnish government, and place names in that language can be found on road signs like this one in the north of the country.

Most of the world's population speak more than one language. 66% of the world's children are brought up bilingually.

Finnish/Sami sign

Keyword: Cynefin

The Welsh word 'cynefin' (meaning 'habitat') has more than one meaning:
- **it can describe something familiar to us** – take a look through the window in your house or in your school. This is a familiar scene (a 'cynefin' scene)
- **it can mean a special place** – an area where birds and animals live and thrive; a place where plants take root and grow; people's usual home or environment; a place of belonging.

The cynefin of sheep

We have a special saying in Welsh: 'cynefin defaid' ('the habitat of sheep'). Many of Wales's mountains are open land. It means there are no fences or hedges, and so there are no fields. Many farms have the right to graze their sheep on this open land (usually in spring and summer). Although there are no fences, these are cynefin sheep. They tend to stay within the same valley and on the same slopes, although they could wander for miles and miles if they chose to.

Sometimes, farmers on one part of the open mountain will want to gather their sheep for washing, shearing etc. Farmers will work together to do this, each starting from a different direction. The sheep of one whole cynefin will be herded into old pens on the mountain – initially to one large, central pen. Each farmer will then move his own sheep to smaller pens, which are like flower petals around the large pen. There are many pens like this on the Carneddau mountains. They are also found in Switzerland, Croatia and Iceland – in areas where many farms share the same open land.

Cynefin pens on the Carneddau mountains

These pens are so similar, even though they are so far apart. They raise the question – did farmers learn from each other when migrating across Europe a long time ago?

The cynefin of bees

Pupils at Ysgol San Siôr, Llandudno, carried out a project on bees and found:
- we share the same cynefin as bees
- without bees to fertilize crops, we would have no food.

The cynefin of salmon
Welsh rivers and the great Atlantic ocean provide a cynefin for salmon

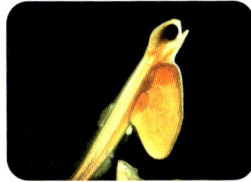  

From eggs buried by salmon at the upper reaches of rivers, small fry will hatch. They will stay there for two years.

At the start of the small fry's third spring, they will swim downstream to the open sea – the Atlantic Ocean. Some will swim as far as Canada – a journey of nearly 3,000 miles.

The salmon will live in the ocean for a year. After growing and gaining weight by the following summer, it will swim the long journey back to the egg burial grounds. The salmon returns to its cynefin, and the cycle of life begins again.

Our Cynefin: What do we see in our cynefin?
Here are some of the things we might see through our windows in Wales:

MOUNTAIN	BIRD	RIVER	STREET	QUARRY	SHOP	BUS
FIELD	CASTLE	RAILWAY	WORKSHOP	TREE	SCHOOL	MARSH
RUBBISH	PLAYGROUND	FARM	FACTORY	ROCK	SEA	MAST

These are all discussed in this book and are part of what geographers observe and study.

Near and far

We can usually see things that are far away and nearby through the same window. We start with things that are familiar and close by, before looking further afield to spot things that are further away. It's all part of the same world.

Local cynefin
Understanding your area, your community – countryside, village, town or city. There is so much to see in your local cynefin.

National cynefin
Different areas of Wales vary greatly. Seas and mountains; lowlands and valleys. Where do people live, and why do they live there?

Global cynefin
What has created the Earth's relief – the rocks, the valleys, the shores? How have people changed and shaped the landscape of the world?

Keyword: Home

In Aberystwyth, there is a house called **Y Nyth** (Welsh for 'The Nest').

In Bontnewydd, there is a house called **Y Gorlan** (Welsh for 'The Pen').

'Cartref' (Welsh for 'Home') is a common name on a house in Wales

House names can provide a lot of information about the location of the house, what the weather is like, the occupation of those who once lived there, what material the house was built from, and so on. Many house names also suggest the warm feeling of belonging.

Y Nyth, Y Gorlan – these are names from the world of birds and animals. But, like the creatures around us, children and humans also have their cynefin.

Living in your cynefin

Several words try to convey 'where you live': house, home, household, locale, area, valley, country.

Each house has a postcode, but we still give houses names to make them more personal, or to say something about the cynefin where the house is located.

'Teg edrych tuag adref' ('There's no place like home') and 'Hawdd cynnau tân ar hen aelwyd' ('It is easy to rekindle an old flame') are two famous Welsh sayings. They convey the warmth we feel when we think about home. 'Bro mebyd' is a Welsh expression for 'the area where we grew up' – and our roots are so important to us.

People in other countries often express warm feeling towards home too, of course. Many a Ty Coz ('the dear old house') can be found in Brittany, like the one pictured (a pub in Montroulez)

But in our own cynefin, there are homeless people

There are some negative attitudes in our society towards homeless people. Very often, it is not these people's fault that they are homeless, but rather:

- poverty and lack of fair wages
- lack of suitable housing in the area
- losing a job
- long-term illness
- relationship breakdown
- mental health problems
- indebtedness.

Airbnb and Tourism

Airbnb is an American company that operates online to provide rented accommodation for travellers, and for visitors in particular. It was established in California in 2008, but now operates worldwide.

The pattern at first was an airbed in a spare room, which is where the 'air' in the name comes from. The idea was that a couple or family could earn money towards their living expenses by letting a room on some nights.

Front door key safe – suggesting an Airbnb in a terraced house, Twthill, Caernarfon

But soon, entire houses were being put on Airbnb – rather than temporary accommodation in a vacant space within the home. Some realised that it was better and easier to let their houses to visitors than to local families. This caused a shortage of rental housing, an increase in rents, and a rise in house prices.

Blaenau Ffestiniog is not regarded as a popular tourist area. Yet there are 321 Airbnb houses there. There are only 322 Airbnb houses throughout the towns and villages of the Lake District in England.

There are many types of homelessness

You do not have to be living on the street to be homeless. Even if you have a roof over your head, you can be homeless:

- if you are in temporary accommodation in a hotel, bed and breakfast, support centre, night shelter or immigrant centre
- if you are sleeping on a friend's sofa, which is common among young people
- if grown children are living with their parents even though the house is unsuitable for them.

There are currently 8,000 people in Wales living in temporary accommodation, including over 2,500 children.

One solution to the problem is to build more social housing of the right type – more single, low carbon units, in line with the local community's needs so that no one has to face homelessness.

Just as we must protect the cynefin of salmon and bees, people must also be allowed live in houses in their own cynefin if they so choose.

What kind of place is my cynefin?

Here in Wales, within one country, there is great diversity. Below are four different types of cynefin where people live in Wales. There are several more, of course.

Solva, Pembrokeshire – the upper village, quay and estuary

Mountainous landscape further from the sea. Dinas Mawddwy in the hills of south Gwynedd

1. Coastal cynefin
There is a great variety of features on the coast: ports, beaches, marshes, cliffs, islands, estuaries, seaside towns, promenades, caravan parks.

2. Hill cynefin
Land further away from the sea. Perhaps there will be a narrow valley, a large lake or marshland, woodland and agricultural land. Welsh place names refer to moorlands, valleys, passes, knolls and slopes.

Glandŵr Street, Abertillery, in a former Monmouthshire coal valley

Swansea – the old St Thomas School and riverside works

3. Mixed cynefin
In the slate areas of Gwynedd and the former mining valleys of Glamorgan, Monmouth and Carmarthen, a combination of rural and urban areas can often be found. There are terraces which housed workers, and populous villages and towns, but also rural hills.

4. City cynefin
This is a cynefin with little countryside – but there are parks and cemeteries. It is mostly tarmac and concrete and buildings of all kinds. Street names include elements such as: markets, squares, banks, chapels, churches, schools.

Dafydd Iwan sings his heart out in the football stadium

Keyword: Land

There is pride in a 'piece of land'. Land can represent a country. Most countries have a national anthem, and very often the anthem describes the special land that belongs to that country.

Anthem

This photo of Welsh fans shows them singing from their hearts. Who cannot feel jubilant when they hear the Red Wall singing the anthem? What do the words of the anthem tell us about what the country is like?

1. Mae hen wlad fy nhadau yn annwyl i mi,
Gwlad beirdd a chantorion, enwogion o fri;
Ei gwrol ryfelwyr, gwladgarwyr tra mad,
Tros ryddid gollasant eu gwaed.

Chorus:
Gwlad! Gwlad! Pleidiol wyf i'm gwlad.
Tra môr yn fur i'r bur hoff bau,
O bydded i'r hen iaith barhau.

2. Hen Gymru fynyddig, paradwys y bardd,
Pob dyffryn, pob clogwyn, i'm golwg sydd hardd;
Trwy deimlad gwladgarol, mor swynol yw si
Ei nentydd, afonydd, i mi.

3. Os treisiodd y gelyn fy ngwlad tan ei droed,
Mae hen iaith y Cymry mor fyw ag erioed,
Ni luddiwyd yr awen gan erchyll law brad,
Na thelyn berseiniol fy ngwlad.

That's right, there are three verses in the Welsh national anthem.

What do we sing about and what are we so proud of?

- the country itself: mountains, valleys
- culture: poetry, music
- the effort to protects these things
- the hope for a future where all this will be still here - 'yma o hyd'.

'Yma o Hyd' is a song that begins with the history of Magnus Maximus ('Macsen Wledig' in Welsh). Macsen was a Governor in Wales on behalf of Rome. In the words of the song, he left Wales 'in the year 383 ... as a whole nation'. Macsen was the first to call Wales a country.

Keyword: Diversity

Between the sea and the mountains, the scenery of Wales changes rapidly. Here's what we can see on one particular journey through Wales.

A journey from Holyhead to Cardiff

Holy Island – one of several islands on the coast
Anglesey – island county with sand dunes, flat land, rocks protruding to the surface, marshes
Menai Strait – a strait with strong tides; there are many towns and villages on both sides
Eryri – Wales's highest mountains, including Yr Wyddfa; rocky area with the largest slate quarries
Llyn Tegid – the largest natural lake in Wales
Lake Vyrnwy – reservoir, forests
River Severn – a river that has its source in Wales and flows into England
Montgomeryshire and Radnor – an area of hills and rural valleys
River Wye and River Usk – two important rivers in south Wales
Bannau Brycheiniog – the highest mountains in the south
Glamorgan Valleys – post-industrial area, lengthy villages in narrow valleys
Cardiff – capital, largest city, one of the main ports

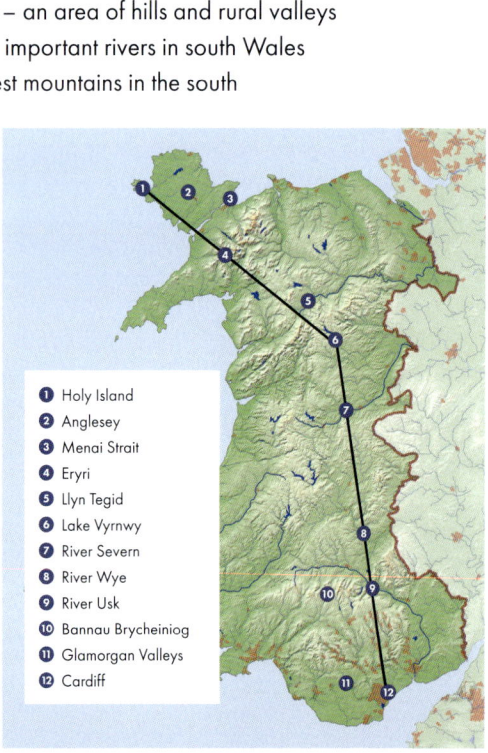

Ynys Llanddwyn off the coast of Anglesey

One of the valleys of Glamorgan: Ferndale, Rhondda Valley

1. Holy Island
2. Anglesey
3. Menai Strait
4. Eryri
5. Llyn Tegid
6. Lake Vyrnwy
7. River Severn
8. River Wye
9. River Usk
10. Bannau Brycheiniog
11. Glamorgan Valleys
12. Cardiff

Diversity of origins, religions, peoples

Norwegian Church, Cardiff Bay

There is a special wooden church in Cardiff Bay. It is one of our capital's most beloved and attractive buildings. It is a Norwegian Church, and would look perfectly natural on the shores of a fjord in Norway. But it is an important part of the port in our capital too. Norwegian sailors erected the church. Their ships carried timber to the coalmines and took away coal exported from Wales. The church keeps alive the memory of people who came here from Norway to work, before becoming part of Welsh society.

Rainbow bucket hat supporting the Welsh football team

Chinese New Year celebrations in west Wales

There is diversity of all sorts – ethnic, religious, linguistic and gendered – among the people of Wales. All types of diversity is embraced, contributing to the country's identity.

All sorts of festivals are celebrated across Wales. The Chinese New Year is celebrated colourfully with oriental dragons in many Welsh towns.

There are many different ethnic groups here, but together they unite to create one country, one nation, which is Wales. According to the 2021 Census, the five largest ethnic groups in Wales are people from Poland, India, Germany, Ireland and Romania. Most of these people, who have chosen to make Wales their home, live in the largest cities of Cardiff, Swansea, Newport and Wrexham. We can therefore have roots in another country, but be proud of our Welsh identity at the same time.

The sense of nationhood is strengthening in Wales today. That is demonstrated in many ways.

Keyword: Identity

 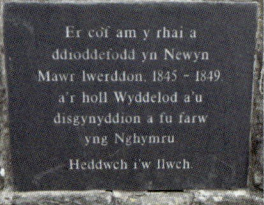

The Irish Famine Memorial in the Irish section of Cathays Cemetery, Cardiff

European grocery store in Wrexham

The Welsh language

For many reasons, not everyone in Wales has had the opportunity to learn and speak Welsh.

Yet again, surveys show that most people in Wales support the language and love it very much.

The Welsh language belongs to the whole of Wales and to everyone who lives here, whether they speak the language or not.

One of the major aims of the Welsh Government is that everyone can learn Welsh and to use the language more often.

The Welsh language is much more prominent in Wales today:
- Welsh schools
- Welsh radio, television, books.

Welsh is used on all kinds of online digital platforms and on social media.

The National Eisteddfod is one of Wales's oldest festivals. The first eisteddfod on record was held in Cardigan in 1176. However, elements such as the chairing of the bard and harp-playing competitions are much older still. Yet again, although traditional in many ways, the National Eisteddfod also reflects the modern world and appeals to a new generation of young people every year.

National Eisteddfod Field, Tregaron 2022

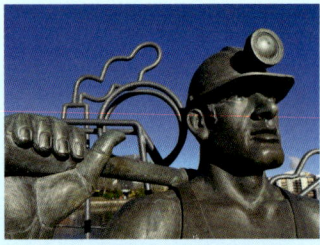

The Welsh Miner: 'From Pit to Port', Cardiff Bay

Work

When working in the same place, strong feelings such as friendship and care for each other are fostered. In the early 20C, there were over 300,000 colliers, quarrymen and miners in Wales. Those industries had a profound impact on our villages, societies and the way we operate as a people. It led to the establishment of brass bands, choirs, and football and rugby teams.

National Flag - small country, big story

The Red Dragon is our national flag. For centuries the Red Dragon has been a symbol of Wales. According to a survey on the Ranker website in 2021, it was also the most popular flag in the rest of the world! The Red Dragon and its mythology are iconic. It is often used to promote the feeling of belonging and Welsh identity:

Welsh produce promoted on the wall of a supermarket in Rhiwbina, Cardiff

- promoting Welsh produce – everything from leeks to cheese, from ice cream to curry
- supporting sport and on the crests of our national teams
- on the emblem of local authorities and the Welsh Parliament
- on road vehicle registration numbers
- Welsh businesses using the Dragon on their logos.

National History - the story of the people who live here

Museums across Wales tell stories of different times and special people who have made a difference to our country. But history is not confined to museums. Look at artwork on the streets, plaques on buildings, stage shows, pub names, monuments – history is alive all around us. This is our story, and it brings us together as one nation. We all share a Welsh identity.

A pub commemorating the prince who founded the first Welsh Parliament

Betty Campbell, the headmistress who boosted the confidence of black communities

Keyword: Governance

Governance means controlling, creating laws, and maintaining order, with the aim of using power to change things for the better. How has Wales been governed past and present?

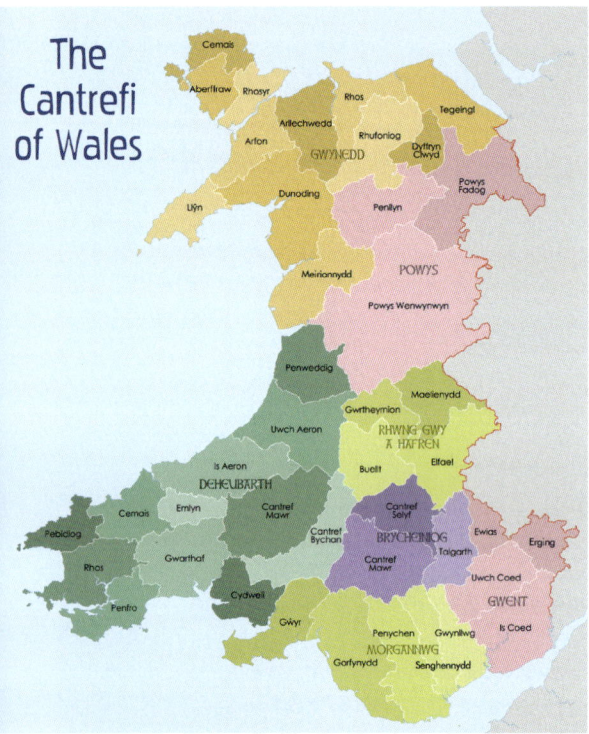

Since 1996, Wales has had 22 counties:

Anglesey
Blaenau Gwent
Bridgend
Caerphilly
Cardiff
Carmarthenshire
Ceredigion
Conwy
Denbighshire
Flintshire
Gwynedd
Merthyr Tydfil
Monmouthshire
Neath Port Talbot
Newport
Pembrokeshire
Powys
Rhondda Cynon Taf
Swansea
Torfaen
Vale of Glamorgan
Wrexham

Where is the county you live in on the map?

Cantref and County

Above is a map of Wales in the Age of Princes (circa 1000–1282). At that time, Wales had an independent government, and the country was divided into units called 'cantrefi' (singular 'cantref'). The word 'cantref' literally means 'a hundred settlements' (family farms). Perhaps the most famous cantref was Cantre'r Gwaelod, but the ancient tale explains why it is not on the map!

When the Normans began to govern parts of Wales from 1284 onwards, local governance was changed, and counties began to be formed. By the time of the Acts of Union of England and Wales in 1536, there were 13 counties in Wales.

Cwmwd

Around 1050, the 'cantrefi' of the princes were deemed to be too large. The population increased around this time. Some 'cantrefi' were divided into two or more 'cymydau' ('commotes'). The word 'cymydau' (*singular* 'cwmwd') derives from the word 'cymydog', which means 'neighbour' – people who lived in the same 'cwmwd' as you. People had better government in a small area. Each 'cwmwd' had its own court, and the princes spent time in each 'cwmwd'.

A court of a 'cwmwd' in Anglesey was the inspiration for Llys Llywelyn which has been recreated in St Fagans National Museum of History

Llan, parish and community council

The 'llannau' (*singular* 'llan') were originally ecclesiastical divisions of land in Wales. They refer to church enclosures. Most of these were established by the saints of the Celtic Church in the 5C and 6C. Under the Normans, parishes were created in Wales on the basis of the existing 'llannau'. They were created by the church to provide services, collect taxes and record population change.

The former church of St Teilo which now stands in St Fagans National Museum of History

Before the 19C, the parishes registered births, deaths and marriages, and collected an ecclesiastical tax (the tithe). In Wales, the parish councils were replaced by the community and town councils in 1972.

Local government today

There are over 730 **Community Councils** or **Town Councils** in Wales, run by over eight thousand councillors. Members are elected to oversee matters such as village halls, playing fields and open spaces, street lighting and benches, and footpaths. Since 2000, these councils have the power to promote and improve the economic, social or environmental well-being of their area.

Community volunteers clean up rubbish in Abergavenny in 2019

These councils are given a share of the local tax, and an officer is appointed to oversee their work (the council clerk). The **One Voice Wales** website gives a voice to the Welsh Local Government Association. Although they work locally, they cooperate nationally.

Key Workers in our Cynefin

The numerous lockdowns during the COVID-19 pandemic (2020-22) led to much talk about our 'key workers'. Some jobs are essential for the public's well-being and safety. Most of that work is carried out by the county council and the Welsh Parliament.

In the community:
Buckley Town Council

Ceredigion County Council buildings in Aberystwyth:
The county councils look after schools, libraries, leisure centres, refuse collection, recycling, bus and public transport funding, social care and planning

National government:
The **Welsh Parliament** looks after health, education, agriculture, tourism, the environment, local government, transport, conservation, economic development, the arts and the Welsh language

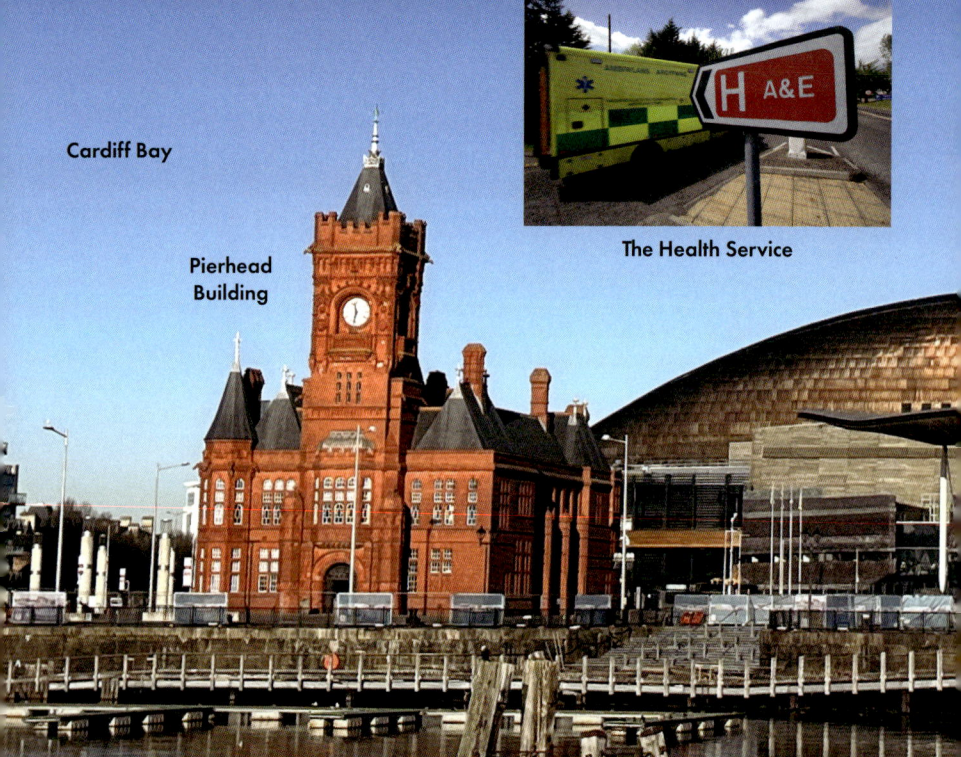

Cardiff Bay

Pierhead Building

The Health Service

The journey to establish a Welsh Parliament

The Welsh name **'Cymru'** began to be used for the country around 1,500 years ago. The literal meaning of the name is 'people who share the same country'. The country is called 'Cymru' and the people are called 'Cymry'.

The provinces of Wales were united under a single leader several times: Hywel Dda, Rhodri Mawr, Gruffudd ap Llywelyn, and Llywelyn ap Gruffudd. A Parliament was established for the first time in an **Independent Wales** under Owain Glyndŵr in Machynlleth (1404).

Cardiff as a Capital

Cardiff became a city in 1905 and the capital of Wales in 1955. In 1913, as coal export from Cardiff reached its peak, it was described as the wealthiest city in the world. Cardiff has a population of approximately 485,000 (2021 Census).

Devolution

Wales voted for devolution and greater powers in two referendums in 1997 and 2011.

This resulted in:

- setting up the Welsh Parliament to try to solve some of today's problems and improve the well-being of the country and its people for the future
- giving the Parliament greater powers to legislate in different areas in a way that suits the country and the people of Wales.

How has devolution made a difference to Wales?
Here are some differences:

- providing free prescriptions for patients
- banning smoking in public places
- charging for plastic bags, followed by banning single-use plastic
- promoting the use of the Welsh language
- managing the COVID-19 pandemic in a careful and responsible way
- considering banning sports that are harmful to animals, such as greyhound racing.

Millennium Centre

Welsh Parliament

Tŷ Hywel (Welsh Parliament offices)

Keyword: State

Sometimes, several nations or countries are part of a single state. In such a state, it is expected that all the countries are equal. **Equality** means that everyone is the same and treated the same. They should have the same opportunities and the same powers to change things. No one has more privileges than others, and no one has more rights than others.

Westminster Parliament, London

The Westminster Parliament was originally formed as a parliament for England in 1295. After the Acts of Union of England and Wales in 1536, Welsh Members of Parliament started attending Westminster. After 1707 and the dissolution of the Scottish Parliament, Scottish Members of Parliament started attending too. From 1801 onwards, there were Members of Parliament for the whole of Ireland as well.

Westminster Parliament in London

In 1922, Ireland (except for the six counties that form Northern Ireland) was given the freedom to establish its own parliament in Dublin. These days, only Members of Parliament from Northern Ireland, Scotland, Wales and England sit in Westminster.

Members of Parliament for each country

Although Wales, Scotland and Northern Ireland have had their own parliaments since 1997, a number of subject areas are not devolved. The individual countries do not have full powers to discuss and legislate on all subjects.

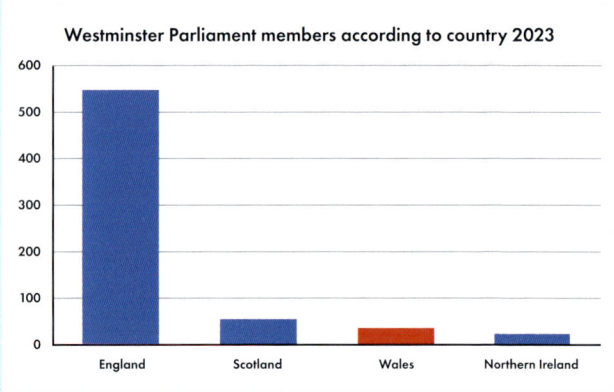

Some decisions on important subjects that affect the other three countries are still made in Westminster, London. English Members of Parliament are in a huge majority in Westminster.

Scottish independence?

By 2023, a strong voice is calling for giving the Scottish Parliament a right to debate all subjects affecting the people and land of Scotland. That means an independent Scotland – a country free to make decisions for its own future.

Scottish Parliament: Holyrood, Edinburgh

What does the future hold for Wales?

The Welsh Parliament has set up a Commission to debate our country's direction and to ensure a better future for Wales, its communities and its citizens. There are many different views on which governing approach would suit Wales best in the future.

Some of the 10,000 people at the YesCymru independence rally, Cardiff, October 2022

Countries still part of the European Union after Brexit

The European Union

A Union was formed between some European countries after the Second World War. The United Kingdom and the Republic of Ireland joined the Union in 1973. Then, in 2020, after the Brexit vote, the United Kingdom left the Union. The map on the left shows a gap where it once was. Wales lost a great deal of funding for projects and income for farmers, and workers in many sectors were lost after leaving the Union.

Ireland is still part of the European Union. In the 1950s, Wales was producing twice as much wealth than Ireland. By the 2020s, the Irish economy was four times that of Wales.

Keyword: United

All countries are part of the same world. To protect all the people and children of the world, the United Nations was established in 1945, at the end of the Second World War.

193 countries are currently members of the United Nations. This organisation defines a 'country' as a state, which is a nation or a partnership of nations with their own independent government.

There are 46 independent countries smaller than Wales in the world. But since neither Wales nor Scotland are independent countries, they cannot be members of the United Nations.

United Nations headquarters in Geneva, Switzerland

International Work

The countries that are members of the United Nations realise that it is not possible to solve all problems independently. For many of the world's problems, countries rely on each other to discuss and resolve things in an equal and fair way. Each United Nations member country has one vote each. It does not matter how big or how small that country is.

Some of the work undertaken by the United Nations includes:
- ensuring peace and security
- promoting better living standards
- protecting human rights and minorities that do not have a government
- delivering humanitarian aid in the face of dangers such as wars and famine
- protecting world heritage
- upholding international law of the International Court at the Hague in the Netherlands
- running the World Bank and the World Health Organisation, and organising the World Food programme.

The United Nations attempting to manage a difficult situation in the Democratic Republic of Congo in 2012

Today's challenge: climate change

COP (*Conference of Parties*) is a branch of the United Nations's work. COP21 was held in Paris in 2015:

- a revolutionary agreement was reached to try to tackle the problem of global warming
- the countries agreed to cooperate to keep temperatures from rising by more than 1.5°C
- each country would create a special programme to 'clean up' its lifestyle in order to achieve the goal of the Paris Agreement.

Wales's contribution

Wales did not attend the conference and had no vote on the subject. However, pollution endangers the future of all human life on Earth. Therefore, the Welsh Government has introduced policies and laws to reduce this pollution. And Wales is having success in:

- **recycling:** Wales's recycling rate is 65.5%, the third best in the world (behind Germany and Taiwan)
- **reaching a high target:** Wales has set a target of recycling 70% of waste by 2024–25
- **reducing landfill waste:** waste going to landfill in Wales was less than 5% by 2020–21.

This is an excellent record and shows that Wales has something to offer and share in international gatherings. But our country does not have a voice in those meetings right now.

Independent countries of the world at COP21, Paris

In 2021, COP26 was held in Glasgow. It led to a 'Climate Pact' to limit global warming this century to 2°C above pre-industrial levels. But none of the world's ten richest countries have met the guidelines they set in 2015. The failure of the leading countries to cooperate is one of their greatest weaknesses.

Today's challenge: food waste

With the world's population set to increase from 8 billion in 2022 to 10 billion in 2050, one challenge faces all countries. The challenge is how to achieve a 70% increase in the Earth's food production without creating more pollution and greenhouse gases, and without turning more of the world's forests and wetlands into farms.

- One third of food currently produced is not consumed. This happens because food is not stored properly. Food is also wasted and discarded instead of being consumed.

A third of the food produced in the world is currently wasted

Today's challenge: children brought up in poverty

In 2023, 34% of Welsh children were being raised in poverty. And this inequity can be seen all over the world.

The gap between 'the very rich' and the 'very poor' is currently becoming greater in Wales and the United Kingdom. In this respect, the United Kingdom has the second worst record in the western world. Here, the wealthiest 10% own 50% of the wealth.

One country – from a cairn in Eryri to a gig at the Eisteddfod

Wales and Future Generations

In 2015, the Welsh Parliament passed the Well-being of Future Generations Act. This act requires Wales to act in a way that considers the future as it finds solutions to today's problems. It must:

- think about the long-term impact of our decisions
- work better with people and communities
- prevent problems such as poverty, health inequality and climate change.

Wales is the first country in the world to have such a law.

Old wisdom in facing a new world

Several cultures in the world have realised that the Earth and everything in it is precious, and that we must protect it:

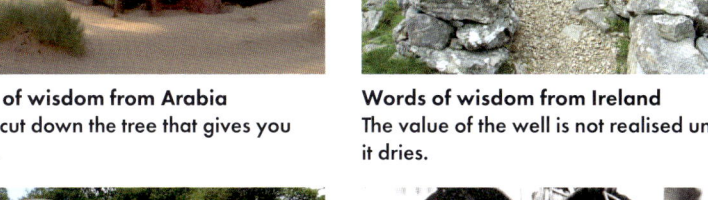

Words of wisdom from Arabia
Do not cut down the tree that gives you shelter.

Words of wisdom from Ireland
The value of the well is not realised until it dries.

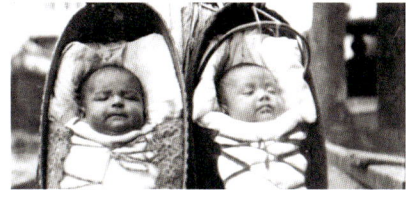

Words of wisdom from Wales
Take care of your garden, and the garden will take care of you.

Words of wisdom from American natives
The Earth is not a gift from your parents but a loan from your children.

What has created Wales's relief?

Geology and tectonic processes

"Why is this happening to us?"

This is often the question when a natural disaster occurs, such as when an earthquake hits, a volcano erupts, or a tsunami strikes.

Turkey and Syria 2023
– destruction and death

- On 6 February 2023 a powerful earthquake (magnitude 7.8 on the Richter scale) occurred in south-eastern Turkey and north-western Syria.
- Thousands of buildings were destroyed, and over 50,000 lives lost.

The impact of the earthquake in Turkey and Syria, 2023

Pilipinas 2020
– deaths, loss of houses, land and sea

- On 12 January 2020, the Taal volcano erupted on one of the Pilipinas (Philippines) islands and swept volcanic ash over towns and villages. Clouds of ash were blown as far as 40 miles north towards the capital, Manila.
- 39 lives were lost to the impact of toxic gases and ash. Thousands of animals and fish were killed. Rice, pineapple and coffee crops were ruined, and the livelihoods of 1,200 farmers and fishermen were affected.

Geologists are scientists who study the Earth and the history of its rocks. They can explain why such disasters happen.

Volcano eruption, Pilipinas 2020

It is because of geology…

The map shows that Turkey and northern Syria lie at a crossroads between the borders of several 'plates'.

The **epicentres** of the 2023 earthquake were located where the Arabian Plate slides past the Anatolia Plate.

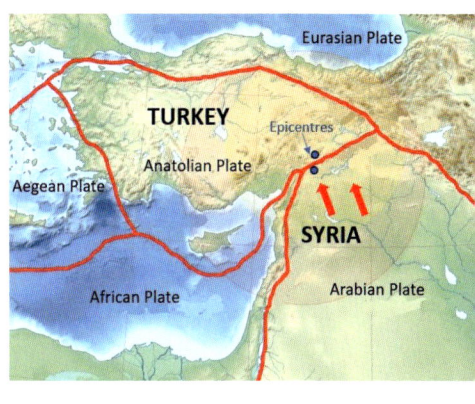

The Taal volcano in the Pilipinas is also in an area where two plates meet. The volcano is part of the 'Ring of Fire' which traces the edges of the plates around the Pacific Ocean. There are over 400 'live' volcanoes here.

What are these plates and why is there so much happening at their edges?

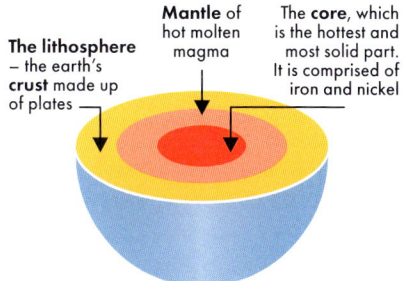

Around 4.5 billion years ago, Earth was a ball of magma, composed of hot and soft rock.

As the Earth cooled, a crust began to form around it like a crust on a loaf.

Deeper underground, it was still hot. This is the mantle, made of molten rock. These rocks are still boiling and churning today.

By 3.2 billion years ago, the churning had caused the crust to crack and splinter like a shell on a boiled egg.

These are the plates.

The plates lie on the surface of the molten **magma** in the **mantle**. They move a few centimetres each year. This causes some of the plates to push against each other, which leads to earthquakes and the formation of volcanoes.

This process is called **plate tectonics**.

The plates are moving!

- As they move, these plates either get closer together, move away from each other, or slip past each other.
- The boundaries of some plates are under continents. Others are under the oceans.
- The map shows the world's tectonic plates, with the red arrows indicating the direction in which they are moving.

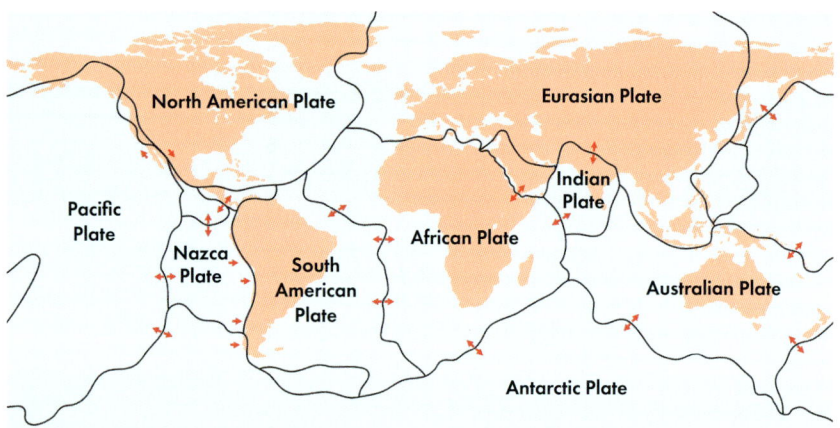

The earthquake in Turkey and Syria in 2023 was caused by two plates sliding past each other. This movement is called **conservative plate movement**.

The Arabian plate is moving slowly northwards, pushing past the Anatolia plate, which lies under Turkey.

When two plates slide past each other in such a way, the friction between them will increase the pressure between the plates. This will eventually cause a sudden movement between the plates – an earthquake.

This tectonic movement has caused earthquakes in this part of the world for millions of years. Aleppo city was destroyed in 1138 and there was an earthquake in the city of Izmit in 1999 that killed thousands of people.

There was an earthquake in Parkfield in the western United States in 2004. The city lies between San Fransisco and Los Angeles. Here, the San Andreas Fault marks where the Pacific Ocean Plate slips past the North American Plate. During this earthquake, the ground moved about half a metre either side of the fault.

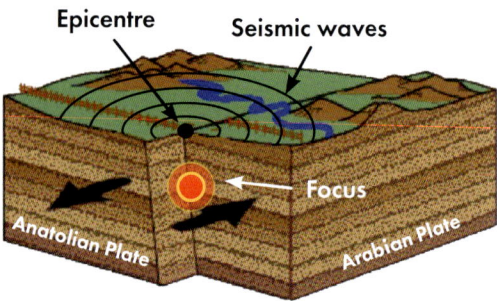

... and are pushing against each other

The edges of plates that are moving towards each other are called **destructive plate boundaries**.

In the case of the Taal volcano, the Eurasian Plate is moving towards the Pilipinas Plate, and is sliding underneath it.

The result is that the oceanic plate is sinking into the mantle beneath the continental plate.

As it sinks into the mantle, the crust melts. In doing so, it forms magma that rises to the surface and erupts in a volcano.

In the eastern Pacific Ocean, the Nazca Plate is moving towards a plate that includes the South American continent.

The continental plate is being pushed up. This is what has created the Andes mountains, and earthquakes are common here.

The world's highest volcano, Nevado Ojos del Salad, is located in the Andes. It is on the border between Chile and Argentina (6,887m).

Italy is the only country in mainland Europe that has 'live' volcanoes. Etna on the island of Sicilia is one of the volcanoes that erupts most frequently in the world.

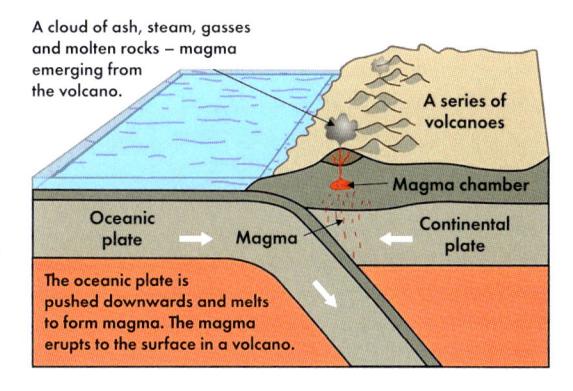

A cloud of ash, steam, gasses and molten rocks – magma emerging from the volcano.

A series of volcanoes

Magma chamber

Oceanic plate → Magma ← Continental plate

The oceanic plate is pushed downwards and melts to form magma. The magma erupts to the surface in a volcano.

In 2022, 79 'live' volcanoes erupted in 28 different countries around the world. There are no live volcanoes in Wales, but there are extinct ones here, including Yr Wyddfa.

The fertile volcanic soils on the slopes of Etna mountain attract farmers who are prepared to risk living there, where they plant vineyards and orchards.

The Vesuvius volcano is located near the city of Napoli (Naples). This is the volcano that erupted in 79 AD and buried the cities of Pompeii and Herculaneum in ashes, killing thousands of people. It is one of the world's most dangerous volcanoes, as more than 3 million people live nearby.

and form new land

Plates can move away from each other. This is the case in the Atlantic Ocean as the North American Plate moves away from the Eurasian Plate. When this happens, magma will rise from the bowels of the Earth to the surface and form new land. Therefore, the edges of these plates are called constructive plate boundaries.

This is what has created a ridge of mountains in the middle of the Atlantic Ocean. Iceland is part of that ridge. It is no surprise that the country is full of volcanic activity and features like hot springs. Between 1963 and 1967, a new volcanic island appeared from the sea southwest of the country, known as Surtsey.

In 2010, aircraft had to stop flying for a while in 20 European countries. There was concern that ash from the Eyjafjallajökull volcano in Iceland would damage the engines.

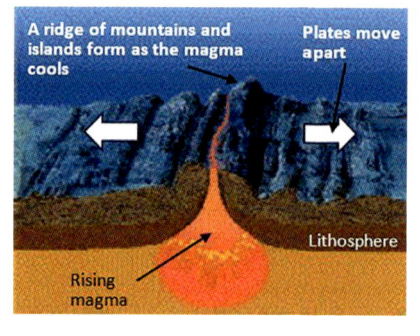

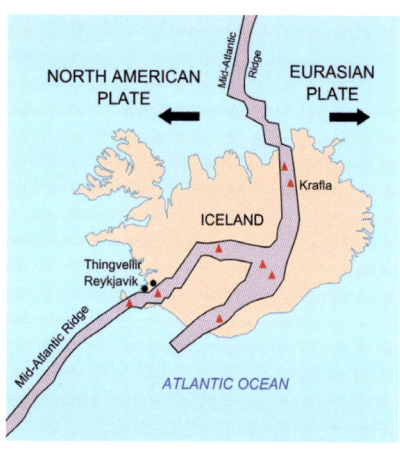

A ridge of mountains and islands form as the magma cools. Plates move apart. Rising magma. Lithosphere.

When two continental plates come together, high mountain ranges are formed. The Alps and the Himalayas were formed in this way.

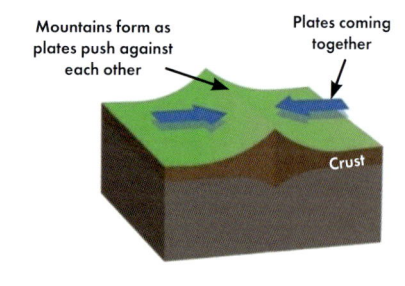

Mountains form as plates push against each other. Plates coming together. Crust.

Hot spring – Geyser Strokkur in Iceland

The impact on people

Natural dangers as tectonic plates shift

Several types of destruction can lead to tragedy, all resulting from the movement of tectonic plates.

Earthquakes can cause:
- landslides and mud flows
- avalanches in the highest mountains
- tsunamis, which are huge waves in the sea that create serious destruction on landfall
- destruction to roads, bridges and other infrastructure, including water pipes and electricity and gas supplies.

Volcanoes can also be devastating. They can:
- spread toxic gases and ash
- cause lava bombs to explode
- cause pollution, including acid rain
- cause mud flows
- destroy houses and farmland.

Ash from volcanoes can enrich the soil, which entices farmers to cultivate the land in dangerous places. Volcanoes are also a tourist attraction, of course.

> Volcanic eruptions and earthquakes still happen today – this shows that the Earth's plates continue to move and that the Earth continues to change.

The damage to Kadonowaki school in Japan following the 2011 tsunami where 20,000 lost their lives.

> One of the most powerful earthquakes happened in 2022 in Papua New Guinea, which is in the Pacific Ocean, north of Australia. The earthquake measured 7.7 on the Richter scale, and occurred where the Australian Plate is moving north-eastwards past the Pacific Plate. 21 people were killed and many more were injured. The earthquake caused many landslides and over 1,000 homes were destroyed. The earthquake impacted the country's electricity supply, including in the capital, Port Moresby.

Fagradalsfjall volcano

The Fagradalsfjall volcano in Iceland erupted on 3 August 2022. The area had experienced a number of earthquakes measuring over 5.0 on the Richter scale during the week leading up to the eruption. Fortunately, nobody was injured and no property was damaged. A few weeks later a 300m fissure or crack opened half a mile from the volcano. Up to 50m^2 of lava per second was pouring from this fissure.

Earthquakes in Wales

The geology of Wales has had a great influence on the development of the country. This can be seen in places such as Criccieth castle, which stands on hard rhyolite volcanic rock, and in slate quarries and coalmines. The geology has also formed Wales's distinctive relief, which supports unique ecosystems and an environment that attracts thousands of visitors.

The impact of tectonic plates moving can be felt even in Wales! But these are very weak earthquakes – less than 2 points on the Richter scale. Millions of such earthquakes occur around the world every year.

Strength (Richter)	Location	Date
1.5	Porthmadog	18 September 2022
1.8	Eryri	11 October 2022
3.8	Llŷn	29 May 2013
2.9	near Nantyffyllon	5 June 2009
2.9	near Llangollen	30 November 2007
2.9	Cardiff	2 June 2002
5.4	Llithfaen	19 July 1984

The Llithfaen earthquake in Llŷn was the largest earthquake to hit the United Kingdom during the 20C. The Daily Post reported that the gable of a house near Aberdaron had collapsed, while a crack had appeared in a chapel in Pwllheli. Chimney stacks had crumpled in many areas.

The Earth's age

How old is the Earth?

This is one of the big questions that has always interested geologists.

In trying to answer this question, geologists in the 20C realised that the Earth was much older than some had previously assumed.

The main reason for this was the discovery of radioactivity and the understanding that radioactive elements in rocks are deteriorating at a constant rate. It therefore became possible to date the very long history of the Earth much more accurately.

Geologists now talk about rocks that are millions or even billions of years old.

To try to better understand these huge time periods, let us compress the history of the world's rocks into a single year.

Imagine then that the oldest rocks in the world, which are 4.5 billion years old, developed on January 1. We must then wait nine months until Wales's oldest rocks, which are 700 million years old, formed in October.

On 24 November, there was great volcanic activity which formed the rocks of Eryri and Pembrokeshire. Towards the end of November, the first plants and animals appeared on land.

In December, thick layers of limestone, common in many parts of Wales, were deposited on the bed of tropical seas. Shortly afterwards, tropical marshes were formed which led to the creation of the coalfields of south and north Wales.

Towards the end of December, the dinosaurs disappeared, leaving their traces in Wales's youngest rocks, for example the cliffs of the Vale of Glamorgan coast.

One big continent

Continental Drift

Have you noticed that the South American continent and the African continent look as if they are part of the same jig-saw puzzle? As if they would fit neatly into each other?

In the early 1900s, a German geologist named Alfred Wegener discovered that similar rocks and fossils were found in South America, Africa, India and Australia.

He concluded that the present continents had been part of one great continent over 300 million years ago. That continent was named Pangaea.

As the Earth's crust cracked and split, the continent of Pangaea began to break up. The plates and continents travelled slowly across the Earth's surface. This is called continental drift, and is shown in this diagram.

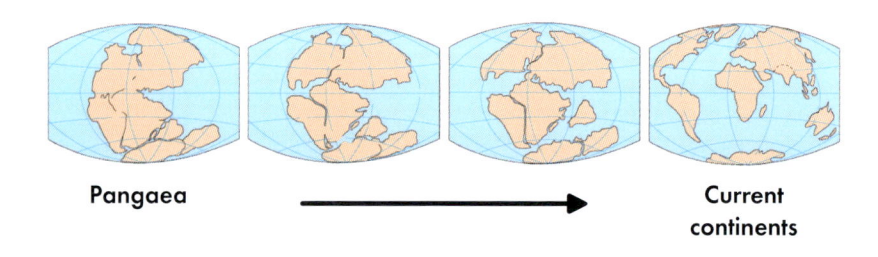

Pangaea ⟶ **Current continents**

Therefore, the location of the continents on the surface of the Earth has changed over time. Like everywhere else, Wales has been on that journey. Wales's journey began at the South Pole between 540 and 560 million years ago.

The rocks of Llanddwyn Island on Anglesey give us an idea of what was going on. At the time, an oceanic plate was moving slowly southwards and sliding under a continental plate that included Wales. On Llanddwyn Island there is evidence that the ocean plate that was swallowed was formed from lava. Lava emerging from the ground beneath the sea squirts out like toothpaste from a tube and as it cools, it forms rocks that are cushion-like. This is called pillow lava and is found on Llanddwyn Island.

Wales's grand tour

Live volcanoes in Pembrokeshire and Eryri

By 465 million years ago, Wales was part of a continent that had broken free from the main continent at the South Pole. The continent moved slowly northwards, with many earthquakes and volcanoes erupting constantly. This is why there is lava called rhyolite in some places in Wales today. The Glyderau mountains and Cadair Idris in Eryri are old volcanoes from this period. So is the Pen-caer area, to the north-west of Fishguard in Pembrokeshire.

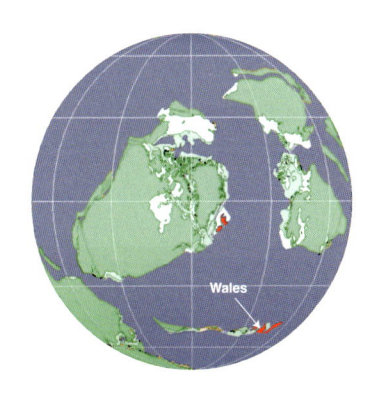

Wales in a desert

When Wales reached the southern tropics, the climate was very dry. Around 380 million years ago, the climate in Wales was similar to the climate you would find in a desert. The sand in that desert formed the red sandstone rocks seen in Wales today. Red sandstone is found in the mountains in Carmarthenshire and on mountains such as Pen y Fan in Bannau Brycheiniog.

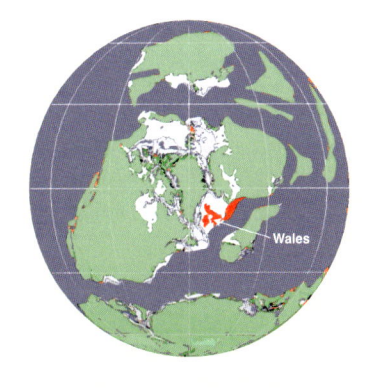

Wales on the Equator

By about 359 million years ago, Wales was part of a shallow and warm sea, just south of the Equator. The climate was tropical – wet and hot. That led to the development of coral and calcium carbonate white sand. This is when limestone was formed on the seabed, which has created some of Wales's most famous landscapes today. Among them are Penygogarth, near Llandudno; the Green Bridge of Wales in Pembrokeshire, and Worm's Head on the Gower Peninsula.

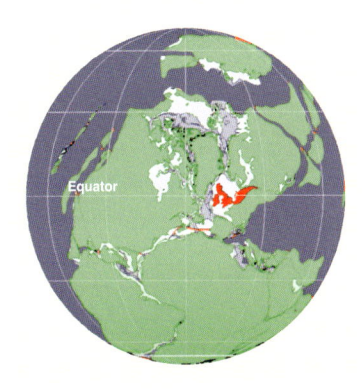

Wales's grand tour

The age of coal

Wales continued on its journey northwards. By 320 million years ago, Wales was on the Equator, home to very wet lands and forests, similar to those in the Amazon today. This is when layers of organic matter formed which slowly turned into layers of coal, common in south and north-east Wales.

Back to the dessert

Between 300 and 200 million years ago, Wales had reached a latitude similar to where the Sahara is today. It was hot and dry once again, and so more red sandstone was formed. Examples of this sandstone can be seen in the Vale of Clwyd. The sandstone can also be found in the Vale of Glamorgan and, amazingly, dinosaur footprints have been discovered here! It is believed that the dinosaur was a type of sauropod, a creature with a large body and a long neck and tail.

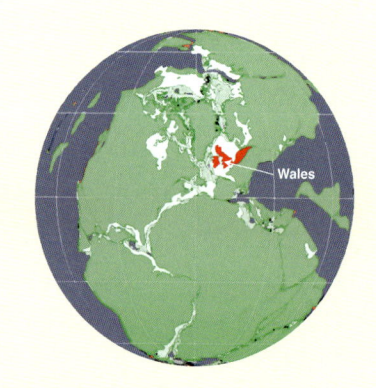

Goodbye, Pangaea; hello, Atlantic Ocean

By 65 million years ago, the dinosaurs had died out and Wales – like the rest of Pangaea – was being torn apart by the forces of tectonic plates as the Atlantic Ocean formed. As a result, fissures were created in the crust and these were filled with magma. There are good examples of this on Anglesey and Holy Island. Wales was now close to its present position on the face of the Earth. The climate was warm until the Ice Age arrived, about 2.6 million years ago.

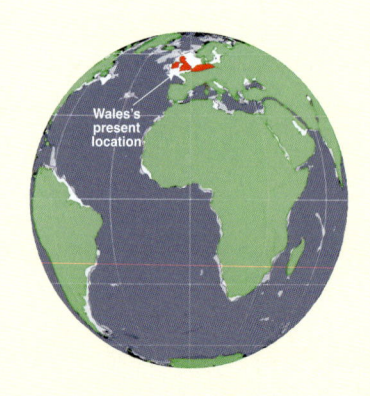

Rock classification

Over millions of years, rocks have experienced all sorts of changes following pressure, folding, faulting (splitting), and heat. Geologists place existing rocks in 3 classes, namely igneous, sedimentary and metamorphic rocks.

Rock	Igneous	Sedimentary	Metamorphic
Formation	Among the Earth's oldest rocks. They form when hot liquid magma slowly cools and crystallizes. The melting occurs deep within the Earth near the edges of active plates. Sometimes it rises toward the surface in volcanoes.	Created by the erosion of older rocks and deposited on the seabed, in rivers, desert marshes or lakes. They form in layers, pressing down on each other and sometimes containing the remains of animals and plants – fossils.	Forms from existing rocks following the effect of heat or pressure. The original igneous or sedimentary minerals will change in form to create new minerals, and their character and appearance will change significantly.
Type	Granite and basalt	Sandstone, chalk and limestone	Marble, slate
Features	Hard and difficult to wear down	Relatively soft rocks	Hard and resilient
Human use	Construction industry and road surfaces	Coal as fuel; lime to create cement and as fertilizer	Slate for roofs, marble for construction
Where in Wales?	Parts of Eryri, and Pembrokeshire	Anglesey, Clwydian Hills, Gower Peninsula	North-west Wales – the areas of Bethesda, the Nantlle Valley, Llanberis, Blaenau Ffestiniog and Meirionnydd

Layers of limestone in Dunraven Bay, Vale of Glamorgan

Basalt

Slate

The geology of Wales

Wherever you find stones on a beach in Wales, you will notice that there are stones of many different colours. This is due to the wide variety of rocks in Wales. The stones could also have been moved to Wales from Ireland or Scotland. Because of all this diversity, the geological map of Wales is an interesting and colourful one.

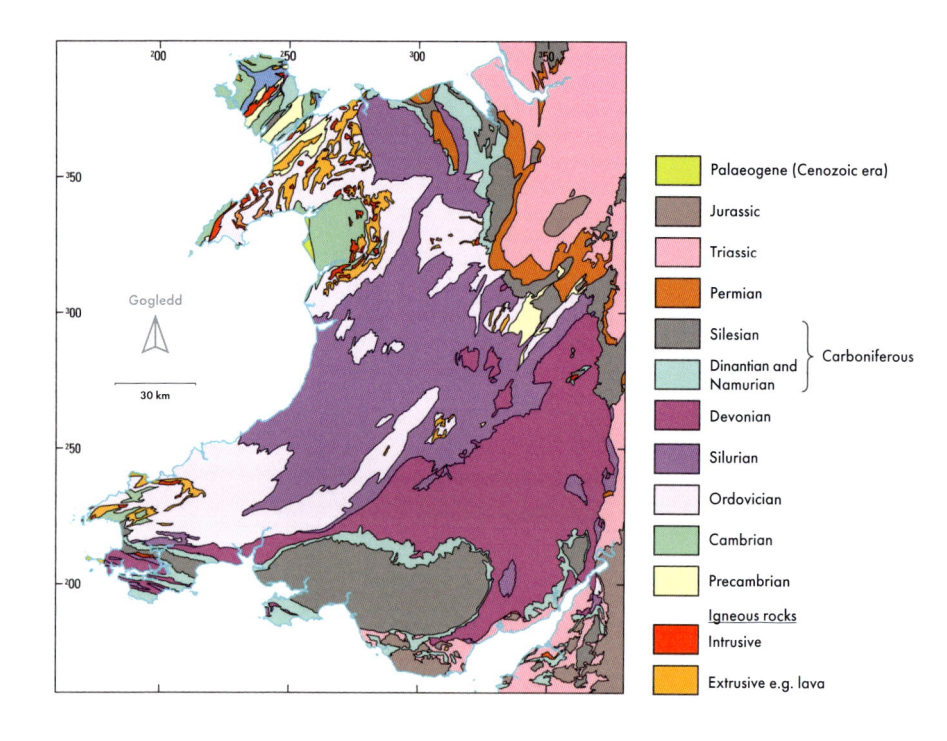

Palaeogene (Cenozoic era)
Jurassic
Triassic
Permian
Silesian ⎫
Dinantian and Namurian ⎬ Carboniferous
Devonian
Silurian
Ordovician
Cambrian
Precambrian
Igneous rocks
Intrusive
Extrusive e.g. lava

Geologists who have studied Welsh rocks for centuries have contributed greatly to our understanding of geology.

The classification of rocks by age began from about 1830 onwards. Welsh rocks have been used as the foundation for much of this work. That is why three very old rock types have Welsh names:

- **Cambrian**: 543–490 million years ago
- **Ordovican**: (the Ordovicians were a Celtic tribe living in Gwynedd) 490–443 million years ago
- **Silurian**: (the Silurians were a Celtic tribe living in Glamorgan and Gwent) 443–417 million years ago.

Geological time chart

This is a geological time chart that set outs the rocks of Wales by their age and period.

Era	Period		Age (Millions of years)
Cenozoic	Quaternary	This period has shaped the relief we see today. It happened as the ice age glaciers left their mark on almost all of Wales's land including valleys, arêtes and moraines. In warmer times between the ice ages, animals such as mammoths roamed the land. The ice of the last Ice Age melted around 10,000 years ago, at the end of the Pleistocene period. This is when humans first appeared.	1.8
	Tertiary	There is little evidence of the existence of rocks from this period in Wales although they may be present under nearby seas.	65
Mesozoic	Cretaceous	No rocks from this period are found in Wales although they may be present under nearby seas.	146
	Jurassic	Rocks from this period are found in the Vale of Glamorgan and are clearly visible on the coast between Ogmore-by-Sea and Barry. Cliffs are found here that contain layers of Jurassic limestone known as lias.	200
	Triassic	The coast between Barry and Penarth and onwards to the English border in Monmouthshire is composed of Triassic sandstone. These rocks are also found further west in the Ogmore-by-Sea and Kenfig areas.	250
Palaeozoic	Permian	Rocks from this period lie below the Vale of Clwyd in the north-east and have been covered by more recent deposition by rivers and ice sheets. These rocks are also found under the sea in the Bristol Channel, Cardigan Bay and the Irish Sea near the north Wales coast.	300
	Carboniferous	Rocks of this period are mainly found in south Wales, from the Wye valley across the coalfield to the Vale of Glamorgan and Gower, and then onwards to south Pembrokeshire. Rocks of the same age and type are also found in north-east Wales and extend along the northern coast to Anglesey. The rocks consist of carboniferous limestone, coarse sandstone and the coalfields of the south and north-east.	360
	Devonian	The rock belonging to this period is old, red sandstone. These rocks extend from the English border through Bannau Brycheiniog onwards to Pembrokeshire. At times, there is harder sandstone at the top, which has created the impressive summits of Pen y Fan, Pen-y-fâl, and the Black Mountains.	415
	Silurian	More of Wales's land is covered by rocks of this period than any other. This includes much of mid-Wales, Monmouthshire, the Clwydian Range and the Dee Valley in the Llangollen area. Extensive areas of central and south Pembrokeshire also contain Silurian rocks. These rocks are mainly sandstone and mudstone.	450
	Ordovician	During this period, a series of sedimentary rocks developed, extending from Pembrokeshire through Carmarthenshire and northwards along the Tywi Valley. In Eryri, Ordovician volcanic rocks are responsible for the rugged landscape, including Yr Wyddfa, which has been created from volcanic ash (tuff) with igneous intrusions and sedimentary rocks all folded in a syncline! Similar rocks make up Cadair Idris and are extensively found on Anglesey and on the Llŷn Peninsula. The Ordovician rocks of Wales are full of folds and faults following numerous ground movements.	490
	Cambrian	Rocks from this period are mostly found in Meirionnydd, including in the Rhinogydd mountains which form part of the Harlech dome anticline. The dome, which has suffered much erosion, consists of sandstone, mudstone and greywacke, which is a type of dark and hard sandstone. Cambrian rocks are also found in north Pembrokeshire, Anglesey and the Llŷn Peninsula.	550
	Pre-Cambrian	Recent pre-Cambrian rocks are very common in Anglesey, Llŷn and Eryri, with some to be found in Pembrokeshire, Carmarthenshire and South Powys. Rocks change when they are exposed to heat and high pressure. Due to such intensive metamorphism, geologists' understanding of these volcanic and sedimentary rocks is limited. Some volcanic rocks on the border with England are thought to be 700 million years old – Wales's oldest rocks.	

Glaciation

How on earth were these giant landforms created?

Y Grib Goch leading to the summit of Yr Wyddfa. 'Y Grib Goch' means 'The Red Ridge', which is as sharp as a knife – an arête

Llyn Cwm Llwch in Bannau Brycheiniog. A lake sitting in an armchair – corrie

Y Cnicht, near Beddgelert in Eryri. Pyramidal peak and the Welsh Matterhorn!

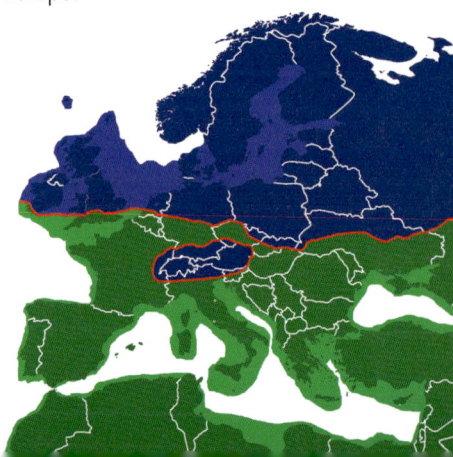

To find the answer, we must go back 10,000 years to the end of the last Ice Age. There have been several Ice Ages in the history of the Earth, but right now we are living in a warm age. The last Ice Age occurred in a period known as the Pleistocene. Global temperatures fell 6°C and it snowed constantly. As snow fell on top of snow, the pressure turned it into ice. Currently, about 10% of the Earth's surface area is covered by ice. But during an Ice Age, 30% of its area is under ice.

In an Ice Age, the sea level falls because the frozen water on land does not return to the oceans. Therefore, during the Ice Age, there was no sea between Scotland and Norway nor between England and France. The British Isles were part of continental Europe.

The red line on the map shows how far the ice reached. The light green and light blue colours show land that are seas today.

Europe during the Ice Age around 15,000 years ago.

46

Glacier and ice sheet

The Pleistocene Ice Age had a great impact on the Welsh landscape. Most of the country was covered by glaciers or ice sheets.

The snow that formed the thickest ice fell on the summits of the highest mountains.

These were the Eryri mountains, Cadair Idris and Pumlumon – located in north-west and mid-Wales. The snow gathered in the valleys to create rivers of ice, or **glaciers**. The glaciers moved slowly down the valleys that existed prior to the Ice Age, completely altering the relief.

This also happened in Scotland and the Lake District in England, which have very similar reliefs to parts of Wales. Glaciers are currently found in the world's highest mountains, for example in the Himalayas, the Rockies, the Alps and the Andes.

In Wales, a sheet of thinner ice covered much of the lowland on the coast and borders. Although traces of the Ice Age are clearly visible in mountainous places such as Eryri, the ice has left deposits all over the country.

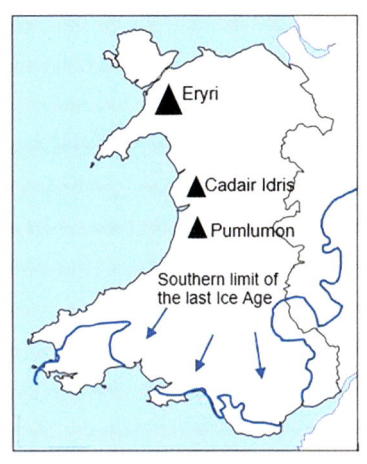

The Pleistocene Age Ice covered most of Wales

In 2022, while exploring a prehistoric cave under Pembroke castle, scientists found mammoth bones. The skeleton was about 10,000 years old. That's right: mammoths, northern deer and other animals living in cold climates could be found in Wales in this period.

The Aletsch Glacier in Switzerland is the largest glacier in the Alps

The Teifi Valley relief – valleys all over Wales were affected by the last Ice Age

Landforms

Glacial valleys and corries are two major landforms created by glacier erosion.

The glacial valley of Nant Ffrancon in Eryri

Penrhyn Slate Quarry, Bethesda

A hanging valley joining the main river

Llyn Dinas – a ribbon lake on river Glaslyn, near Beddgelert

The glacier moves slowly down the valley, eroding rocks from the sides and floor. Gradually, the valley that used to be V-shaped will change into a-U shaped valley. After the glacier melts and recedes, a river will flow through a wide valley which it did not form itself. Tributaries will be left high above the sides of the deep valley. These are called hanging valleys, and the tributaries will cascade down the steep slopes to the bottom of the U-shaped valley to join the main river.

Tributary flowing into the main valley

Main valley – V-shaped

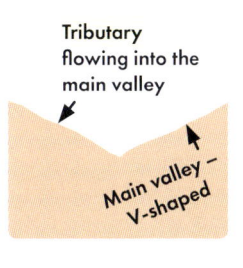

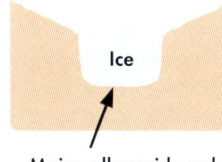

Ice

Main valley widened and deepened by the glacier

Tributary above the main valley – Hanging valley

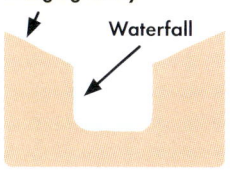

Waterfall

U-shaped glacial valley

Steep sides

The A5 road

Flat floor. A ribbon lake may have existed here once. The lake was later filled by river deposits.

River Ogwen – a small river in a big valley!

Cwm Cau, a corrie on the southern slopes of Cadair Idris in Gwynedd

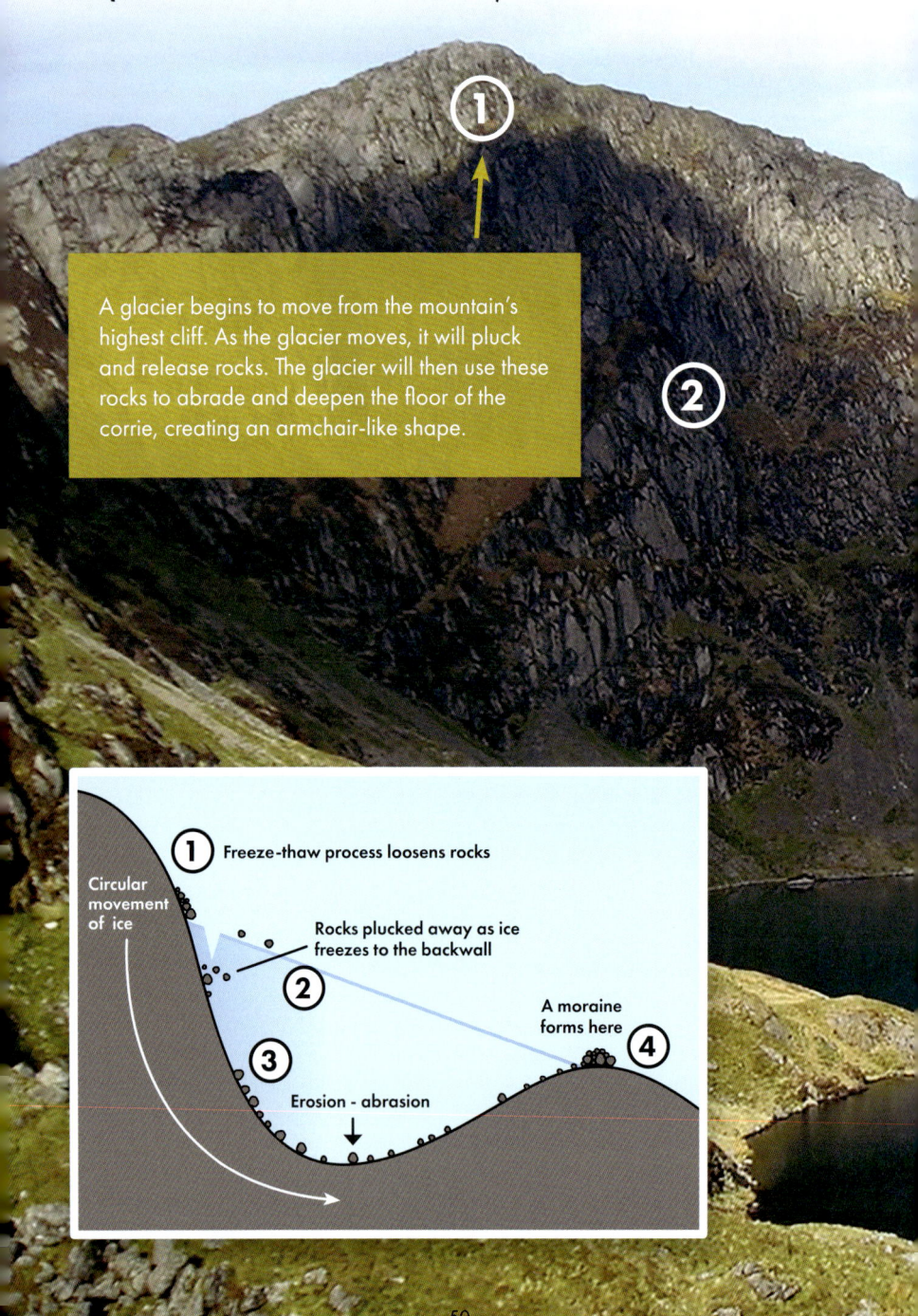

① A glacier begins to move from the mountain's highest cliff. As the glacier moves, it will pluck and release rocks. The glacier will then use these rocks to abrade and deepen the floor of the corrie, creating an armchair-like shape.

②

① Freeze-thaw process loosens rocks

Circular movement of ice

② Rocks plucked away as ice freezes to the backwall

③ Erosion - abrasion

④ A moraine forms here

Llyn Cau below the summit of Cadair Idris (893m), near Dolgellau in Gwynedd. The lake sits in a cwm or corrie 470m above sea level, with cliffs on three sides. The only open side is the eastern side, where Nant Cadair flows out of the lake and into the river Fawnog. In turn, this river flows into Llyn Myngul in the Tal-y-llyn valley below – the southernmost ribbon lake in Wales.

Corries are very common in Eryri, including Llyn Glaslyn on the slopes of Yr Wyddfa and Cwm Idwal at the upper end of the Ogwen Valley. There are also corries further south, including Llyn y Fan Fawr, Llyn y Fan Fach and Llyn Cwm Llwch in Bannau Brycheiniog.

After the Ice Age, the ice melted and filled the valley with water to create a lake – Llyn Cau. A moraine will sometimes be deposited at the head of the cwm or corrie.

Tundra

Next to the ice sheets, there were extensive areas of ponds and mosses. Such reliefs are called Tundra.

These areas are found in the Earth today in northern places and on high mountains.

Deer and other animals could easily travel from Europe to south Wales as the ice sheet retreated northwards. As it warmed, and as poor-quality soil became more fertile, shrubs and then trees grew. Other animals came to Wales, and soon families of hunters arrived from Europe. The fact that people were beginning to live in Wales was a sign that the Ice Age was over.

As more ice turned into water, sea levels rose. Britain turned into islands again. Without the weight of the thick ice sheet, some of Wales's rocks, compressed by the ice, began to rise slightly.

The tundra in Siberia

PROCESSES

Weathering

Several processes were involved as the ice eroded the land, shifted the debris and then deposited it as the ice melted.

When rocks are broken up by the weather and biological processes, this is called weathering.

If temperatures vary around freezing point, then freeze-thaw weathering will be a common process. Water will find its way to a crack on the rock face. As it freezes, it expands and opens the crack, causing pieces of rock to fall from the cliff.

Scree forming on the slopes of Moel Hebog, near Beddgelert. Rocks have fallen following weathering on the cliff above

The loose pieces of rock can fall to form a scree at the base of the cliff. This process continues to affect the landscape in Eryri and other parts of Wales.

Plucking and abrasion

These processes were occurring during the Ice Age when glaciers were moving slowly from the mountains towards the lowlands:

- Plucking occurs when the glacier freezes to the rock and the clefts within it. As the glacier moves, it plucks away pieces of rock

- Abrasion occurs when frozen stones at the bottom of the glacier scrape and chip the ground and rocks as the glacier moves over them. This process will leave marks on the rocks called striations. These striations can indicate in which direction the glacier was moving. These are sometimes found on sheepback rocks (roches moutonnées) on the valley floor. 'Roche moutonnée' means 'fleecy rock', as the eroded side of the rock looks like sheep lying on the ground.

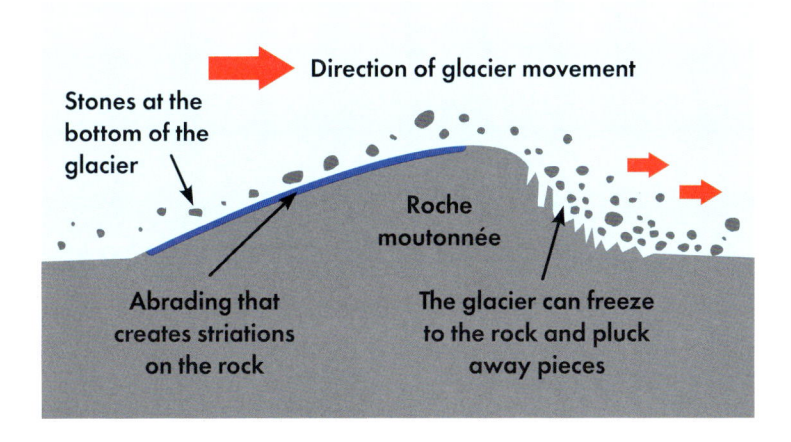

Roche moutonnée on the floor of the U-shaped glacial valley in Nant Ffrancon

Glacial landforms in mountain regions

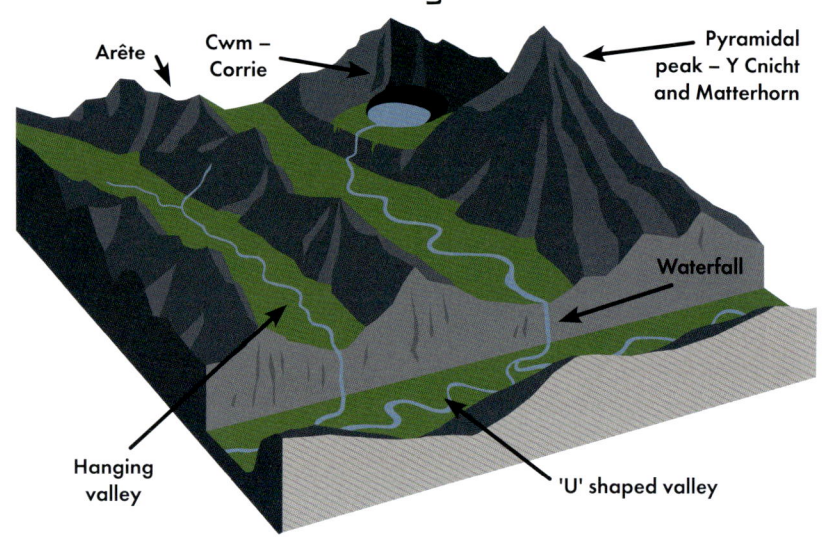

This is how the relief of the uplands looked following the Ice Age. Narrow arêtes formed where valleys and corries back on to each other. When glaciers originate in close proximity to each other and move in several directions, a horn or a pyramidal peak will form, as happened on Yr Wyddfa.

Glacial deposition

At the end of the Ice Age, as temperatures rose, the ice began to melt. The glaciers retreated back up the valleys. As it melted, the glacier would deposit and leave many traces that are still visible today. Traces of erosion are most common in the uplands. Deposits by ice sheets and glaciers, however, had a bigger influence on the Welsh relief in the lowlands. Most of Wales was covered by boulder clay containing sand, clay and rocks of varying sizes, all mixed together.

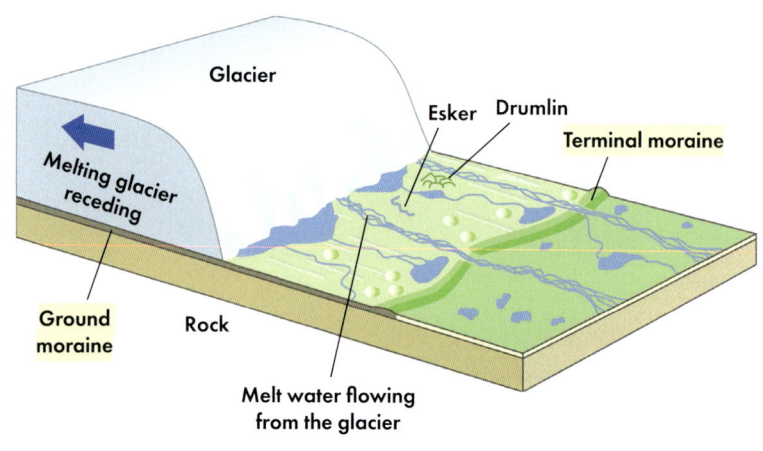

Some of the landforms that emerge following deposition include:

- **moraine** – a heap of deposits that were a mixture of mud, sand, gravel and pebbles. A terminal moraine is a mound of deposits across the valley, showing the furthest point to which the glacier travelled. A moraine can create a dam for a ribbon, glacial lake.
- **esker** – a ridge of stones deposited by the meltwater in the glacier
- **drumlin** – a low hill of glacier sediment, similar to a basket of eggs!
- **erratics** – large rocks, dumped higgledy-piggledy by the glacier as it melted. These stones do not belong to the rocks they lie on.

King Arthur's Stone on the Gower is now a summit stone on a cromlech. But before Bronze Age builders found this new use for the stone, it was an erratic carried from afar to the moorland on the peninsula.

There are many unusual stones like this all over Anglesey, Pembrokeshire and the Gower Peninsula.

Submerged land

When sea levels rose at the end of the Ice Age, the land was submerged in some places.

Where U-shaped glacial valleys existed, fjords were formed which are common on the coast of Scotland and in Norway.

In south-west Wales, some of the low lying valleys that had not been affected by the ice were submerged. This created rias. The port of Milford Haven is in a ria.

Solva in Pembrokeshire – the valley was drowned when the sea level rose after the ice receded.

Geirangerfjord, Norway

Rivers

Without water, the Earth would be a desert. It would look like the surface of the moon. Water is one of Wales's most valuable resources. It is part of our cynefin, culture and heritage. A reliable supply of clean water is important for human health, while rivers provide a cynefin for many animals, fish and plants.

Water has been an important part of the economy for centuries, offering a convenient means of transport and energy from river flows. This led to the establishment of towns, villages, mills and industries on the flat land of the sheltered valleys.

Unfortunately, pollution affects the water standard of many Welsh rivers, including the river Wye. This pollution destroys natural life and makes the rivers less attractive to visitors who use them for fishing, canoeing and other activities.

An old mill and water-wheel on the river Teifi in Cenarth

Blaen and Aber

There are several places in Wales that contain an element of the word 'blaen' in their names, which means 'head'. These places are usually at the upper ends of valleys – Blaen Rhondda, Blaenavon and Blaenau Ffestiniog, for example.

There are also many towns in Wales and other Celtic countries that include the word 'aber', meaning 'estuary'. These towns are on the coast, or where two rivers merge, or where a river's journey ends. For example, Abertawe (Swansea) in Wales and Aberdeen in Scotland.

The upper reaches of the river Tywi near Moel Prysgau

The longest river that has its source in Wales is the river Severn (354km), which begins its journey on the slopes of the Pumlumon mountain. It flows eastwards into England before reaching the sea near Chepstow in Monmouthshire. The longest river flowing within Wales itself is the river Tywi (120km). It has it source in the Cambrian Mountains and flows southwards and into the sea at Carmarthen Bay.

But the length of Welsh rivers cannot compare with the world's longest rivers. For example, the Amazonas (Brazil), the Nile (Egypt) and the Yangtze (China) are all over 6,000km long!

River catchments and erosion

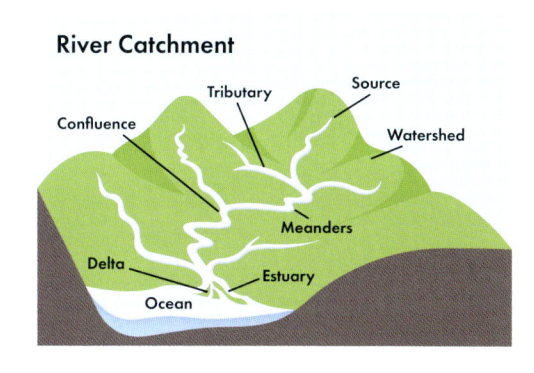

The water flowing in our rivers and streams has changed the relief, and continues to do so constantly. Rivers have their sources in the mountains, and they flow from here down along the valleys before reaching the sea. The river expands and widens along its route, joining other rivers or tributaries (confluences). As it approaches the end of its journey, it will meander across the floodplain towards the estuary. The whole land or area over which the river and its tributaries flow is called the river's **catchment**. The hills around the valley create a boundary between the river's catchment and the catchment of the next river.

River Catchment

Interlocking spurs on the river Gill in the Lake District, England

Travelling along the A470 between Talerddig and Carno, you will cross a **watershed**. Talerddig's streams flow west into the catchment of the river Dyfi, while Carno's streams, a few miles to the east, belong to the catchment of the river Severn.

Welsh rivers have their **sources** in marshes or lakes in the uplands. The terrain near the source is steep. At the beginning of its journey, the river will flow around interlocking **spurs** in narrow 'V' shaped valleys.

As it moves, the water in the river contains energy. This energy releases gravel and stones, which collide with the bed and banks of the channel, causing erosion. This process, which deepens and widens the channel, is called **corrasion**.

Sometimes, the flow of the river uses gravel and stones to chip hard chunks of rock on the riverbed, creating rounded forms called **potholes**. These features, which form over millions of years, are common in some of Wales's mountainous streams and rivers.

Potholes in the upper reaches of the river Elan, Powys

Waterfalls and gorges

This is Pistyll Rhaeadr, near Llanrhaeadr-ym-Mochnant in north Powys. It is Wales's highest waterfall, where the water descends 80m from the top to the plunge pool below. There are numerous waterfalls on our rivers. 'Sgwd' is another Welsh name for a waterfall, used commonly in the upper parts of the river Tawe – for example, Sgwd Henrhyd.

A plunge pool will form at the bottom of the waterfall. Here, the river will use stones to further erode the soft rock, causing the top of the waterfall to collapse. This process is called undercutting. Over time, the waterfall's position will move back up the valley forming a narrow valley, called a gorge.

Niagara Falls on the border between Canada and the United States of America is one of the world's largest waterfalls.

Waterfalls are common landforms in the upper part of the river course, where the riverbed suddenly descends. This often happens at the boundary between rocks of different hardness. Hard rock is better able to withstand erosion than the surrounding soft rocks.

1
River
Hard rock
Soft rock

2
Soft rock erodes faster and creates a step

3
Undercutting
Plunge pool

4
Following constant undercutting, the edge of the waterfall will move back up the gorge

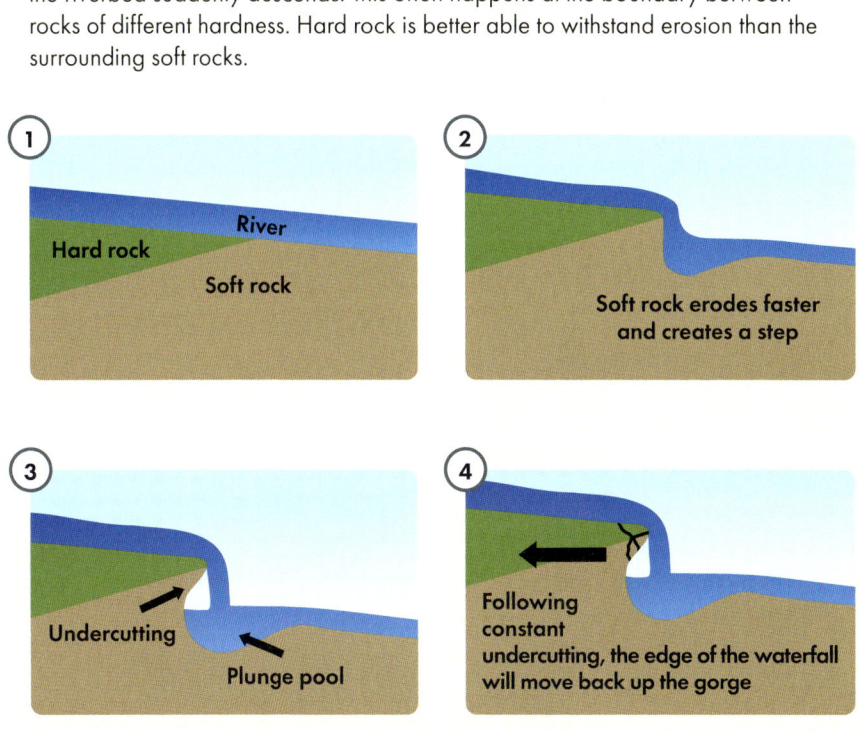

Meanders and ox-bow lakes

As we move seaward, the upland valleys will open out, widen and become flatter. Here, the Welsh landscape has been heavily influenced by the Ice Age and the shape of the valleys has been mainly influenced by glaciers.

A meander forms as a river twists and turns across the flat valley floor. This is a meander on the river Tywi, near Llanarthne in Carmarthenshire.

DEPOSITION

EROSION

Neck narrowing

EROSION

Erosion and deposition processes are underway here, with the deepest water (shown by the red arrows) on the outward side of the bend flowing faster and therefore possessing the energy to erode the riverbank. On the inner side, the water flows more slowly and therefore deposits the load. If the river continues to erode the sides, the river will break through the narrow neck. This will leave an ox-bow lake, with the river now taking a new route.

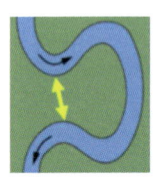

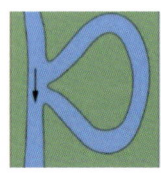

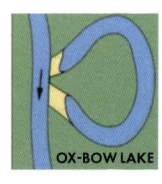

OX-BOW LAKE

EROSION

EROSION

Slip-off slope – deposits of gravel and pebbles

DEPOSITION

DEPOSITION

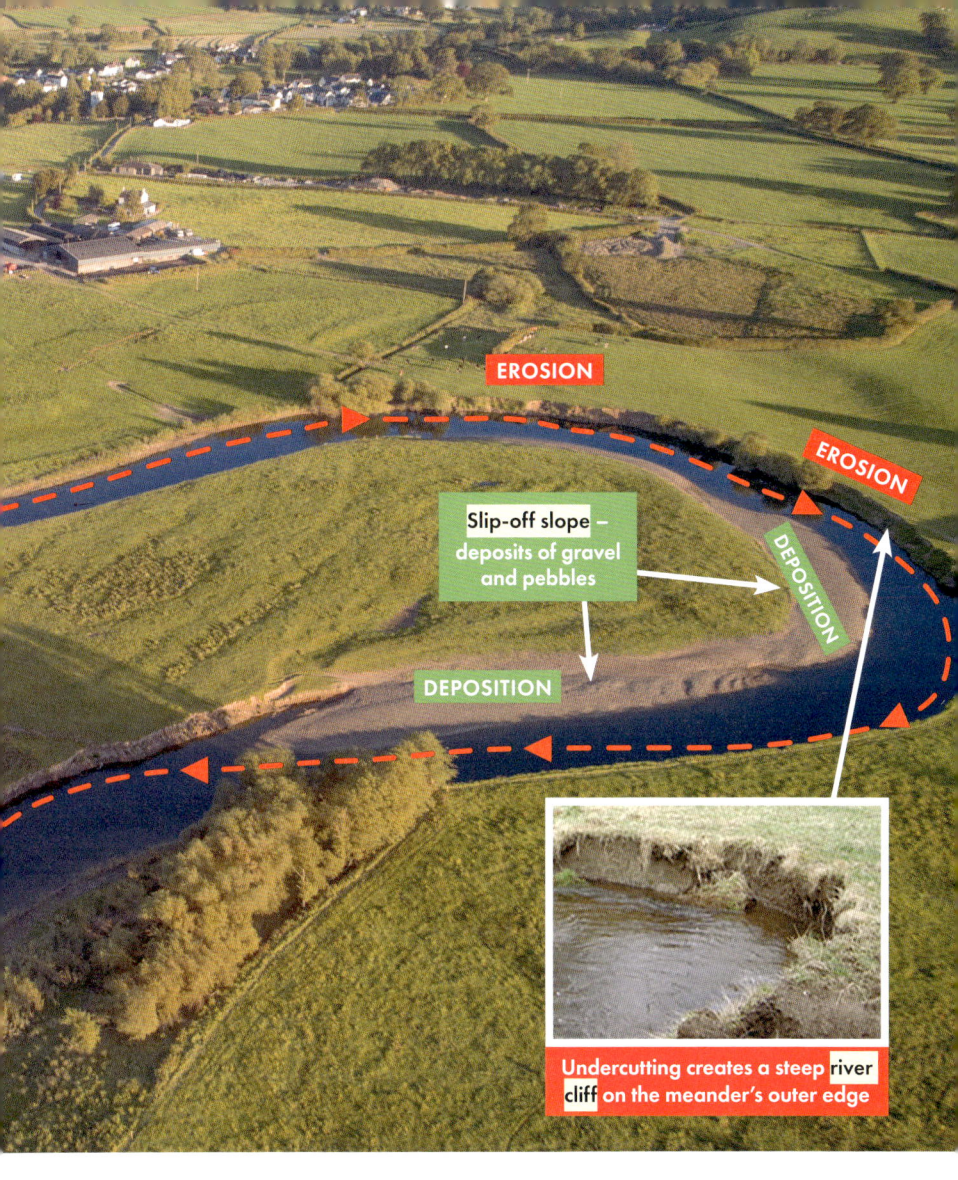

Undercutting creates a steep river cliff on the meander's outer edge

Meanders on the river Teifi at Newcastle Emlyn. This Welsh castle, built around 1240, is situated within the bend of the river. Why is this type of site well suited to a castle?

Location of the castle within the meander

Delta and deposition

As it reaches a still body of water, a river loses its energy, drops its load, and deposits. This can happen in the sea or in a lake. At times, a delta will form, as seen at the mouth of the river Nile in Egypt. The name 'delta' comes from the fourth letter of the Greek alphabet which is in the form of a triangle − Δ

Vegetation on the river Nile which flows northwards into the Mediterranean Sea

River deposits

Llyn Myngul at Tal-y-llyn, Gwynedd

This occurs in many Welsh lakes, including Llyn Myngul in Tal-y-llyn. You can see where deposits from rivers are gradually filling the glacial lake. Eventually the lake will disappear.

The remarkable estuary of the river Dee

The mouth of the river Dee in north-east Wales is a vast and wide estuary. The estuary is far too large for the size of the river. Geographers believe:
• that either rivers such as the river Severn and the river Mersey flowed through this estuary until the ice sheet locked up the land, forcing the rivers to change course
• or that the Irish Sea ice sheet moved southwards, eroding this coastline in doing so. There is a lot of glacial sand and gravel here, mixed with river deposits.

Today, the estuary is a haven for wildlife. However, it used to be a busy place with several small ports. On the Welsh side there are many industrial remains and ports such as Greenfield near Holywell, Mostyn, Flint and Connah's Quay.

Chester was an important river port since Roman days, with ferries departing to Ireland until the early 1800s. But the river was choked by deposits. To dry out the flat land near the estuary (Sealand) and deepen the river, a straight, narrow channel was cut in 1737. This was called the 'New Cut'.

In Wales, on the east bank of the river, Shotton steelworks is still in operation, and employs around 800 workers.

The Airbus company has a factory on the banks of the river in Broughton. Until recently, the company exported the wings of the giant Airbus A380 aircraft along the river. A quay was built near the works, and special boats would be used to transport the wings to Mostyn docks to be transferred to ships.

Ships then transported the wings to docks near Bordeaux in the south of France. There, boats would take them along the Garonne river to Toulouse, where the planes were being built. After 16 years the practice ended in 2020 when Airbus stopped building the A380 to focus on smaller aircraft. It is possible to fly the wings for those smaller aircraft to Toulouse in a special aeroplane.

In 1998 a new bridge was opened to cross the River Dee near Connah's Quay. The bridge is called Flintshire Bridge, and improves links between Wales and the Wirral, and onwards to Merseyside and Liverpool.

Flintshire Bridge with Connah's Quay's gas power station in the background.

People, droughts and floods

People and rivers

It was natural that people created their cynefin on the banks of streams and rivers, as they provided water to drink and wash. Fish and shellfish from the river could feed communities, and the water could be used to irrigate and grow crops on dry lands.

The waters of some rivers, such as the Ganga in India and the Jordan in Israel (photo on the right), are considered sacred by the people who live on their banks. On these banks, religious services and funerals are held, and the water is used for baptism.

In Vietnam, people live on the river, while markets are held on the river Kwai in Thailand. Rivers are also important for trade and tourism.

For centuries, people have learned to use the power of the current to generate energy. It is usually a waterwheel in a mill that turns the might of the river into power for industry. Such a waterwheel continues to work at the National Wool Museum in Dre-fach Felindre, Carmarthenshire.

River water irrigating crops

When Welsh people emigrated to establish a colony in Patagonia, they found that the land of the Camwy valley was dry and infertile. However, a young man named E. J. Williams set about planning a network of canals and ditches. Each farmer was responsible for opening a channel to direct water to his own land. They managed to grow wheat on the barren lands – this is a photo of the Welsh harvesting the crop at Drofa Gabets in 1905.

Drought as a result of climate change

The river Po in Italy is the country's longest river (652km). It is usually in full flow, carrying waters from the uplands in the mountains of the Alps. This enables farmers to grow all kinds of abundant crops on the plains of northern Italy.

In 2022, the Po Valley experienced the worst drought in 70 years, following three years of low rainfall and warmer temperatures. Electric power stations were shut down and the use of pipes for irrigation was forbidden during the day as the water **evaporated** before reaching the ground.

During the summer of 2022, the source of the river Thames in England dried up for the first time ever. This led to discussions about diverting water from Wales to the river Thames to supply the densely populated area of London and south-east England in times of great drought. One such scheme was to transfer water from the Lake Vyrnwy reservoir at Powys along the river Severn, and then via a new pipeline or restored canals to the river Thames. Could rain perhaps be considered the 'oil of Wales' in the future, bringing significant income to the country?

Lake Vyrnwy Dam, Llanwddyn, Powys

Reservoirs and flood management

Although **floods** bring fertile deposits to fields, in some valleys this can be dangerous to animals and people. Reservoirs are built in the upper reaches of some rivers to manage flooding – such as Llyn Brianne (1973) in the upper reaches of the river Tywi, and Llyn Clywedog on the river Severn.

20% of the world's dams are in China, and nearly half are used to irrigate low-lying lands. The Three Gorges Dam is the world's largest hydroelectric power station – but 4 million people had to leave their homes in order to build it.

Three Gorges Dam, China

Borders and bridges

Rivers separating countries

In South America, more kilometres of international borders mirror the courses of rivers than anywhere else in the world. Rivers separating countries include:

Amazonas: Colombia, Peru and Brazil
Iguazu: Argentina and Brazil
Bermejo: Argentina and Bolivia
Catatumbo: Colombia and Venezuela
Paragua: Brazil and Paraguay
Paraná: Argentina and Paraguay
Uruguay: Argentina and Uruguay and Brazil

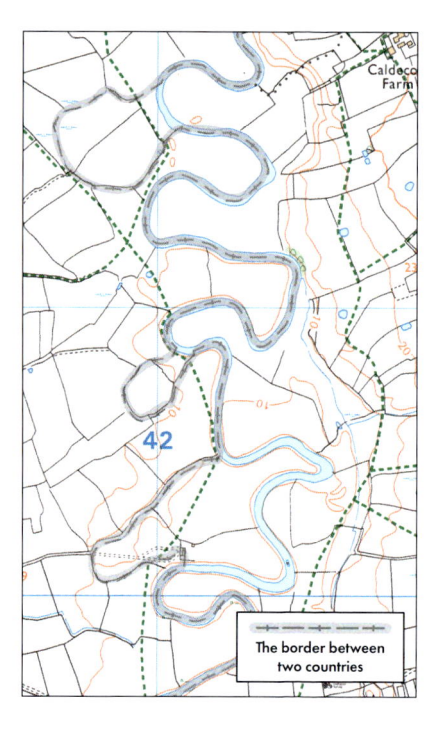

The border between two countries

Various rivers also mark the border between England and Wales, including the rivers Dee, Vyrnwy, Teme, Monnow and Wye. The Ordnance Survey map above shows a section of the river Dee to the east of Wrexham. You can see that the Welsh border sometimes follows the present course of the river, but diverges at other times. After reading the last few pages, can you perhaps explain why?

Paying to cross the border

Two bridges now cross the Severn estuary between England and Wales. Until 17 December 2018, all vehicles had to pay a toll for crossing these bridges. As the bridges were on the border between England and Wales, it meant that people had to pay to travel from one country to another. The tolls were then abolished and the toll gates demolished, following an agreement between the Welsh Government and the UK Government. 25 million journeys are now made over the bridges each year.

Fords, causeways and bridges

The oldest way to cross a river was to look for a convenient and safe place where there was shallow water and a firm riverbed. Such places are called fords.

If the river crossing was a footpath, stones could be placed on the riverbed to protrude above the water when there were no floods. That enabled walkers to leap from one stone to the next without getting their feet wet. Such crossings are called causeways.

Then, bridges began to be built. The earliest bridges may have been wooden footbridges.

A ford on the river Wye

A causeway across the river Braint, Anglesey

A bridge across the river Wye between England and Wales at Chepstow

Pontcysyllte **aqueduct**, near Acrefair, which carries the Llangollen **Canal** across the Dee Valley. It is one of the UNESCO World Heritage Sites in Wales

Some bridges in Wales

Pont Fawr at Llanrwst was built in 1636. Half the cost was paid by Caernarfonshire and the other half by Denbighshire. Both counties realised the importance of having a bridge between the two sides of the river and between the two counties. It was instrumental in establishing Llanrwst as one of north Wales's leading market towns – the 8th largest town in Wales in the 18C.

There are also:
- railway bridges
- canal bridges
- bridges that have become visitor attractions, demonstrating the craft and ability of the engineers who built them.

The coast

Do rising sea levels threaten Wales?

Storms have left extensive damage on the Welsh coast during this century. Aberystwyth has been hit many times.

- There is more damage on the Welsh coast due to rising sea levels.
- Across the world, sea levels have risen 8–9 inches (21–24 centimetres) since 1880.

Why are sea levels rising?

- As the ice melts in the poles and the sea warms and swells, experts expect sea levels to rise again – as much as 12 inches (30 cm) by 2050.

Improving defences in Rhos-on-Sea

The coastal road and parts of 'Afon Ganol', in the old Conwy valley near Rhos-on-Sea, are below sea level. In summer 2023, improvements were made to the defences to protect this area from the impact of storms and high waves as the sea level rises.

Will this be the first village lost to the sea?

Experts believe Fairbourne in Meirionnydd will be the first village in Wales to be submerged if sea levels continue to rise.

The county council is considering removing everyone from the village by 2050 ...

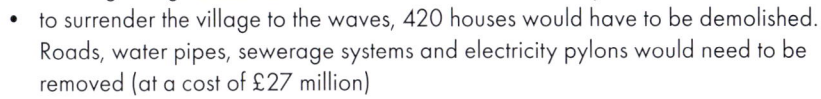

A plaque to mark the construction of a sea wall to protect Fairbourne in 1981 – but the sea level is now higher than the sea wall.

- about 850 live there
- building a huge **sea wall** would be unattractive and costly (around £115 million)
- to surrender the village to the waves, 420 houses would have to be demolished. Roads, water pipes, sewerage systems and electricity pylons would need to be removed (at a cost of £27 million)
- some are keen to save the village by building cheaper defences.

Fairbourne holiday camp and village built on a **salt marsh** at the mouth of the river Mawddach. The beach is 2 miles/3 km long. The land is between 2 and 2.5 metres above the sea, which is lower than Aberystwyth's prom!

Concrete tetrapods

Defences?

Above Fairbourne beach, remains of World War II defences can be seen, and beyond them, the sea wall built in 1981. Will the construction of a concrete tetrapod bank mark the final effort to save the village, or will the people of Fairbourne be the United Kingdom's first climate refugees?

What kind of coastline does Wales have?

The coastline is the border between land and sea, and it is a boundary that is constantly changing. The sea surrounds Wales to the north, west and south, and the coastline covers 1,680 miles / 2,688 km.

The coastline contains various types of cynefin, such as:
- beaches and inlets
- vast sand dunes
- cliffs and rocky headlands
- estuaries and salt marshes
- islands
- seaside towns and ports.

Wales has a footpath along its coastline, called the Wales Coast Path. The route can be walked from the Dee estuary in the north-east to Chepstow in the south-east – a distance of 870 miles / 1,392 km. The path was opened in 2012.

Llwybr Arfordir Cymru
Wales Coast Path

The Llŷn Peninsula, a plateau of volcanic rocks, with high cliffs and sandy coves

Anglesey, the largest island in Wales

Penygogarth, a headland of limestone cliffs

The broad Dee estuary which is an important bird sanctuary

Irish Sea

Liverpool Bay

Caernarfon Bay

The sand dunes of Morfa Harlech

Sand spits of the Mawddach and Dyfi estuaries on the coast of the bay

Cardigan Bay

The high and rugged cliffs of north Pembrokeshire

St. David's Head and Ramsey Island nature reserve

The ria of Milford Haven

Carmarthen Bay

Northern Gower and Pembrey salt marshes

Bristol Channel

The Severn estuary, which has one of the largest tidal ranges in the world

The broad beaches of Pendine and Cefn Sidan

Glamorgan's heritage coast, cliffs with remains from the Triassic and Jurassic periods

Y Ro Wen sand spit

The view southwards along the sand spit of Y Ro Wen with the estuary of the river Mawddach in the foreground.

Sand spits have formed in the estuaries of the rivers Dyfi, Mawddach and Dwyryd in northern Cardigan Bay. The sand spit of Y Ro Wen, pictured, has developed as eroded deposits from the cliffs to the south are transported northwards by currents known as longshore drift. These are then deposited in the mouth of the river Mawddach. Over a long period of time, the river has deposited its load in the sheltered waters behind the sand spit, where Fairbourne village stands today.

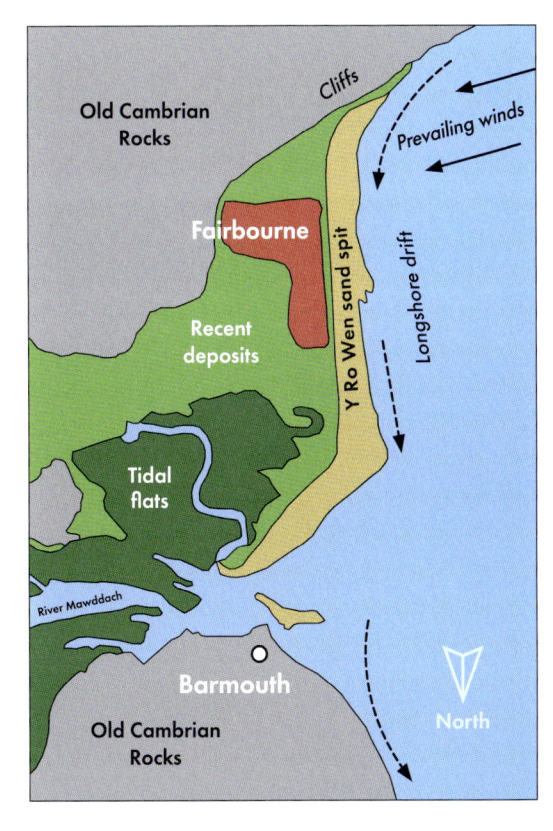

Green Bridge of Wales

Geology, and especially the hardness of rocks, has a great impact on the shape of the coast. Notice the layers in the cliff – these are sedimentary rocks.

The Green Bridge of Wales is located in south Pembrokeshire, where there are carboniferous limestone cliffs. Over time, storms have caused sea waves to hurl pebbles at the cliffs, eroding the weakest parts of the surface and creating caves (1). This process is called corrasion, and corrosion, which is chemical erosion, takes place here as sea water dissolves the limestone. Caves on headlands can sometimes merge together to create an arch (2). When the roof of the arch falls, a stack will form (3). Sometimes this stack is further eroded to form a stump (4).

Carreg Bica, Llangrannog – a stack that still stands. Perhaps it once supported a natural arch.

How does the sea erode?

We have seen that the Welsh coast contains a great variety of landforms, including the Green Bridge of Wales and the sand spit of Y Ro Wen.

Some of the landforms have been created by the sea eroding and others by the sea deopsiting

Erosion on the coastline is caused by the force of the waves. In stormy weather, and in high winds, the waves will have enough force to throw stones or pebbles at the cliff, releasing chunks of rock. This process is called corrasion.

The base of the cliff will be eroded to create a wave-cut notch that will cause the rocks above to fall into the sea in due course.

Sometimes, the strength of the waves themselves will cause erosion while some rocks, such as chalk and limestone, will dissolve in the saltwater.

Waves will then remove eroded material from the cliffs and transport it along the coast. This material can be deposited elsewhere to form pebble or sand beaches.

Erosion usually occurs on headlands, and deposition occurs in the bays, inlets and estuaries.

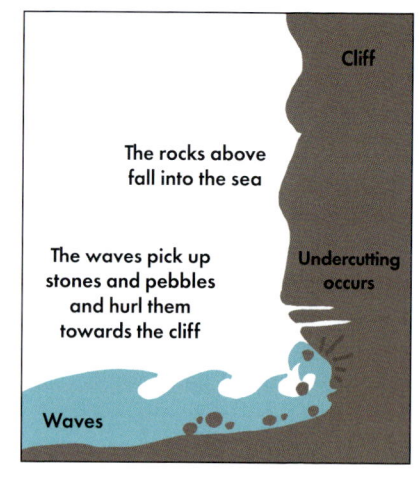

Cliffs near Llanrhystud in Ceredigion

How does the sea deposit?

The movement of deposits along the coastline is known as longshore drift. Longshore drift moves in the same direction as the prevailing winds. This is the direction the winds blows most often.

The waves usually reach the beach (the swash) at an angle, depending on the wind direction. The water then returns to the sea in a straight line (the backwash) due to gravity. This means that deposits move along the beach in the same direction as the winds, from **A** to **D** in the diagram. You can follow the trail of one small stone from **A** to **B**, **C** and **D**.

In Cardigan bay, longshore drift will move from south to north as the prevailing winds come from the south-west (see the map of Wales).

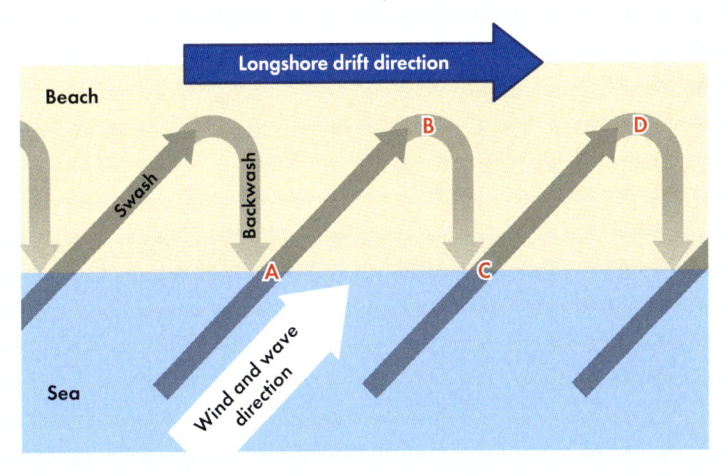

Deposition can change the form of the coastline fairly quickly. Harlech castle, built in the late 13C, was once much closer to the coast than it is now. A long staircase extends down from the castle so that ships could deliver goods to the castle. Due to deposition by the sea and other processes, the castle is now about half a mile from the sea, as seen in the photo.

Harlech Castle looking westwards towards Cardigan Bay

The ebb and flow of the tide

The tide is a natural, rapid change experienced on the coast. Two flood tides and two ebb tides (low tides) occur every day.

These tides are caused by the force of gravity between the Earth, Moon and Sun.

Gravity causes the water to surge in the part of the Earth facing the Moon and the part facing away from the Moon.

High tides occur in the light blue areas on the diagram. As the Earth rotates, everywhere will experience a high tide twice every 24 hours.

Water will be drawn to create tides on the Welsh coast from the direction of the Atlantic Ocean in the south-west. The tide reaches Wales through the Celtic Sea, and through the gap between Cornwall and Ireland, where it moves north along the coast. Therefore, Pembrokeshire's high tides occur more than an hour and a half before the high tides of the Llŷn Peninsula. This flood tide meets another tide that enters through the gap between Northern Ireland and Scotland.

- Every day, the Menai Strait has four high tides rather than two. There will be two high waters coming from the direction of Caernarfon and two from the direction of Conwy. A whirlpool can be found in the middle of the Menai Strait, between the two bridges. Here, the water swirls dangerously as different currents meet.
- Between several Welsh islands and the mainland, sounds of seawater with dangerous currents can be found. These are created by the ebb and flow of the tides.
- The Bristol Channel has the second-largest tidal range in the world. The tidal range is the difference between the low and high tides.

The tide rushing through the sound between Ramsey Island and the mainland in Pembrokeshire

People who walk on beaches every day will notice that the patterns in the sand look different each time.

The wind also causes rapid changes on the coast, whipping up sand and creating dunes. That is what threatens to bury the church of Llandanwg, near Harlech.

Trade and ports

Having a suitable coastline for merchant ships is important to the development of a country and its economy. From this map, it is evident that the coast of France and Brittany has:
- enough sheltered inlets to create safe ports, for example Brest, Nantes, Bordeaux, Cherbourg, Calais and Marseilles
- wide rivers in low valleys so that smaller vessels can transport goods from the port along the estuary to towns in the interior of the country, for example along the Loire, Seine, Rhône and Garonne rivers
- coastlines on various seas, including the English Channel, the Atlantic Ocean and the Mediterranean Sea. This allows France to trade in many directions – northwards to England, Ireland and Wales; westwards to North and South America, and southwards to Mediterranean countries.

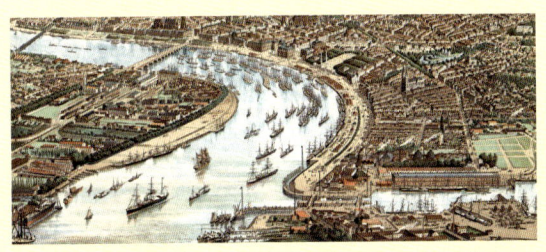

Bordeaux Harbour in 1899 – there may be ships carrying Welsh slate or coal in this picture

Some of the advantages of the French coast can be found on the Welsh coast as well:

- Wales is in western Europe, open to connections across the sea with the west of the continent and the rest of the world. Wales does not border on more enclosed seas like the Baltic Sea or the Mediterranean Sea
- there are a number of sheltered areas to develop harbours, for example Holyhead, Porthmadog, Milford Haven, Swansea, Cardiff and Newport
- Wales does not have many rivers to transport goods far inland, but nowhere is further than 50 miles from the sea.

The sea surrounds Wales on three sides as well

Many Welsh quarries were close to the coast and used ships to transport the heavy loads. There used to be a busy quay here in Porth-gain, Pembrokeshire. Stone to build roads and slate was exported from the quarries nearby. Later, a brickworks was also built there.

Human effort
Defences

There is evidence along the Welsh coastline of human effort to protect the land from erosion by the waves and wind. They include:

- installing wood, concrete or stone groynes on beaches
- building barrages to prevent flooding and to recover land from the sea
- planting trees and marram grass that take root and protect sand dunes from the wind.

Wooden groynes prevent longshore drift and protect sand on the beach at Machroes, near Abersoch

The coastline at Tremadog Bay in Gwynedd has changed a lot in the last two centuries. A gentleman named William Alexander Madocks built a number of barrages to reclaim land from the sea and create a safe route across the estuary of the river Glaslyn. The largest of these barrages is the 'Cob', completed in 1811. Following the construction of the sea wall, the port and town of Porthmadog developed.

The Cob sluice-gates continue to keep the sea out of Traeth Mawr, protecting the town and thousands of acres of agricultural land.

The Cob sea wall, Porthmadog

Natural Resources Wales is working to restore and maintain Wales's sand dunes. The dunes are a cynefin brimming with life, including plants, butterflies, birds and a wide variety of insects.

Merthyr Mawr sand dunes, near Bridgend

Impact of global warming

Sea level change

Due to global warming, the ice in the poles is melting. This is causing sea levels to rise by almost 4mm a year, on average, worldwide.

At very low tide, the remains of old forests emerge on the Welsh coast. These are found in Ceredigion and Trearddur Bay on Anglesey, and they provide evidence that sea levels have risen. The legend of Cantre'r Gwaelod, about the drowning of Maes Gwyddno, is one of Wales's most famous tales. Do these features suggest that it is based on some truth?

In 1607 more than 2,000 people lost their lives in flooding along the banks of the Bristol Channel. Records show the flooding stretched from Carmarthenshire up to Gwent, and the Cardiff area was one of the worst hit.

The road has fallen into the sea following erosion in Skipsea, East Yorkshire

The sea to this day continues to threaten coastal dwellers, eroding soft cliffs and beaches, and flooding lowlands. One village that suffers from this is Skipsea on the east coast of England.

As a result of erosion by the waves, the campsite at the top of the cliff is losing up to 10 caravan pitches a year. This situation is common along the east coast of England where there are cliffs of soft, glacial boulder clay, which erode very quickly.

Borth sunken forest, Ceredigion

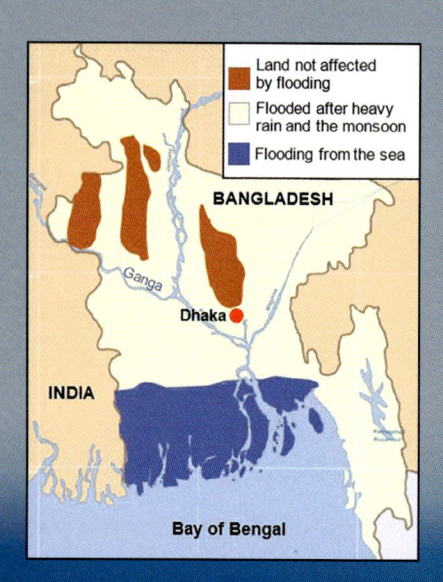

Floods and destruction

Flooding from the sea is a major problem for countries like Bangladesh in the north of the Bay of Bengal. It is an area of low-lying land, where many rivers flow into the sea through the delta of the river Ganga. It is one of the countries with the highest population density in the world. The people are used to living with seasonal floods. But because sea levels are rising, the flooding lasts longer. As a result,

267 million people in the world live on land that is lower than 2m above sea level. If sea levels rise a further 1m by the year 2100, millions of people will face devastation. 62% of these lands are in the tropics, and some of the world's poorest countries are located here.

South Tarawa, where the capital of Kiribati is located

saltwater damages the lands and crops grown there.

The Republic of Kiribati is a series of islands only a few metres above sea level. The islands are in the Pacific Ocean, north-east of Australia. Residents are concerned that no one will be able to live there by the end of the century if sea levels continue to rise.

Some residents have already migrated from the country, while others are trying to protect their lands and homes with higher embankments or by moving further away from the sea. But the sea continues to threaten, submerging the land, polluting freshwater stores, killing crops and damaging homes. Kiribati may be the first country in the world to be submerged by the waves due to climate change.

Weather and climate

The weather keeps changing, and it is a frequent topic of conversation. What is the weather like – hot or cold, wet or dry, calm or windy? We have many sayings about the weather.

Some sayings about the weather in Wales:
Rainbow in the morning gives you fair warning
Clear moon, frost soon

So what is climate?
The climate is the average weather pattern over a long period of time – usually 30 years or more. The weather is what happens on a day-to-day basis.

How is the weather affecting us?
The weather has an impact on how we travel:
- flooding can impede transport after heavy rains
- ice makes roads dangerous
- if there is too much wind, traffic will be controlled on high bridges such as the Severn Bridge or the Britannia Bridge across the Menai Strait.

The impact of the weather is mostly felt by those working outdoors – farmers, for example. Farm work will change from season to season due to the impact of the weather on land, animals and growth of the crops.

Measuring and forecasting the weather

Weather measuring stations have been installed all over Wales as the weather varies from place to place. Some schools also have weather stations.

The photo above shows a weather station run by the Met Office. It uses different tools to gather information.

Weather stations collect information about the current weather. The information is stored because keeping a record of the weather is important to determine whether climate patterns are changing.

The tools used are:

- **rain gauge** to measure precipitation (rain, snow, sleet, hail)

- **thermometer** to measure temperature – including highest and lowest temperatures

- **windvane** and **anemometer** to indicate wind direction and strength

- **barometer** to measure air pressure

- **sunshine recorder** to measure how sunny/cloudy it is

Information will also be sent to Wales from other weather stations – some located on ships at sea, some high up in the atmosphere, and some even in space. Meteorologists study the clouds, atmosphere, wind and temperature to try to predict what the weather will look like.

After studying all the information, we get weather forecasts on our mobile phones, on computers, on radio and television, and in newspapers. This prepares us for the weather ahead. Perhaps more importantly, it prepares emergency services to respond to dangers caused by the weather.

Atmosphere

The atmosphere, which is the covering of gases that surrounds the globe, extends 50km above the Earth. Aeroplanes fly at an altitude of about 15km above the Earth.

Precipitation

Precipitation occurs when drops of rain in a cloud become too heavy and fall to the ground in the form of rain, snow or hail. This often happens when water vapour in warm air rises and cools. This will cause it to condense, turning into droplets of water that then fall as precipitation.

Relief rainfall

Mountains cause air to rise as winds move over them. The air will then cool, condense, and precipitation will occur. This is clearly seen when the prevailing winds – which are winds blowing most frequently – cross the mountains of north Wales from the south-west.

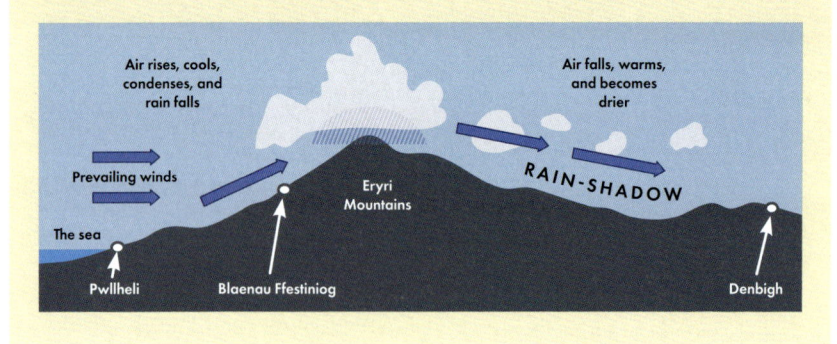

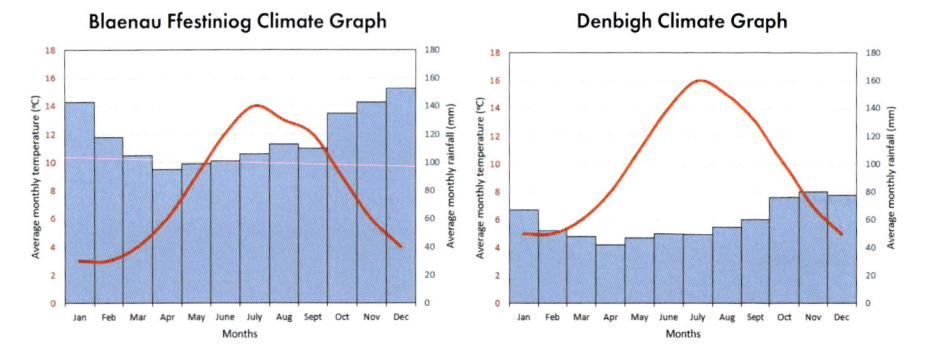

Convectional rainfall

The Sun heats the Earth causing moisture to evaporate and rise. As this happens, the air cools, condenses and forms tall cumulus clouds. As the drops of water form, they fall as heavy showers of rain – sometimes during thunderstorms. This can happen in Wales, but it is more common in tropical countries.

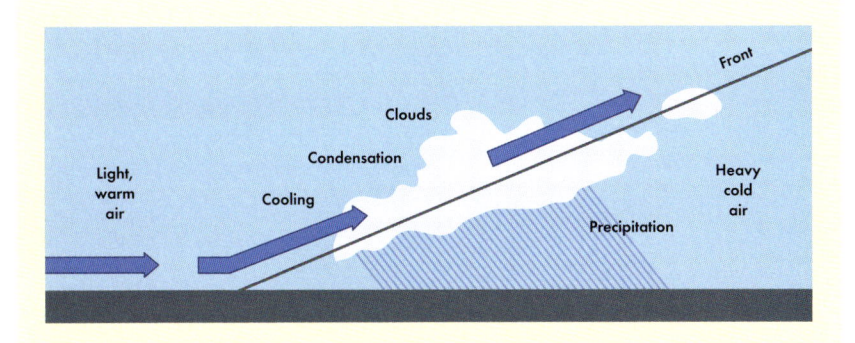

Frontal rainfall

This is the most common type of rainfall in Wales. It will occur along fronts, as moist air rises, cools, condenses and forms clouds, leading to precipitation.

Recording the rainfall

In late April 2022, Phil Thomas from Penrhyndeudraeth climbed up Cadair Idris to measure the month's rainfall for the final time. What was remarkable was that he had done this voluntarily for exactly 20 years. The rain gauge on Cadair Idris, a copper bottle, is large enough to hold a month's worth of rainfall.

Rainfall is vital to the nature reserve on Cadair Idris (it gets 200 days of rain every year). Rainfall supports gorges, forests and various rare mosses. During his visits, Phil kept an eye out for litter and erosion as well. Although he has retired, the work continues.

Airmass

The air or airmass moving over the country has a major influence on the weather. An airmass is a body of air that contains similar characteristics, for example humidity and temperature. Because of Wales's location, our weather is influenced by a number of different airmasses.

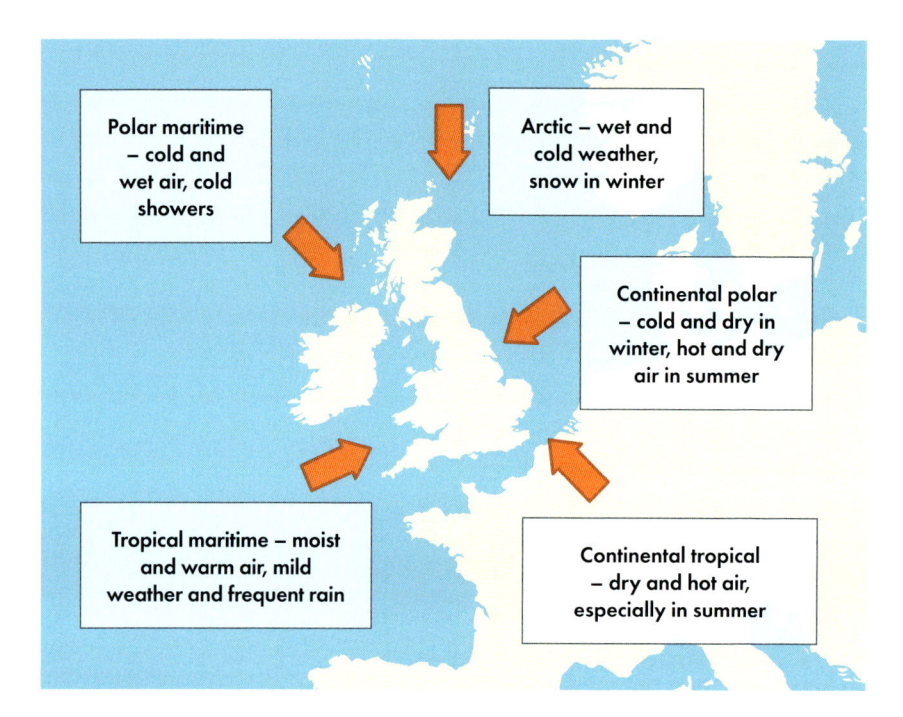

Polar maritime – cold and wet air, cold showers

Arctic – wet and cold weather, snow in winter

Continental polar – cold and dry in winter, hot and dry air in summer

Tropical maritime – moist and warm air, mild weather and frequent rain

Continental tropical – dry and hot air, especially in summer

The airmasses bring different weather in summer and winter. Airmasses from the north (Arctic and polar airmasses) bring cold weather, and those from the south (tropical) bring warmer weather. Airmasses that have travelled over the sea (maritime) are more humid than those that have travelled over land (continental).

Depressions and anticyclones

Air pressure is another major influence on our weather. The air around us has a weight that creates pressure on the ground. When warm, light air rises from the ground, the pressure will be low. This is called a depression. But when cold air sinks towards the ground, the pressure will be high. A high pressure system is called an anticyclone.

It is this difference in air pressure that creates wind. When there is a depression over Wales, we get volatile and rainy weather. But if there is an anticyclone over the country, the weather will be stable – hot and dry in summer, cold and dry in winter.

Warm fronts and cold fronts

Depressions moving over Wales from west to east contain fronts where different airmasses meet. As the air of a warm airmass rises over the heavier air of a cold airmass, it will cool, condense, and form clouds. Rain will then fall. The process is similar to what happens during convectional rainfall. Along the fronts, therefore, the weather is unsettled. There will be changes in temperature, strong winds and rainfall.

Warm front

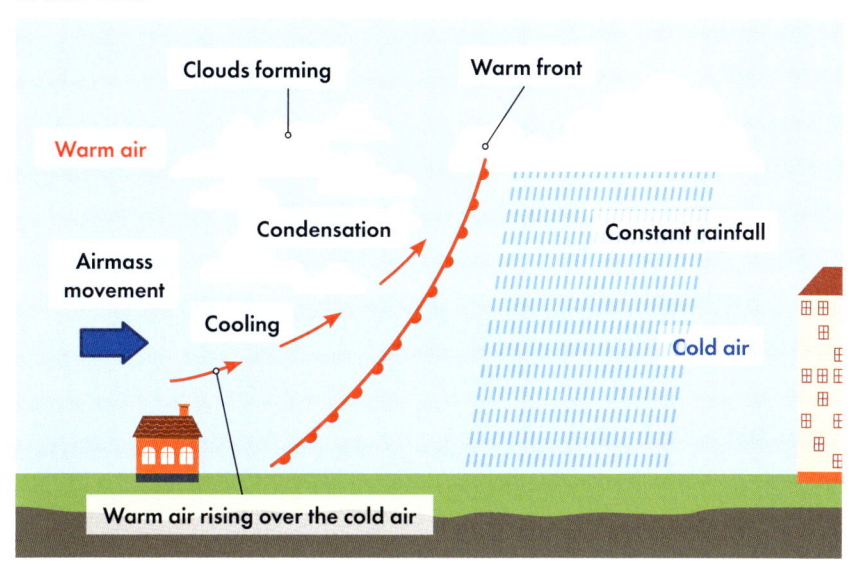

Cold front

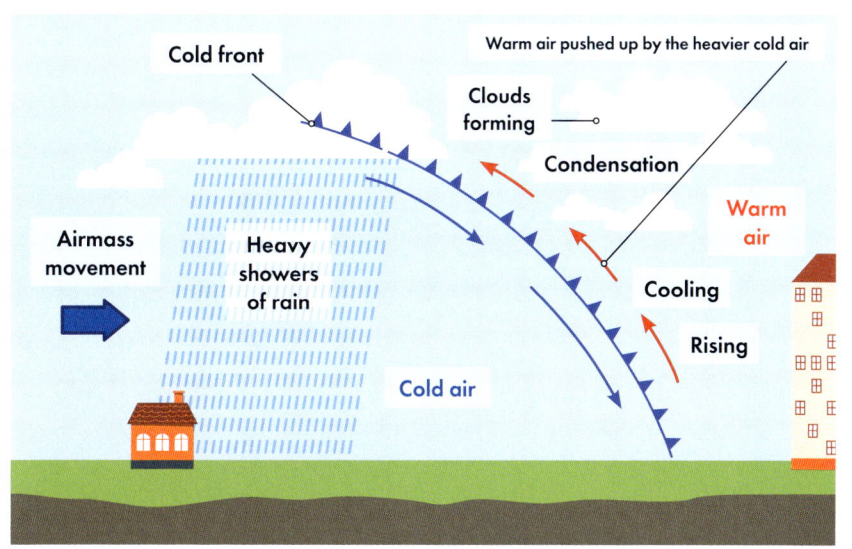

A depression in a photo and on a weather map

Low pressure weather systems are called depressions.

In this satellite photo, clouds are seen rotating around the depression.

On a weather map, the location of the depression is indicated by the pattern of isobars, which are lines connecting places that share the same pressure. Pressure is measured in millibars, and you can see that the centre of the depression here measures 976 millibars. The location of the warm fronts (red) and cold fronts (blue) is shown, where clouds will cause rain to fall. The isobars in depressions are fairly close together, so there will be strong winds.

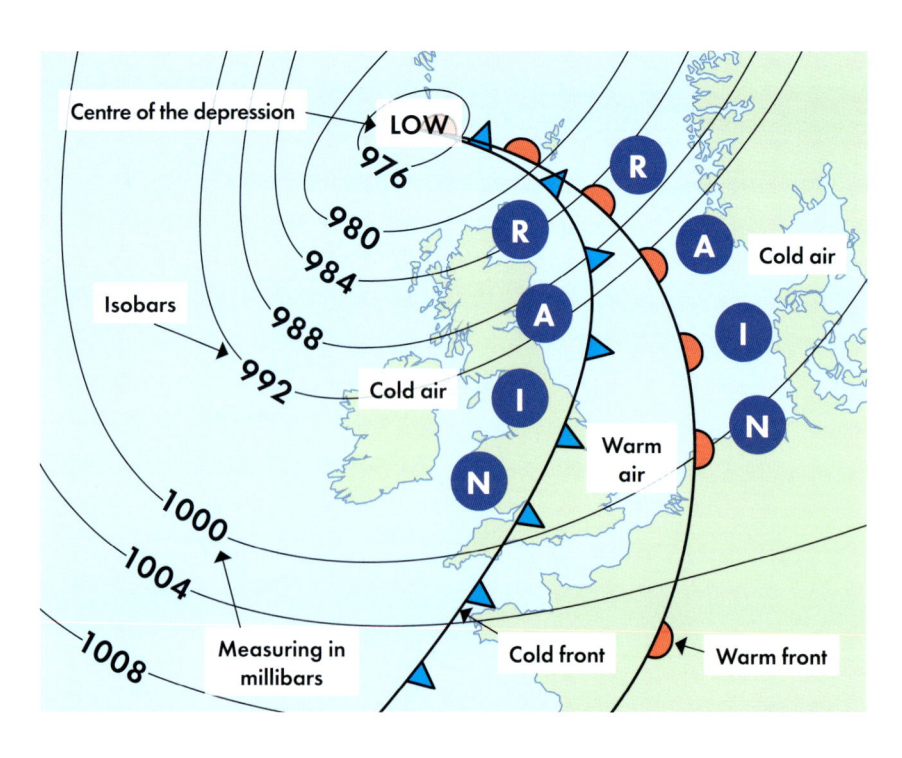

An anticyclone in a photo and on a weather map

High pressure weather systems are called anticyclones. Anticyclones form when cold air in the atmosphere sinks towards the ground, causing high pressure.

The isobars in anticyclones will show the highest measurements in the centre. Note that the isobars are further apart, so the wind will not be as strong. In summer, the weather will be stable, dry and sunny. In winter the weather will be very cold and dry.

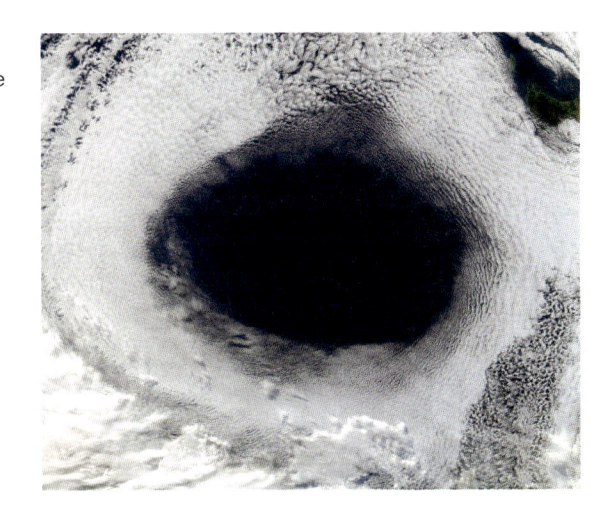

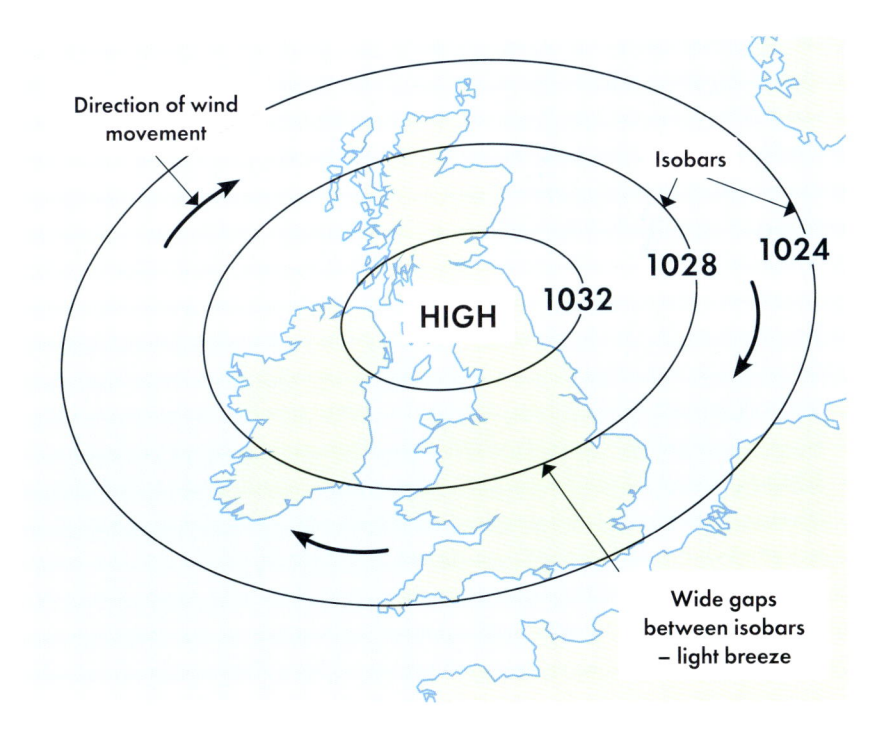

Direction of wind movement

Isobars

1028 1024

HIGH 1032

Wide gaps between isobars – light breeze

How does location impact the weather and climate?

1. Distance from the Equator
The Equator is the latitude line around the centre of the world. The places on Earth closest to the Equator are usually the warmest places. This is because the Sun shines directly above the centre of the world all year round. The climate here is tropical – a hot climate. When moving away from the Equator, the shape of the Earth means that the Sun's rays are spread over a larger area, and so they do not heat that area to the same degree.

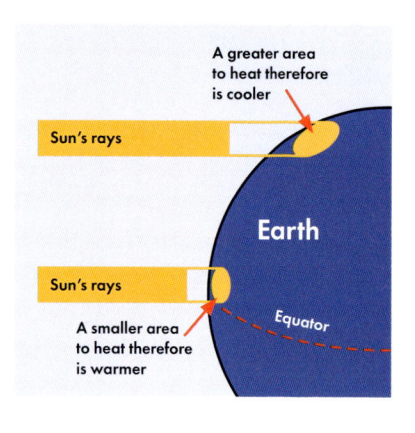

2. Land altitude
Altitude is measured above sea level. Altitude is important for the climate as air cools when it climbs higher – it cools at around 6 degrees per 1,000m. Therefore, the climate of a mountainous area is cooler than that of low-lying lands. A good example of this is Kilimanjaro mountain, which is near the Equator in Africa. Despite this, snow can be found on its summit all year round. This is due to its altitude – it is 5,895m above sea level.

3. Distance from the sea
The sea warms up more slowly than land. But it retains its heat longer. Therefore, the sea keeps the land nearest to it cooler in summer but slightly warmer in winter.

The **North Atlantic Drift**, which is a jet of warm water that forms part of the **Gulf Stream**, reaches the shores of Wales. The maritime climate keeps Wales from experiencing climate extremes compared to countries further from the sea.

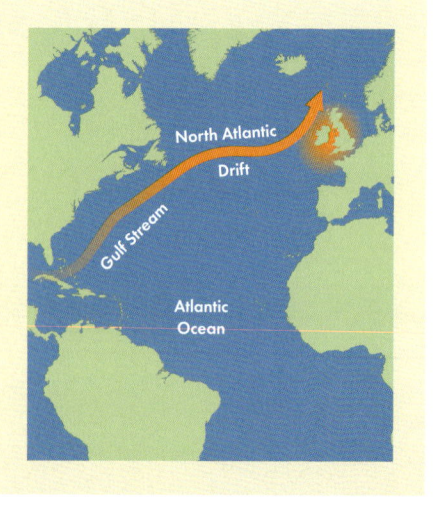

4. Wind
Wind direction also affects the climate. Wales's prevailing winds come from the south-west, which means they have crossed the Atlantic Ocean. The winds pick up moisture as they cross the ocean and bring a lot of rain to Wales. Wind direction is important for temperature. It can warm us in winter and cool us down in summer.

The world's climate regions

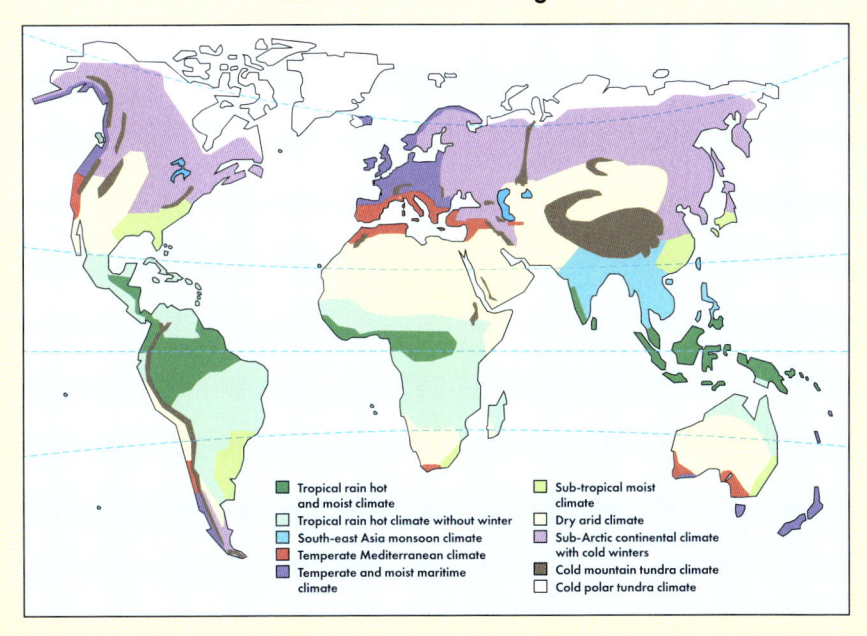

Tropical rain hot and moist climate
Tropical rain hot climate without winter
South-east Asia monsoon climate
Temperate Mediterranean climate
Temperate and moist maritime climate
Sub-tropical moist climate
Dry arid climate
Sub-Arctic continental climate with cold winters
Cold mountain tundra climate
Cold polar tundra climate

The main types of climate in the world

Hot climate – hot, tropical climates are found in the regions close to the Equator. Some regions will be hot and wet (areas of tropical forests) and other regions hot and dry (areas of desert).

Temperate climate – areas like Wales have this type of climate. This is the climate between the tropics and the poles. Within this area, however, there is great variation in weather conditions. In the Mediterranean region, summers are hot and dry while the winters are mild, similar to south Australia and to California in north America. As Wales is in the higher latitudes, it is colder and wetter here.

Continental climate – areas far from the sea. The climate is drier here, with very hot summers and very cold winters.

Polar climate – cold all year round. These are the areas of the Arctic Circle in the North Pole and the Antarctic Circle in the South Pole.

Where do the people of Wales live?

Population

The population of Wales and the World

The population is the number of people who live in a particular place. Every ten years, the UK Government conducts a census containing a number of questions for each household to answer.

The 2021 Census figures showed that the population of Wales was 3,107,494 – the highest total since official censuses began in 1801.

By November 2022, the population of the world was over 8,000,000,000 (8 billion).

The five countries with the largest populations in 2022

Population	Country
1,425,855,853	1. China
1,421,176,657	2. India
338,941,839	3. United States of America
276,231,354	4. Indonesia
237,723,284	5. Pakistan

Population of the United Kingdom and Wales in 2022	
67,603,541	The United Kingdom
3,107,500	Wales

China and India are way ahead in terms of total population. But India was set to become the world's most populous country after 2023.

The world's five most populous countries, together with the UK and Wales

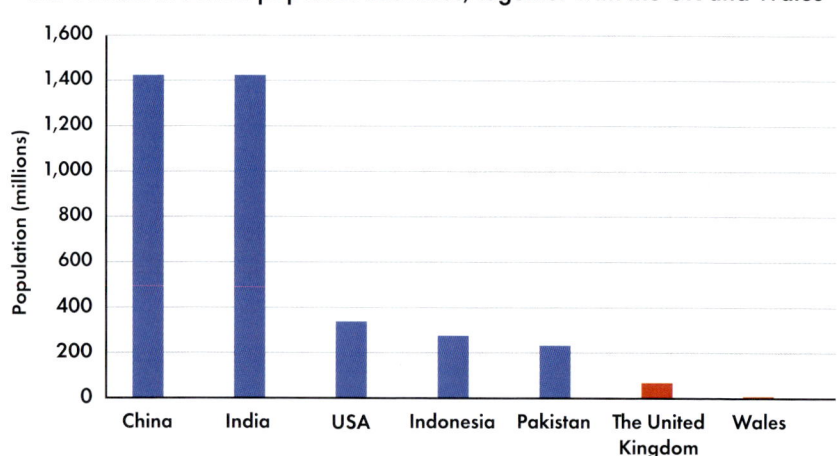

Country	Population (millions)
China	~1,400
India	~1,400
USA	~340
Indonesia	~280
Pakistan	~240
The United Kingdom	~68
Wales	~3

Population density

Population density is the number of people living within a particular unit of land. The population density of cities is high, but in the countryside the population density is low.

Cardiff local authority's population density is around 2,600 people per km². On average, only 98 people live in each km² on Anglesey.

The average population density across Wales is around 150 inhabitants per km². On average, in England 434 people live in each km².

There is an uneven pattern to the distribution of the population in Wales.

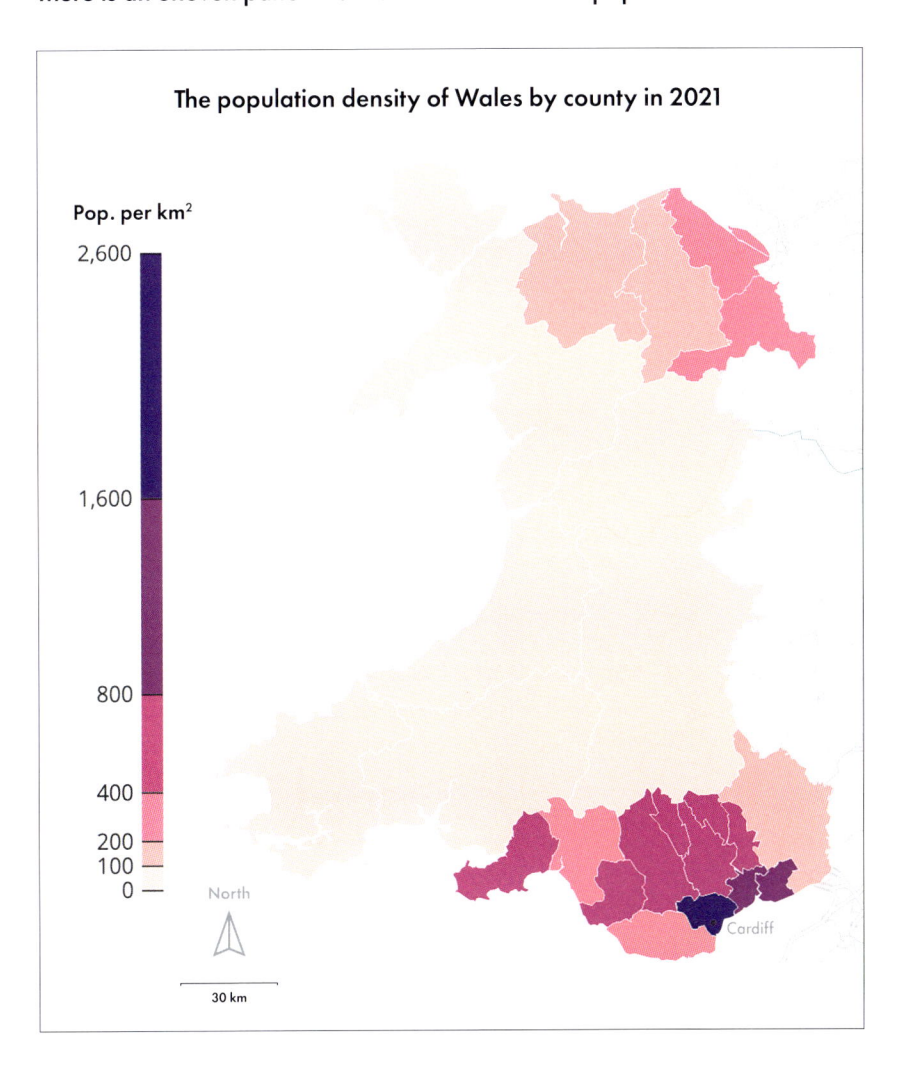

The population density of Wales by county in 2021

Population change

The population of countries, cities, towns and villages is constantly changing.

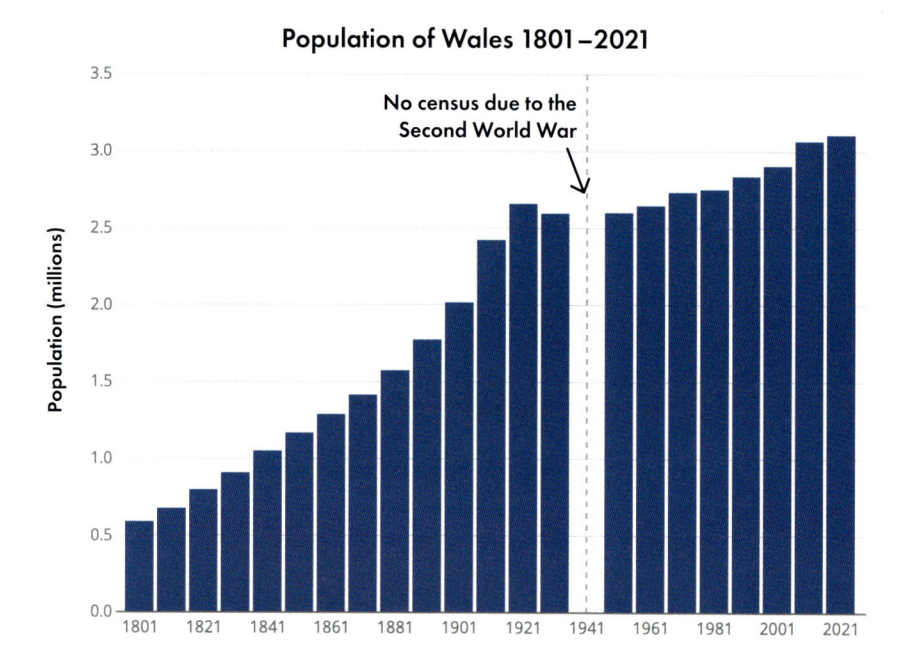

Population of Wales 1801–2021

No census due to the Second World War

The 2021 Census showed a 44,000 increase in the population of Wales since the 2011 census. Almost six times more people lived in Wales in 2021 compared to 1801.

The graph shows that the increase in population has been steady, apart from a decline between 1921 and 1961. During that period, many coalmines, steelworks and tin plants closed. Many people emigrated from Wales as a result.

The population of a country can change due to birth rates and death rates. These are the number of births and the number of deaths per 1,000 people.

If the birth rates are higher than the death rates, the population will increase naturally. But if more die than are born, the population will decrease.

Wales's birth rates have been falling since 2010. The table shows the natural change in Wales's population in 2021 and half a century ago in 1971. Look at the numbers of births and deaths in 1971 and 2021.

Year	Population	Number of births	Number of deaths	Increase or decrease	Birth rate (per 1,000)	Death rate (per 1,000)
1971	2,740,000	43,056	34,817	8,239	15.7	12.5
2021	3,107,494	28,781	36,141	-7,360	9.3	11.6

If the natural change indicates that there were more deaths than births in 2021, what is causing Wales's population to increase?

Population structure

Population pyramids are used to study population structure.

A population pyramid is a horizontal bar graph showing the population distribution by age and gender.

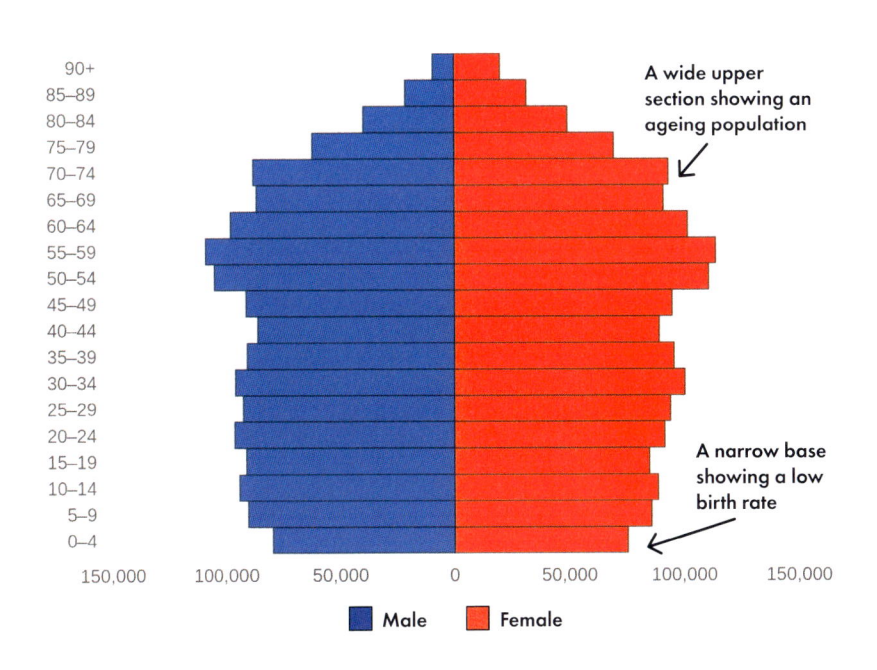

Where do people live?

Wales is a country of small towns. Towns with fewer than 10,000 people are considered rural.

However, in Wales there are:

- 3 major cities – Cardiff (348,000), Swansea (170,000) and Newport (131,000)

- 6 towns with between 57,000 and 40,000 people. From largest to smallest, these are Barry, Bridgend, Cwmbrân, the city of Wrexham, Llanelli and Neath

- 19 towns with over 15,000 people, including Merthyr Tydfil, Port Talbot, Rhyl, the city of Bangor and Carmarthen

- two very small cities, namely St Asaph (3,400) and St Davids (1,300).

Living in an urban area in Wales (Cardiff)

Wales's population distribution

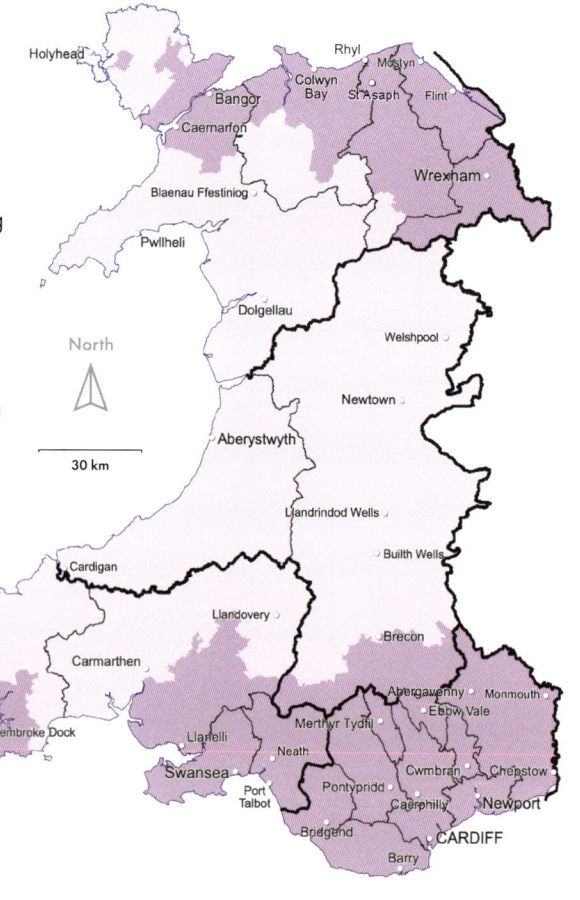

Rural-urban distribution
- Less sparse
- Most sparse

The map on page 96 shows that central and west Wales are more sparsely populated and more rural. The southern and northern areas are less rural. Not all rural areas are similar. Gradual change occurs when moving further from the largest towns and cities to the more remote areas of mid and west Wales.

In the rural areas near the large urban areas, there are people who have moved out into the countryside to live. They commute back into the towns to work. People living in these rural areas will travel to the urban centres to do their shopping and for entertainment.

Such areas include the Vale of Clwyd in the north and the Vale of Glamorgan in the south.

Moving further from the densely populated centres to the more remote areas of west and mid Wales, the population becomes sparser. Often, the population is older as young people leave to get education and find work. People come to these rural areas on holidays and to retire. With the development of broadband internet connection, more people can work in these rural areas despite living far from the big towns and cities.

Living in rural Wales

35% of the population of Wales lives in rural areas.

Like everywhere else, Brexit, the COVID-19 pandemic and climate change are creating problems. Despite this, new opportunities exist with many people managing to make a living in the countryside.

While the countryside can be a lovely place to live and raise a family, there are issues:

Hay harvest on a farm in Powys

- agriculture, the main industry, being under pressure
- a lack of economic opportunities in other fields
- a lack of transport and public services
- an increase in poverty, loneliness and anxiety
- ageing housing stock
- houses that are expensive to buy

Who lives in rural Wales today?

Here are two families who live in two different areas:

Williams family, Cerrigydrudion, Conwy

Family members:
4 children, parents; grandparents living in a cottage on the farm

Parents' work: Farming

Distance to school:
Primary: 1 mile; Secondary: 16 miles

How many cars does the family have?
3 cars and 1 pick-up

Where do you go shopping?
Bala, Ruthin, Denbigh and Llanrwst

What do you buy online?
Clothes, food, resources for the farm and poultry shed

Nearest railway station?
Chirk, 30 miles away

Leisure / social life?
Members of the local drama company and Côr Cerdd Dant Llangwm, supporting local activities / concerts, hiking

Holidays?
Visiting areas in Wales, the Eisteddfod, skiing

In what ways has your daily pattern changed in the last 20 years?
Although we still raise sheep and cattle, the new poultry shed provides the farm's regular income. Sustainable energy: solar panels, windmill, manure methane and the lake are used to heat the shed and house

Groe/Lansdown Davies Family, Banwy Valley, Montgomery

Family members:
4 children and parents

Parents' work:
Farming / working for the Mudiad Meithrin – working from home and across Wales; Grandfather also helps out on the farm

Distance to school:
Primary: 1 mile; Secondary: 1 mile

How many cars does the family have?
One car and one farming truck ... and several tractors!

Where do you go shopping?
Mostly to Welshpool

What do you buy online?
Too much!

Nearest railway station?
Welshpool (15 miles away)

Leisure / social life?
Cultural and arts events, going for walks, spending time with friends, reading

Holidays?
A week at the Eisteddfod, and a few weekends in various places

In what ways has your daily pattern changed in the last 20 years?
Relying too much on cars; Mum works full time; a mountain of farm-related paperwork and Government rules

Leaving and returning to the countryside

The 2021 Census figures show that the number of young people aged 20+ living in the Cardiff area is increasing.

Even so, research shows that people are leaving the city for the countryside, particularly in the 30–40 age group. This is common in cities around the world: between 2011 and 2021, 550,000 more citizens migrated from London than migrated to it. The same pattern is found in cities in the United States of America: New York, Miami, Chicago and Los Angeles.

Fidler family
– from Felinheli to Cardiff

Family members:
2 children and parents
Why move to the city?
In search of work – a lack of choice at home at the time
Work?
Mum: Head of Communications, Food Standards Agency
Dad: Project Manager in the National Health Service
How do parents travel to work?
Both work from home but sometimes go into the office
How do you stay fit?
Running, tennis, football, walking, netball
Nearest railway station?
Between two stations in the city!
City attractions?
Season ticket to watch the Cardiff City football team; a great museum; countless parks
Countryside attractions?
Walking and discovering country parks, for example Porthkerry Park in the Vale of Glamorgan, the Wales Coast Path, the mountains of Bannau Brycheiniog

Pryce family
– from Cardiff to Carmarthenshire

Family members:
2 children and parents
From where originally?
Mum – moved from Bow Street to Cardiff (1989–2005), then to St Clears
Dad – from Cardiff
Why move to the countryside?
To raise our sons in west Wales – an area similar to where Mum was brought up, with a garden and near the coast
Work?
Mum: Journalist
Dad: VT television engineer
How do the parents travel to work?
Mum: the car is essential; the office is 8 miles away but works from home 2 days a week
Dad: mainly car, train to get to Cardiff
How do you stay fit?
Electric bike, walking the dog
Nearest railway station?
The station at St Clears is due to reopen soon!
City attractions?
The clothes shops! (A number of Carmarthen's shops have closed)
Regular, public transport
Countryside attractions?
Tranquillity, beaches, great walking paths, a wide selection of Welsh language societies; cheaper parking, less traffic and queuing

Cities are getting bigger

More fields, forests and rural areas on the outskirts of cities are being used up for construction:
- there is a demand for modern, urban housing to replace unsuitable old terraced housing
- new industries and jobs attract migrant workers.

Industrial estates, business parks, bypasses, and new shopping centres are all causing urban areas to sprawl. This is currently evident in west Cardiff.

In 2022, Cardiff Council confirmed a 10-year development plan that would include building 4,000 houses on 60 sites around the city. 2,800 of these will be council housing. At the time, the Council had 8,000 applications on its waiting list for housing.

Pentref Rhostir, Llangyfelach – expansion of Swansea

A 'new community' is being developed over the next 15–20 years off junction 48 of the M4 motorway, near Swansea. The 280-acre site will include:

- 1,950 new homes, 15% of which are affordable housing
- a new primary school
- a shopping centre; a hospitality centre – food and drink
- medical and community centres, nursery

Artist's illustration of the Rhostir development

- 100 public open spaces: children's parks and recreation spaces
- a network of cycling and walking paths, and a link road approximately one mile long.

How the relief impacts on developments around urban areas

It is more practical to develop urban areas and transport links on low-lying, fairly flat land. In such places, it is possible to build:
- good roads, motorways, railway networks, airports
- industrial estates and factories that rely on goods that can be conveniently moved on the transport network
- housing estates for the workforce
- low-lying, flat land is often close to the coast. Urban developments benefit from being close to the coast.

Lack of housing for local people in rural areas

Since 2006, the provision of housing in rural areas has been a policy priority in Wales. Here are some obstacles that have emerged:
• a shortage of land with planning permission
• a lack of funds to build affordable housing
• a shortage of suitable social housing
• a lack of accurate waiting lists as the community loses hope that houses will become available.

Homelessness and hidden homelessness (e.g. living with one's parents/living in a caravan) have also been found to have increased significantly in rural areas. There are as many homeless households in rural areas as there are in the urban areas of Wales (although 80% of the population lives in urban areas).

By the end of 2021, house prices in some rural areas of Wales had increased significantly:
• immigrants selling their houses in towns or cities and retiring to the countryside
• immigrants moving to rural areas to 'work from home'
• immigrants buying a second home as a holiday home; 7.2% of Welsh homes were sold as holiday homes (the percentage across the UK is 1.7%) and as many as 6,000 of the housing stock in Gwynedd are not available as homes to local people.

Bro Machno – a rural area in the county of Conwy

Although this rural area has a strong community spirit, there is serious concern for the future of the community and what awaits the next generation. According to a 2021 survey of the 446 homes in the area:

• there were 88 second homes
• there were 61 self-catering holiday homes
• there were 17 empty houses
• 51.5% of the local population could not afford a home in the area.

Terraced houses in Bro Machno

Global facts – urban and rural areas

Most people in the world live in urban areas, and this trend is expected to increase. In 1950, only 30% of the world's population lived in urban areas. That is expected to double by 2030.

North America is the most urban continent in the world, with over 80% of residents living in urban areas. The least urban continent is Africa, with only just over 40% living in urban areas. However, there is great variation from country to country on this continent.

The fastest growing urban areas are in Asia and Africa. And the urban population of these continents is expected to triple by 2050.

Urban areas attract residents from the surrounding rural areas. Immigrants from other countries want to live in urban areas too.

The twenty cities with the largest number of immigrants in the world are: Beijing, Berlin, Brussels, Buenos Aires, Chicago, New York, Hong Kong, London, Los Angeles, Madrid, Moscow, Paris, Seoul, Shanghai, Singapore, Sydney, Tokyo, Toronto, Washington DC and Wien.

In most of the world's major cities, immigrants from other countries make up over 20% of the population.

In some countries, migration from rural to urban areas is responsible for over half the increase in the urban population. Countries where large numbers of people are moving from rural areas to urban areas include China, Thailand, Rwanda, Indonesia and Namibia.

The rapid development of the Pudong district, Shanghai, China over the last fifty years.

Comparing the Welsh population with that of Tibet

Most of Earth's land is 'rural', with a low population. Tibet, a country in the Himalayas, is one such example. 6.7 million people live there, but only 3 people per km^2.

Yamdrok Lake in central Tibet

Living in the Himalayas

Around 50 million people live in the largest mountainous area in the world – the Himalayas. The peaks rise from the lowlands of northern India and consist mainly of three countries: Nepal, Tibet and Bhutan.

Some people migrate there – in search of tranquillity and a more spiritual life in the wonderful landscape. Tourism has increased there over the past half century.

The natives have a culture of embracing and loving peace. They have adapted to living on the scarce resources of the high ground. They know a lot about medicine and architecture, but tourism creates:
- litter and air pollution
- a shortage of water.

Tibet's location

Technology in the cowshed

High-speed internet connections transforming rural areas

Opportunities in rural areas
As the Welsh Government takes responsibility for ensuring that 95% of Welsh dwellings and businesses have a high-speed internet connection, rural life has been transformed during this century:

- **ordering food and household goods:** food can be ordered from local shops or supermarkets that offer a delivery service. A number of local producers now offer a home delivery service as well

- **keeping in touch:** it is easier to talk – and see – friends and family, and to chat regularly

- **in emergencies:** it is possible to ask for practical help (e.g. from a plumber or a garage) and request a service.

- **working:** during the COVID-19 pandemic lockdowns, many workers commuting to urban offices realised they were able to do their jobs from their homes, using services and information shared on the web

- **promotion and marketing:** rural producers do not have to have a shop or an urban market to sell their goods or services. By using websites and social media, they can display and promote their products, and arrange for their sale and transportation.

Goods are delivered everywhere today

Wales Air Ambulance

Wales Air Ambulance is a voluntary charity costing £8 million a year to run. It has provided an extremely important service since 2001, at a time when the National Health Service ambulance service is under severe pressure.

The helicopters responded to nearly 2,000 calls in 2021.

This service – and efforts to install defibrillators across the countryside – has certainly given confidence to many people living in rural areas.

Wales Air Ambulance

The Health Service in Llŷn

The Llŷn Peninsula is an agricultural area in north-West Wales that attracts many tourists. It is a peninsula with many narrow, difficult roads for emergency vehicles.

Only three medical centres serve the west of the peninsula: Botwnnog, Pwllheli and Nefyn. The main hospital is at least 30 miles away in Bangor. The roads are narrow and traffic is heavy during the holiday season and at weekends. To get specialist treatments, people must travel over 100 miles to Liverpool or Stoke-on-Trent. Still, there is much demand for health services in this area:
- **farm accidents:** the agricultural industry is one of the most dangerous in terms of the number of human accidents
- **accidents at sea:** the sea fishing industry is the most dangerous of all when it comes to the loss of life. Many visitors will get into difficulties because they are unfamiliar with the tides, and the weather can change suddenly
- **road accidents:** heavy traffic on poor roads
- **ill health among older people:** there are many older people in the area and they often need emergency health services. The voluntary effort to install defibrillators in the area is a major step forward.

A defibrillator in Llwyndyrys, Llŷn

Migration

"Why do people migrate?"

Migration means moving to live to another area or country.

Migration to save lives

Some people are forced to migrate to flee famine, war or natural disasters such as floods.
- Most of those fleeing such dangers are women and children.
- Lives are often lost as people migrate. We constantly hear news about fragile boatloads of migrants being lost at sea. Those pictured above have just been rescued by a warship on the Mediterranean.

But not all migration is forced, and sometimes people choose to migrate. Some will also migrate and stay within the same country or area – internal migration. Migration can therefore take place over small distances, with people moving from village to village or from the countryside to town – rural-urban migration.

Migration from rural to urban areas and vice versa

Two farmhouses – South Tyrol, Italy (left) and the Vale of Glamorgan. The families have chosen to leave their homes in search of a better future in an urban area.

Other families choose to leave urban areas and hope to find a better life in the countryside, living closer to nature.

Terraced housing for miners' families in the Rhondda Valley

The people of Wales have migrated

As in many other countries, the people of Wales have moved for hundreds of years.

As the population increased, and as work became scarce, some people emigrated from one area of Wales to another to find employment. Usually, they moved from rural areas to industrial areas such as the coal valleys of south Wales, the slate areas of Gwynedd, and Flintshire. Others would move to new countries. Some were fleeing oppression and seeking religious freedom, the right to live their lives through the medium of Welsh, and the right to new land, property and opportunity. That is why people

Welsh people went to America to get the freedom to practice religion away from the Church – here is a Welsh name in 'Lower Meirion' Pennsylvania

emigrated from Wales to Patagonia in South America in 1865.

Other people emigrated from Wales to America to get freedom to practice their religion or to find work when life in the coal fields became hard.

Immigrants

Economic immigrants are attracted to other countries in search of work and a better life.

Immigrants who must leave, or sometimes flee, their countries because they do not feel safe there are called refugees or asylum seekers. These people have been forced to move and they are looking for support and somewhere safe to live.

A recent development is that people are forced to migrate due to the effects of extreme weather events – these are called climate refugees.

Migration on the continent of Africa

Economic migration

Most migration takes place within the continent as migrants move from country to country in search of work – they are called economic migrants. Countries such as South Africa, Côte d'Ivoire, and Nigeria attract a lot of such migrants. Therefore, 80% of Africa's migrants do not leave the continent.

Climate change

Natural disasters, such as prolonged droughts, heavy storms and floods, contribute to increased migration. In the last ten years 2.5 million people in Africa have been forced to migrate by such natural disasters.

Climate change will force more people to migrate. The steady rise in world temperatures due to climate change means that it will not be possible to live in parts of Africa in the future. Water shortages, extreme heat and illnesses are factors that cause people to move.

Violence and oppression

In 2023, there was an alarming increase in violence by armed groups in the Democratic Republic of Congo. 5.8 million people were forced to flee in the east of the country. They are now living in camps and in need of humanitarian aid.

More than a million people from the Democratic Republic of Congo are refugees or asylum seekers in the countries that it borders. These include Uganda, Burundi, Tanzania, Rwanda, Zambia, Congo and Angola.

The cities on the continent's coast are growing rapidly – Lagos, Luanda, Dar es Salaam, Alexandria, Abidjan, Cape Town and Casablanca. If sea levels rise, it could create further problems for these cities in the future.

Kiwanja refugee camp on the border between the Democratic Republic of Congo and Uganda and Rwanda

Immigration to Wales

People have been moving into Wales too. In the past, seeking a better future for their families was people's main reason for coming to Wales:
- Irish people fleeing starvation arriving in Cardiff docks
- Spanish and Basque people fleeing Spanish Fascists
- Italians spotting an opportunity to open cafes in south Wales
- Somalis working on Cardiff coal ships.

Italian café in one of the coal valleys

Refugees to Wales

Wales has a long tradition of welcoming refugees:
- Belgians at the start of the First World War
- Germans and Jews who fled Hitler and the Nazis
- Afghans in 2021
- families from Ukraine in 2022.

Many refugees have contributed to Welsh life:

- introducing new languages and cultures and creating diversity
- doctors, health workers and carers supporting services
- cooking new foods, opening restaurants and selling street food
- contributing to rebuilding after the damage of the Second World War. Families from the Caribbean (the *Windrush* ship generation) did much to reconstruct Cardiff and Swansea after they were heavily bombed during the war.

Greek flavour in Gwynedd

Cindy from Vietnam and Stavros from Corfu migrated to Blaenau Ffestiniog. They brought with them their love of gardening, as well as their ability to be self-sufficient and to recycle and re-use materials. On a single allotment in the slate region, they are:
- growing vines, figs, and ground pears under glass frames
- collaborating and sharing, in the tradition of their countries
- teaching and training Welsh gardeners, and sharing techniques. They regard the Blaenau Ffestiniog region with its wet weather and mild winters as an excellent area to garden.

According to one estimate, there will be 1.2 billion climate refugees by 2050. Sharing food-growing skills with immigrants will be extremely important.

Language and culture

The Census and the Welsh language

The number of Welsh speakers is important to the Welsh Government, as it aspires to reach one million speakers by 2050.

Every ten years since 1901, the Census records the number of people who can speak Welsh. The graph shows a pattern where the number of Welsh language speakers is steadily decreasing. But since 1961 there has been little reduction.

According to the 2021 Census, the percentage of people who can speak Welsh fell between 2011 and 2021. The percentage in 2011 was 19.0%, but by 2021 it had fallen to 17.8%.

There has been a decrease in the number of Welsh speakers in the Welsh-speaking heartlands in the west.

Percentage of people in Wales aged three years or over who can speak Welsh, shown every 10 years

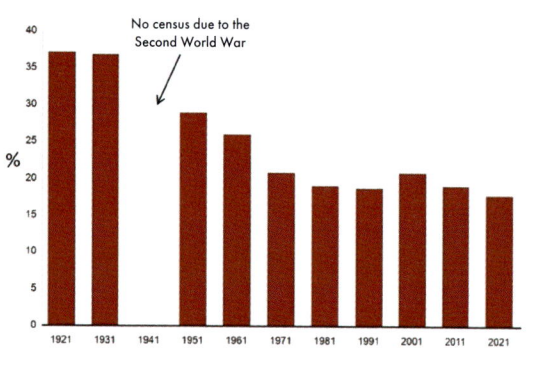

No census due to the Second World War

Carmarthenshire was the local authority with the largest reduction in Welsh speakers.

But there has been an increase in the number of Welsh speakers in other places. The 2021 Census showed that there were 42,750 Welsh speakers in Cardiff. This is a record number with 12.2% of the capital's population able to speak Welsh.

Where are the largest numbers?

The number of people aged three years or over who can speak Welsh per settlement, 2021.

This map shows the number of Welsh speakers in each town and village.

Are you able see your cynefin? The map helps to show where development is needed – for example, where to open the next Welsh-medium schools.

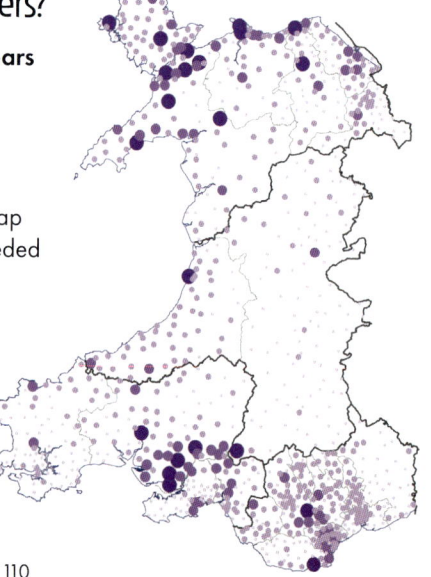

Number of people (aged three and over) able to speak Welsh, by settlement

- ● More than 3,000
- ● 1,500 - 3,000
- • 300 - 1,499
- · Less than 300

110

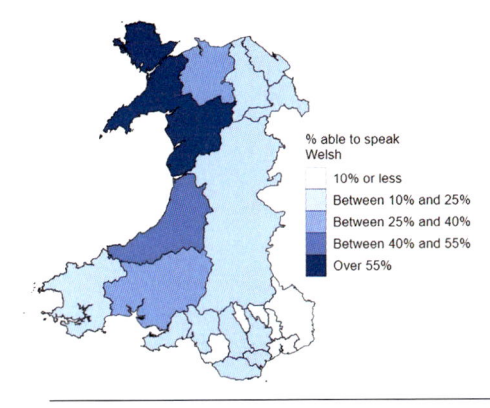

Percentage of people aged three years or over who can speak Welsh by local authority, 2021

This map shows the percentage of the population in each county in Wales who can speak Welsh.

In which part of Wales are the counties with the highest proportion of Welsh speakers?

% able to speak Welsh
- 10% or less
- Between 10% and 25%
- Between 25% and 40%
- Between 40% and 55%
- Over 55%

The change in the percentage of Welsh speakers between 2011 and 2021 per local authority

The map shows that the percentage of Welsh speakers has decreased in most of Wales's local authorities.

Where in Wales has there been an increase?

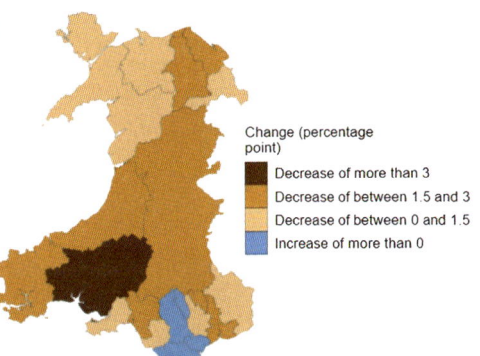

Change (percentage point)
- Decrease of more than 3
- Decrease of between 1.5 and 3
- Decrease of between 0 and 1.5
- Increase of more than 0

There is an emphasis from the Welsh Government on providing more opportunities for people to use the language every day. Of course, there are now more Welsh language activities and more opportunities than ever to use and enjoy the language. These opportunities need to be promoted and built upon.

Welsh language education

The first Welsh-medium independent primary school was established by Urdd Gobaith Cymru in Aberystwyth in 1939. By 2020 there were 65,000 children receiving Welsh-medium primary education.

Welsh for Adults

Welsh for Adults is supported by the Welsh Government to help adults who want to learn Welsh.

Mentrau Iaith

The Mentrau Iaith (meaning 'Language Initiatives') are local organisations who run Welsh language events. They promote the language and help people to use Welsh. There are 23 such initiatives in Wales. Menter Cwm Gwendraeth, established in 1999, was the first of its kind.

Urdd Gobaith Cymru

The Urdd was founded in 1922 as a youth movement in Wales. It provides opportunities for children and young people to socialise and take part in activities though the medium of Welsh. Today more than 50,000 children and young people between the ages of 8 and 25 are members of the Urdd.

Welsh language entertainment

Eisteddfodau, S4C, Radio Cymru, the publishing sector, the rock scene, apps, blogs and the internet all contribute to life through the medium of Welsh.

Different backgrounds but a single identity

Over 55% of people in Wales described themselves as 'Welsh only' in the 2021 Census. Now that ethnic diversity can be found in all parts of Wales, it is interesting to see how they feel in terms of belonging and identity.

A very common response is: "We are from an ethnic background, and are very proud of our family history. But we feel we are part of Wales and have a Welsh identity like everyone else here."

Urdd Gobaith Cymru organised an online Jamboree where a quarter of a million children sang along to 'Yma o Hyd'. This was to support the Welsh football team at the 2022 World Cup. Children from diverse backgrounds sang with one voice, for one country – 95% of all Welsh school children.

Welsh Youth Parliament

When the Welsh Parliament was established in 1999, a Young People's Education and Engagement Service was set up. This gave children and young people in Wales the opportunity to learn about and participate in the work of the Welsh Parliament. Tens of thousands of children and young people from across Wales have now taken advantage of this.

60 members were elected to the first Welsh Youth Parliament in December 2018. From the beginning, the objectives have been to work for a better future, with better education and skills and a greener, healthier world. In the future, there will be discussions about increasing the powers and subject areas of the Welsh Parliament.

The Welsh language belongs to everyone in Wales

Language crosses all boundaries, all faiths, all ethnic backgrounds. The Welsh language belongs to everyone who lives in Wales (and everyone who speaks it outside Wales too).

During the COVID-19 pandemic lockdowns, more people were learning Welsh as a new language than any other language in the world.

Whether we speak Welsh or not – the language is still part of us, and part of our lives:
- most place names in Wales are in Welsh
- Welsh is one of the two official languages in Wales
- Welsh is the language of the national anthem and many other songs.

Welsh and the web

Increasing the use of Welsh is closely linked to the language's visibility on the internet. By 2019, 93% of homes and businesses had access to superfast broadband. There are more connections between all corners of Wales and more connections with the rest of the world.

The Welsh language on Adidas trainers, 2022 World Cup

What will the future hold for Wales?

Will Scotland choose Independence soon?
Will Northern Ireland merge with the Republic of Ireland?
What will happen to 'England and Wales', GB and the UK?
Who will make decisions and take responsibility for the future of Wales and its people?

Living on the border today

Carreghofa School, Llanymynech

A little over a hundred years ago, Llanymynech's school was in England. In 1911 a new school was built for the area – and that school is in Wales. The border between the two countries runs through the centre of the village. Half of the children are from Wales and the other half from England. Even so, it has one single school. Being in Wales, the school uses the Welsh language and follows the Welsh Education Curriculum.

Some situations are funny when you live on the border. "When Mum cleans the inside of the windows of our home in Bradford Terrace, she's in England," says a Year 5 girl. "But when she cleans the outside, she's in Wales. The thickness of window glass is the difference between two countries in our house!"

The village's golf course has some holes in Wales and some in England. The border can be interesting at times. But the children get to consider the differences the border represents as well.

"The school is in Wales and I think we have better opportunities in a small country. There are so many things we can do. We have just been taking part in the Books Council of Wales competition."

But the differences can be frustrating at times. During the COVID-19 pandemic, Wales introduced different rules to those of England to protect the public.

Sometimes, one country's new tarmac will end abruptly when crossing the border into the other country.

"The children here learn two languages and they are taught Welsh and English history and culture," said Tom Roberts, the teacher. "Down the road in Shrewsbury, they are only taught English and English history.

"Children living in Wales get their secondary education at Ysgol Llanfyllin – where they can choose to continue their education in Welsh or English. The girl who chairs the Welsh Club at Carreghofa School lives in England. If she decides to cross the border to attend secondary school in Wales, she will not get free transport. Her only option is to attend school in Oswestry – but the Welsh language will not be taught and there will be little mention of Wales there."

Loss of cynefin, loss of language

Every 40 days, one of the world's languages dies. One of the main reasons for the current loss of languages is that people are forced to leave their cynefin due to the effects of extreme weather events – rising sea levels, storms, droughts and famine. As they become climate refugees, the society these people had in their cynefin collapses. They find themselves in an unfamiliar place. No one else speaks or understands their language.

The boundaries are shifting for some people. Across the Earth, people who lived in a safe cynefin a few years ago are now living among dangers or are having to flee. Without a cynefin, their language dies. Half of the world's 7,000 languages may have disappeared by the end of the century. The languages most under threat are those in the Pacific Islands and in areas near the Equator. Pictured are some of the people of Vanuatu, a small island in the Pacific Ocean where there are currently 110 languages.

How is the economy of Wales changing?

Connections

'Connections' – in Geography – are 'ways of 'connecting with each other across land, sea and air'. Since prehistory, people have travelled. Today, we travel to go to school and work, to deliver goods, to buy food, to go on holiday – and some will be forced to travel to flee famine or dangers.

Barriers to connecting?

There are several challenges in trying to connect effectively between different areas in Wales:

- high mountains across country and near the coast
- narrow valleys, with flooding and marshes in the lowlands
- a lack of flat land
- deep and wide rivers and estuaries.

But what about the landscapes of Norway, Switzerland and parts of Italy – are these problems impossible to solve?

Early routes

The earliest people arrived in Wales by sea. From the coast, ancient trails can still be seen leading from the shore to the higher ground deeper inland.

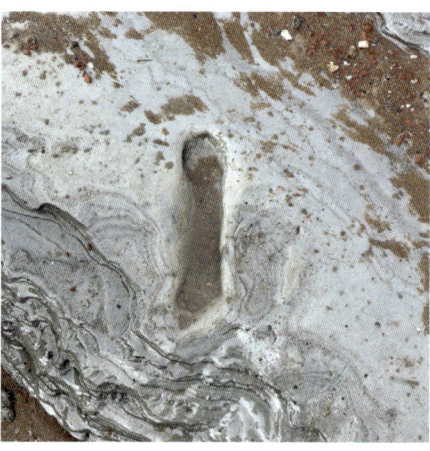

This is a footprint hardened in clay. Many can be found on the Gwent coast. They are evidence of trails in use between 5,000 and 10,000 years ago.

A mountain railway in Switzerland that successfully cuts through the landscape

Roman Roads in Wales

The Welsh word 'pont', which means 'bridge', comes from Latin, the language of the Romans. The same is true of many other words used in technology and construction. The Romans built a network of roads through Wales, linking military forts with copper, gold, lead, iron and silver mines. These roads were meant to maintain peace and foster wealth, but as a result, the country had well-paved, straight roads.

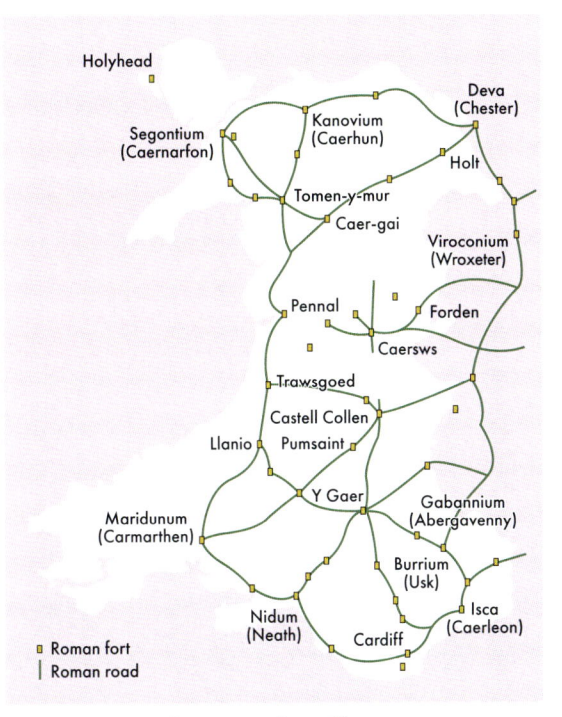

Roman fort
Roman road

Roman roads and forts

Remains of an old Roman road above Trawsfynydd

Roads connecting the whole of Wales

Apart from Pembrokeshire and Llŷn, the Roman road network reached all parts of Wales. Their major towns were in the Welsh Borders: Deva, Viroconium and Isca.

The A48 and M4 highways (Carmarthen to Chepstow) follow the route of the Roman road across south Wales.

The Romans proved that connecting different parts of Wales was not difficult. However ...

Today, a 180-mile car journey from Bangor to Cardiff takes between 4 and 5 hours. The train is not much quicker as it meanders through England. From Bangor, you can travel far more quickly to London than to the Welsh capital!

Who were the early travellers?

- Armies (e.g. Romans, Welsh princes)
- Saints and preachers
- Drovers taking cattle and sheep to markets. From the late Middle Ages to the advent of the railways, the drovers took stock from Wales as far as London.

Early vehicles: Llanfaches turnpike

Better roads were needed as more carriages began to use them. Tollgates were built to get people to pay money for using the turnpike roads. The charge – or toll – was meant to be spent on maintaining the road in a good condition.

The Stagecoach: Waterloo Bridge

When the stagecoach began carrying the mail, it had to keep to a timetable. Some roads were improved to meet this demand. The A5 was an important road for the stagecoach, leading from Shrewsbury through Eryri to Holyhead. It carried the mail to Ireland.

Welsh Canals

In the industrial age, to transport heavy loads from inland areas to the ports, canals such as this one were built: the Monmouthshire and Brecon Canal.

Before it was tarmacked, the mountain road seen below was an old trail. It was used by farmers and by drovers who would take their animals on long journeys to market.

Mountain road to Machynlleth

Heads of the Valleys dual carriageway

This road recently benefitted from extensive investment from the Welsh Government and the European Union. It crosses high hills and connects the industrial and densely populated areas of the Valleys.

How do Welsh connections overcome relief problems?

1932 tunnel through Penmaenbach rock

The cutting of the Talerddig railway in mid-Wales was the deepest in the world (37m) when the line opened in 1862.

Barmouth railway bridge – opened in 1867, restored in 2022-24

Hengoed **Viaduct**, Rhymney Valley. A viaduct is a series of arches strung together into one long bridge to cross a valley.

Local travel

The Welsh Government prioritises active travel which includes walking and cycling while travelling locally.

Ysgol Hamadryad's travel plan

Travelling to school by car contributes to:
- climate change
- childhood obesity
- traffic congestion
- poor air quality.

Since 2016, Ysgol Hamadryad (a school with over 450 children in Cardiff Bay) has developed an active travel plan. The scheme includes:
- creating a school safety zone: no parking within 100m of the school
- introducing a 'walking bus' from Havannah Street car park to the school, with a rota of supervisors and free parking for 20 minutes
- encouraging parents to walk or cycle to school with their children
- providing cycling and scootering lessons from Year 1.

Ysgol Hamadryad's walking bus, south Cardiff

National Cycle Network Wales

There are over 1,200 miles of paths on the national cycle network in Wales. As well as providing leisure and exercise opportunities, the network is within a mile of 60% of the population of Wales. It is therefore an opportunity to use green, healthy and inexpensive transport to travel to school, college and the workplace.

Better facilities for cyclists in the capital

By 2023, there were parking spaces for 1,000 bikes in Cardiff. The aim is to create 4,000 spaces in the future, maintaining new cycleways to protect cyclists from other transport.

Regional travel

The Welsh Government's plans include:

- **Buses** – developing integrated regional and local bus networks to increase the number of people who travel on buses.
- **Metros** – a 'Metro' is a system that links or integrates bus and train timetables. This makes travel arrangements easier and encourages travel that is good for the individual and the environment. The plan is to develop a Metro for the South East, the South West and the North.
- Building infrastructure that includes sufficient charging points. This will encourage drivers to use electric vehicles.

New cycleway in central Cardiff

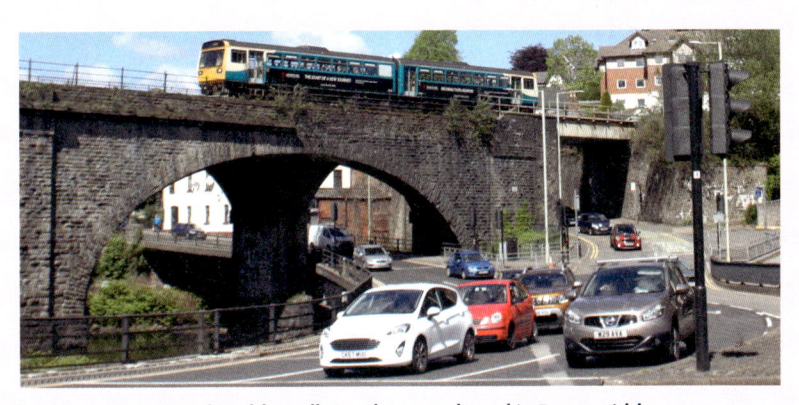

The Rhondda Valley railway and road in Pontypridd

South East Metro

Cardiff and the Valleys

There are plans to introduce a programme of work to try and improve integrated transport in the south-east. The aim will then be to replicate this throughout Wales.

Some issues in the south-east:

- long queues at Cardiff train station
- shortage of carriages on Valleys trains and passengers forced to stand
- inconvenient timetables.

Improvements – some plans:

- improving Cardiff station's capacity to deal with large crowds and events in the capital
- opening the Cardiff Bus Interchange, a brand-new bus station with plenty of bays, cafes and shops
- improving stations in the Valleys, including two new stations and electrification.

National travel

Getting to Cardiff

When Wales was given its own Parliament, it became more important for people to be able to travel from all parts of the country to the capital. As well as to discuss political issues, people need to travel there:
- to support sport teams in the national stadiums
- to enjoy cultural performances and festivals
- to visit national museums and the Urdd centre
- to be involved in various educational and commercial projects.

It is also important to be able to get to all other parts of the country from Cardiff.

Cardiff Central Station

Welsh railways today

In the 1960s, many Welsh rail lines were axed, and the tracks removed. Today, some of these lines are cycle paths. But efforts are underway to improve rail services.

- In 2016, the Welsh Government established a train company to serve Wales and the Borders: Transport for Wales. New faster, greener trains were then purchased to raise the standard of rail travel.

- A new station was opened in Bow Street, on the outskirts of Aberystwyth. The station has a large car park where people can now leave their cars and travel by train to Aberystwyth. This reduces traffic problems on the town's streets.

- The map illustrates how the Wales and the Borders railway looked in 2022, showing links with ports and airports.

- There are clear gaps: there is no link between the north-west and the south-west of the country; neither is there a connection between mid-Wales and the north-west and Cardiff.

The new Bow Street station, Ceredigion

TRAFNIDIAETH CYMRU
TRANSPORT FOR WALES

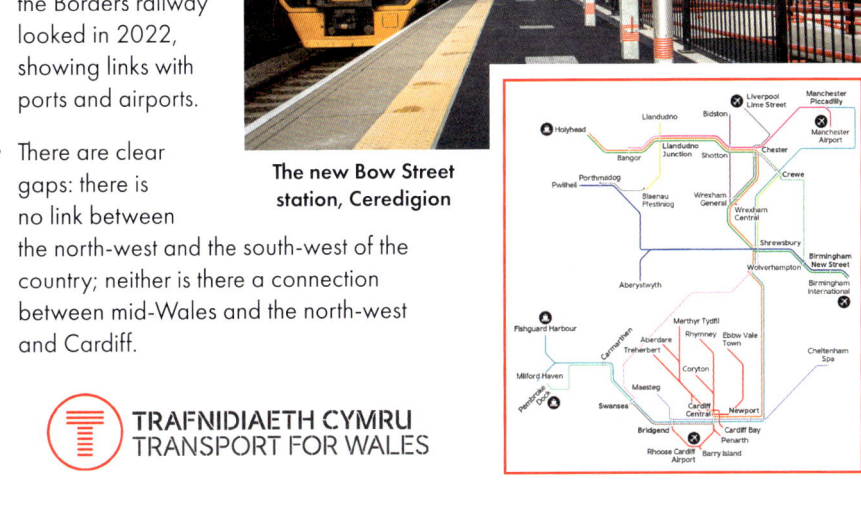

Roads linking Welsh regions

The A55 is a dual carriageway along the northern coast linking Holyhead with Chester.

The A40 and M4 follow old eastbound routes across south Wales.

But these are roads leading out of Wales into England. How much do they contribute to connecting the Welsh regions?

The dual carriageway (A55) and the Holyhead– London railway along the northern coast

In 1978, 186 miles of road between Llandudno and Cardiff were designated the A470 to serve as a 'south–north highway'.

There are not many plans at present to improve the condition of the A470 or to introduce more roads to bypass some of the towns and villages along the route.

Since early 2013, the Welsh Government does not support the construction of any new roads that will lead to an increase in the number of cars travelling and add to carbon emissions.

Although there is a need to reduce transport that burns fossil fuels, road use remains the best method of getting around in Wales.

Heavy traffic cannot pass each other on these two turns: on the A470 highway in the Conwy Valley

123

New bypass at Caernarfon

These were the arguments in favour of the Caernarfon bypass, which opened in 2022:
- the air service from Anglesey to Cardiff has stopped
- bus and train services between south and north Wales are limited, and the journey is long
- improved roads would help to deliver Welsh produce to Welsh markets, improve the local economy and reduce the carbon footprint of doing so
- avoid traffic jams created by visitors heading to Llŷn.

The new 6-mile Caernarfon bypass – opened in 2022

International travel

In 2013 the Welsh Government purchased the largest shareholding at Wales International Airport, Cardiff. But there are problems in trying to develop it into the country's main airport:
- getting back and forth between the capital and the airport is not easy – and it is difficult to get there at all from most parts of Wales
- the Welsh Government does not currently have the powers to reduce aviation taxes, and the UK Government is using this to protect airports in England.

Cardiff airport during lockdown in 2020

Ports

Holyhead's ferry port is the second busiest in the United Kingdom, second to Dover. But changes that came about after leaving the European Union have hit its trade very badly. Holyhead and Fishguard saw a 30% reduction in their trade with Irish ports.

At the moment:
- time is added to each trip as loads have to be inspected and paperwork examined at the border
- ships take loads from Ireland direct to ports in France rather than taking them through England and Wales
- more of Northern Ireland's trade goes through Scotland and Liverpool than through Dublin and Holyhead.

Holyhead Port

Despite all these efforts, car use is on the rise

Transport is responsible for 14% of Wales's greenhouse gas emissions. And the Welsh Government believes that people use too many cars. Use has increased by 9% since 2003.

The Welsh Government's vision for the future

The Government wants to reduce our reliance on cars. This will help to solve the climate crisis:
- fewer cars mean safer roads for pedestrians and cyclists
- fewer cars mean fewer carbon emissions.

Method	%	Increasing or decreasing
Car	81%	↑
Walking	8%	↓
Bus	4%	↓
Train	4%	↑
Bike	2%	↑

However, there are current barriers to achieving this:
- Wales's rail network is poor and outdated, with several connections cut since the 1960s
- there is a lack of progress in creating a network of electric car charging sites in Wales.

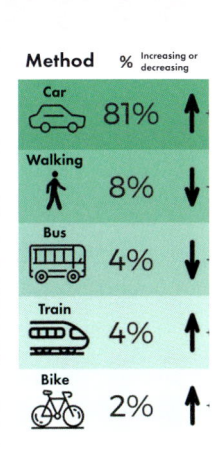

The rail network in the future

Across the world, railways are the best mode of transport because they are:
- **greener**, and create minimum environmental harm
- **faster**, with a number of innovative projects in France and Japan
- **cleaner**, by using electricity from sustainable sources or energy from green hydrogen
- **safer**, by using sensors and drones to control them.

Underground and overground, networks of effective railways are being built in several countries. Experts predict that trains will become more important than ever for travelling during this century.

The end of diesel engines

While travelling on diesel trains is substantially greener than air travel, the trains of the future will have to contribute to creating cleaner air. Two hundred years ago, 3% of the population lived in cities. By 2050, 75% of the world's population will live in cities. One of the UN's climate change targets is to scrap all diesel trains by that year. In Europe and parts of Asia, many railways have already been converted to run on electric power. But this pattern varies widely from country to country:

Bullet train in China, a country where every region has an express train

- Switzerland: 100% electric railways since 1916
- India: 80% (52,247km in 2022)
- British countries (combined): 50%
- England: 45% (5318km in 2020)
- Scotland: 25.3% (711km in 2022)
- Wales: 1.6% (29km of 1783km of Transport for Wales's railways in 2020).

Cardiff Central Station, electrified since 2021

Modern electric trains arrived in Wales in 2020 when the 29km of railway through the Severn Tunnel to Cardiff was electrified. Transport for Wales is electrifying the core railways of the South Wales Metro, creating a new electric train hub at Taff's Well. There will be an additional 170km of electric railways in Wales by 2024 (11% in total).

Hydrogen trains

Other railways are beginning to use green hydrogen produced in renewable electric power stations. In 2018 French company Alstom launched the world's first hydrogen train to carry passengers.

A hydrogen train carrying people in France

When Wales was at the forefront...

The trains for the HS2 line in England

The first railway in the world to carry paid passengers was the Swansea and Mumbles Railway, from 1807 onwards. The carriages were horse-drawn until 1877; steam engines were then used up to 1928. The railway was then powered by electricity until the company ceased operations in 1959. It was therefore the first railway in Wales to be electrified.

The need to invest in Welsh railways

In 2019 the Welsh Government called for developing the railway network in Wales. The aims were:
- to improve the connections between the country's regions
- to use fewer diesel engines through electrification
- to invest in railways rather than roads to create green transport.

But there are barriers to improving Welsh railways:
- while 11% of the UK's railways are in Wales, only 1% of rail modernisation funding from the UK Government has come to Wales
- at the same time, the HS2 high-speed railway between London and the north of England is being developed by the UK Government. The project will cost over £100 billion but Wales will not receive any equivalent funding which would be worth over £5 billion. However, the section of the project between Birmingham and Manchester was scrapped in October 2023 with high-speed trains therefore ending their journey at Birmingham. The UK Government's intention is to invest in smaller transport projects, including a promise to electrify the north Wales line between Crewe and Holyhead.

Case study
(a country roughly the size of Wales)

SLOVENIA
Area: 20,273km²

A mountainous, wooded country, with the land rising near the Alps in the north

Population: 2.1 million

Slovenian is the official language

The land has been part of several empires from the days of Rome to the Yugoslav state

Independent country: 1991

The country has developed with a strong economy, and the income disparity between the richest and poorest is among the smallest in the world

The country's **water quality** is among the best in Europe

The cynefin varies greatly, with conservation rules applying to 12.5% of the land

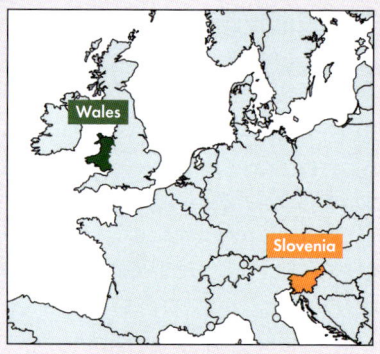

Slovenia's location
The Mediterranean Sea to the south-west
The border with Italy to the west, Austria to the north, Hungary to the north-east and Croatia to the south-east

While there are many old mining industries and chemical plants here, there are now manufacturing companies as well

There was substantial investment in the country's infrastructure in the early 21C. There are particularly good railways and motorways here, despite it being mountainous terrain.

The economy has recovered from financial difficulties and saw a 5% growth in 2017. Tourism is on the rise, but on a sustainable scale. According to National Geographic magazine, **Slovenia has the most sustainable tourism in the world.**

Electricity is generated using hydropower. Over 50% of

Slovenia's 1,209km of railways had been electrified by 2016.

284,355 people live in the capital, Ljubljana.

The capital, Ljubljana – with the Alps visible on the horizon. This is the challenge the country faced in creating a network of roads and railways after gaining its independence.

Electric cars in a green country with clean electricity

Cycling in Slovenia

Triglav is the highest mountain in Slovenia (2,864m above sea level; height of Yr Wyddfa: 1,085m).

The country is very proud of its mountains, and the summit of Triglav can be seen on the country's national flag. But the mountains are no barrier to good roads and railways in Slovenia.

Work

What kind of jobs are in our cynefin?

Work in the town of Machynlleth

Most people in industrialised nations get some kind of a job in order to sustain themselves and their families.

The workplace, which is where people undertake tasks for their employers, can be in the outdoors, or indoors in an office, school, shop or factory floor.

This variety is seen in jobs in the Machynlleth area.

How many different types of work can you see in the photos?

Travel is a part of the work of many people in Machynlleth because there is a railway station and bus company in the town.

Railway station and the garage of a local bus company

In some industries it is possible to work without going into the workplace at all, such as in this home business that produces cakes. Small businesses like this are very common in Wales.

There was a major increase in the practice of working from home using communication technology during the COVID-19 pandemic, and this pattern has continued in many roles.

Working from home

As they manufacture and produce goods and offer services, workers contribute to the country's economy. People will then spend their salaries buying goods and services, and this again benefits the economy.

The town's industrial estate sign

Where do the people of Wales work?

The two Welsh companies that employ the most people are the Admiral insurance company and the Iceland food company. These companies have their headquarters here in Wales. Two other Welsh companies that employ many workers are GE Aviation and Redrow, a company that builds houses.

The four largest companies with their headquarters in Wales (2020)

Company	Type of business	Location	2020 Turnover	2020 Employees
Admiral	Insurance	Headquarters in Cardiff and other offices in Swansea and Newport	£3.4 billion	10,829
Iceland	Food supply	Headquarters in Deeside and over 900 shops throughout the UK and beyond	£3.2 billion	15,759 (many outside Wales)
GE Aviation Wales	Aircraft maintenance	Nantgarw, near Cardiff	£1.7 billion	1,171
Redrow	House building	Ewloe, Flintshire	£1.3 billion	2,364

Large companies

These four companies are major employers. There are other non-Welsh companies that employ many workers in Wales. They include Tata Steel Company, whose headquarters are India, and Airbus, the aviation company, whose headquarters are in the south of France.

In 2024, Tata Steel Company employed 4,000 workers in Port Talbot and a smaller number at its plants in Llan-wern, near Newport; Trostre, near Llanelli; and Shotton on Deeside. In Broughton, Flintshire, Airbus has the largest factory in the world producing aircraft wings, where it has 4,000 employees.

Even so, Wales is mainly a country of small companies and businesses. The economy depends mainly on small local companies employing few workers. Only 14% of the workforce are employed by the 300 largest companies in Wales.

The Airbus factory and a Beluga plane that transports the wings from the works

The waffle factory in Llandysul

Small companies

Tregroes Waffles is an example of a small company in rural Wales. Kees Huysmans from the Netherlands founded the company in 1983. He set about producing waffles by hand at his home and selling them at local fairs and markets. As demand for the product increased, a purpose-built factory to produce the waffles opened in Llandysul in 1994. The company currently employs about 20 employees, who all live locally. Following much marketing work, the company now produces 4,000 waffles per hour! The waffles are sold in most of the leading supermarkets and in many independent grocery stores and cafes throughout Wales and beyond. They are also exported. The company now produces savoury biscuits as well.

Self-employment

Miriam Jones creates all kinds of woodturning work on the family farm in Llŷn. She took an art and design course in Manchester and is the fourth generation – but the first woman – in her family to do carpentry. The farm and the Welsh countryside are an inspiration to her. She started working in the garage, but then in 2018 built a new, purpose-built workshop on the farm. It is convenient and effective, and a pleasant place to work.

Miriam Jones

She sells her work in various galleries across north Wales – and a few in England too. She now offers less choice of goods as it is difficult to keep sufficient stock. She receives many commissions – for awards, weddings and so on. She has collaborated with other artists – such as Joe Roberts (who works with metal) on the light trail project at Tŷ Newydd, Llanystumdwy. She also creates lamp bases for the Gola company in Felinheli.

How did Wales develop into an industrialised country?

It is impossible to travel around Wales today without coming across the remains of heavy industry. Some images are still very much alive in our national consciousness:

- miners descending in cages to the depths of the Earth
- quarrymen hanging by a chain, piercing the rock
- steelworkers sweating in front of hot furnaces.

Wales became an 'industrial country' around the middle of the 19C. What that means is that it had more industrial workers at that stage than those who worked the land. Many of the early industries were based on the abundance of natural minerals that can be found in Wales's rocks.

COPPER

Landore, near Swansea, was another early industrial area. By 1823, nine copper works in the lower Swansea Valley produced a third of all the world's copper. The area was known as 'Copperopolis'. The Hafod plant was the world's largest copper plant at the time, employing over 1,000 workers.

Remains of a copper furnace, Hafod Morfa, Swansea

The copper industry in Swansea grew because:

- there was a convenient port here for importing the copper ore from Parys Mountain and Cornwall, and for exporting the finished copper
- there was a coalfield nearby – 4 tonnes of coal are needed to produce 1 tonne of copper.

Parys Mountain copper mine, Amlwch, Anglesey

IRON

Iron production requires iron ore, lime and coal. The iron industry developed in places such as Blaenavon and Merthyr Tydfil where these raw materials were found close to each other. In Merthyr Tydfil, four ironworks were built at Dowlais, Cyfarthfa and Penydarren. The iron industry employed the largest number of industrial workers at the time. In 1851 Merthyr became the largest town in Wales.

Blaenavon ironworks, Torfaen

COAL

In the second half of the 19C, the coal mining industry developed rapidly. Coal became 'king' in Wales.

The main coalfield was in the south. But coal was also mined in the north-east, in the Wrexham area. And there are traces of mines even on Anglesey and in Pembrokeshire. Coal from valleys such as the Rhondda was carried along the new railways. By 1913, Cardiff and Barry were exporting more coal than any other port in the world. The industry continued to grow until the outbreak of the First World War (1914–18).

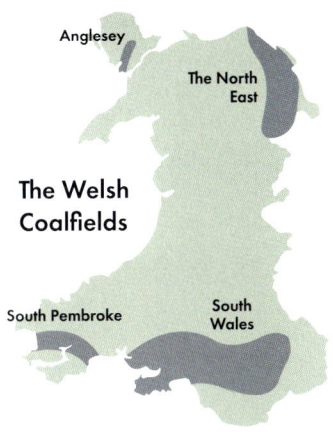

In 1913, 57 million tonnes of coal were produced in Wales in more than 600 pits – a record amount. One in three workers in Wales at the time worked in the coal industry.

After the Second World War, coal mining began in large, open pits on the surface – a process known as opencast mining. The largest working opencast mine in south Wales is Ffos-y-frân, near Merthyr. The plan is to stop mining there soon. Will this be end of the 'coal age' in south Wales?

The Welsh Coalfields

SLATE

Slate mining was an important heavy industry in north Wales. The industry grew rapidly until the late 19C, with the establishment of large quarries and pits at Bethesda (Penrhyn Quarry), Llanberis (Dinorwig Quarry), Nantlle Valley and Blaenau Ffestiniog. The slate was exported worldwide through ports such as Port Penrhyn in Bangor, Felinheli and Porthmadog. Purpose-built railways linked the quarries with the ports.

Dinorwig slate quarry

INDUSTRIAL DECLINE

There was less demand for Welsh slate after the 19C, with cheap roof tiles becoming more popular. The Swansea valley copper works closed in the early 20C as they faced competition from overseas and the practice of smelting near the mines where the copper ore was located.

The coal industry also experienced decline, and by 1950 only 171 deep pits remained. Other types of fuel, such as oil and gas, were gaining in popularity. Therefore, there were only a few working mines left by the end of the 20C. This led to widespread unemployment in the Valleys. The last deep pit closed in 2008. This was the Tower Colliery, near Hirwaun – a co-operative pit managed by the workers.

Heavy industry

Port Talbot steelworks is an example of a heavy industry in Wales. Heavy industry often means pollution. To protect the environment, these industries need to be much greener.

Facts about Port Talbot steelworks

Opened	beginning of the 1950s
Owner	Tata Steel – a company from India
Product	slabs and strips of steel
Employs	4,000 (as many as 18,000 worked here in the 1960s)
Iron ore	imported from Canada and several other countries
Coal	imported, mainly from the United States of America and Australia (before its closure, some coal came from the Ffos-y-frân opencast mine, near Merthyr)
Integrated plant	all processes that create the steel take place on the same site. It is the largest such site in the United Kingdom.

The steel industry was nationalised in the late 1960s and came under Government control. A number of large, new plants were established on the coast – in Port Talbot and Llan-wern near Newport in the south, and the John Summers plant on Deeside in the north. Two new tinplate works (thin layers of tin-coated steel) were also established at Trostre, near Llanelli, and at Felindre, near Swansea.

Advantages of the Port Talbot steelworks site
- on level ground with plenty of space
- on the coast, with a port nearby for importing raw materials
- good road (M4 motorway) and rail links to transport the steel for processing
- plenty of workers locally, and a tradition of working in the steel industry
- plenty of local companies to service the works.

Creating a green steelworks in Port Talbot

- **Pollution** – because of the need to protect the environment, the biggest challenge at present is to produce steel in a much greener way. This steelworks with its blast furnaces is the biggest polluter in Wales, producing 5.8 million tonnes of carbon a year which is 22% of the total carbon output for Wales.
- **New technology** – in 2023, the UK Government offered Tata Steel £500m to support the development of electric arc furnaces in Port Talbot. With this support Tata Steel are planning to replace the old blast furnaces with new electric arc furnaces which are less harmful to the environment.
- **Employment** – fewer workers are needed to maintain the electric furnaces, which means that up to 2,500 jobs could be lost at the steelworks. Many could also lose their work in those industries and businesses that rely on the steelworks.
- **Demand** – many are critical of these plans and what has been done to protect steel production at the Port Talbot plant. Within a green economy there may be an increase in demand for steel to produce windmills and other types of equipment to generate renewable energy. Will the works be able to meet this demand, or will more steel be imported from other countries?
- **Creating an economic strategy for Wales** – some are now asking would it be better if the Welsh Government's responsibility for economic development included powers to develop industries in Wales?

What happened as heavy industry declined in Wales?

As the heavy industries declined, new factories were set up to bring new jobs to the old industrial areas. Many of these were companies from outside Wales. They took advantage of:

- Government grants for moving to Wales
- cheap land for factory construction
- a cheap workforce accustomed to receiving low wages.

As travel links improved – particularly roads – moving to Wales became more attractive. Industrial estates were established at Treforest, near Pontypridd; Fforest-fach, near Swansea; in the Wrexham and Deeside area in the north-east; and later in Newtown in mid-Wales. By 1975 these new factories employed more workers than the coalmines and the steel and tinplate plants combined.

Hoover Factory, Merthyr Tydfil

In Merthyr Tydfil, Hoover set up one of the largest washing machine factories in Europe, employing 4,000 workers. Several companies that manufactured car components came to south Wales. Ford built a car axle factory in Swansea, employing 2,000 people. After the oil refineries were developed in Milford Haven, chemical plants came to Baglan Bay, near Swansea. Ford later built a car engine factory in Bridgend, and the Sony company was attracted to nearby Pencoed. On the shores of the Menai Straits, the Ferodo factory was built.

These experiences were mixed, and many of the multinationals turned their back on Wales in a few years' time. Some of the reasons for this were:
- the grants expired
- there was a cheaper workforce available elsewhere
- the demand for goods fell and there was competition from elsewhere.

Friction Dynamics Factory, near Caernarfon (previously Ferodo)

Industrial tourism

Wales's industrial heritage attracts many visitors to different parts of the country, meaning the past is now a new industry. Experiences include:

- national museums for the coal, slate, wool and coastal industries
- industrial transport – small quarry trains carry passengers today
- the remarkable history of some areas, for example the UNESCO slate landscape in Gwynedd
- an adventure with a view on a zipline or an exciting trail for mountain biking.

There are now 11 million overnight visitors to Wales each year, and some areas are extremely busy during the summer. The Government and some in the industry hope to see an increase in these figures, with visitors attracted throughout the year. This will offer permanent employment to workers. More than half of the sector's employees are seasonal workers.

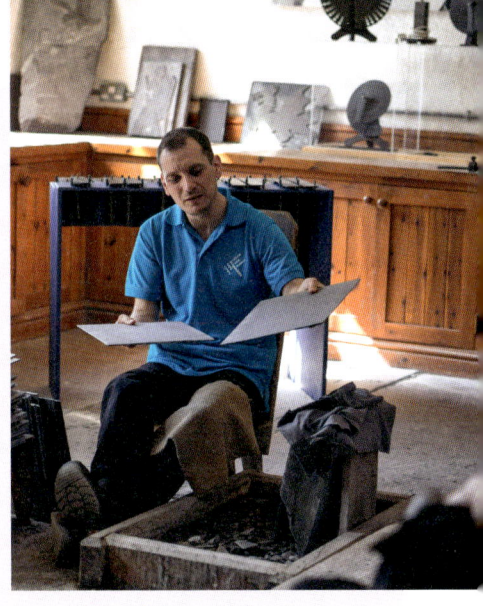

Slate splitting and dressing demonstration at the National Slate Museum

Creative industries

Wales's creative talents are renowned, especially in acting and singing. And there are now skilled people creating television and film programmes here. There are animators and creatives using technology to produce interactive games. An increasing number of international films are also being attracted to filming locations in Wales. Major organisations such as the BBC are producing Dr Who and other popular series at their new studios in Cardiff Bay. And there are small independent companies that employ freelancers based all over Wales. S4C recently moved their base from the capital to Carmarthen. This means people are not forced to move to Cardiff to work in the creative industries.

Filming Torchwood in Cardiff

What different types of work are available?

Employment can be classified into four sectors:

Take a look at these various jobs:

1. **Primary**: industries such as mining, farming, fishing and forestry that make use of the Earth's natural resources

Workers in a quarry

2. **Secondary**: industries that process raw materials to create other products. These include iron and steel plants, oil refineries and food processing factories. Factories producing finished goods such as cars, electrical appliances and furniture also belong to this group

Workers at a clothing factory in Bangladesh

3. **Tertiary:** includes occupations that offer advice, support and services to others. These include office workers, transport workers, shop workers, and professionals working in the health service, education or communications

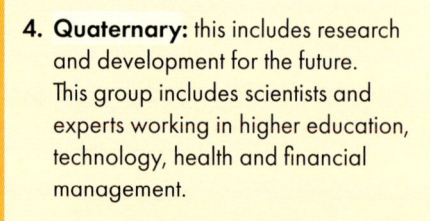

Workers collecting waste for recycling

4. **Quaternary:** this includes research and development for the future. This group includes scientists and experts working in higher education, technology, health and financial management.

A scientist undertaking research at a university

The pie chart shows that the majority of people in the United Kingdom work in both the secondary (25%) and tertiary (70%) sectors. These are industries that produce something or provide services and support to people. This is also true in Wales, with the companies that employ the most workers belonging to the tertiary sector.

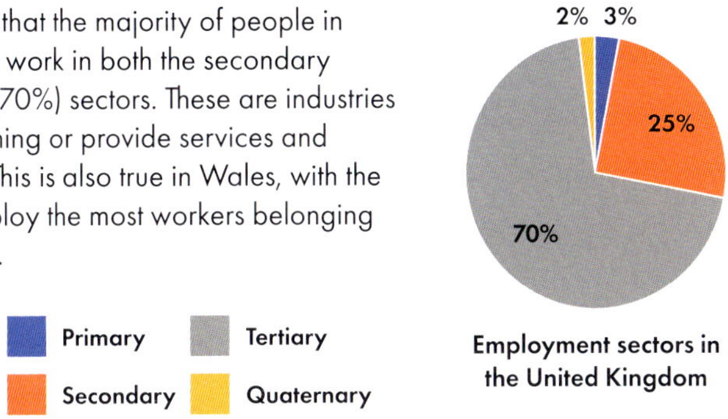

- Primary
- Secondary
- Tertiary
- Quaternary

Employment sectors in the United Kingdom

2% 3%
25%
70%

But this is not how things were in the past. The graph shows that primary workers were the most common type in the United Kingdom in 1800. This was before the Industrial Revolution, the period when many people left jobs that worked the land to work in industry. The post-industrial pattern shows that most jobs these days are in the tertiary sector.

Employment sectors in the United Kingdom during the past 200 years

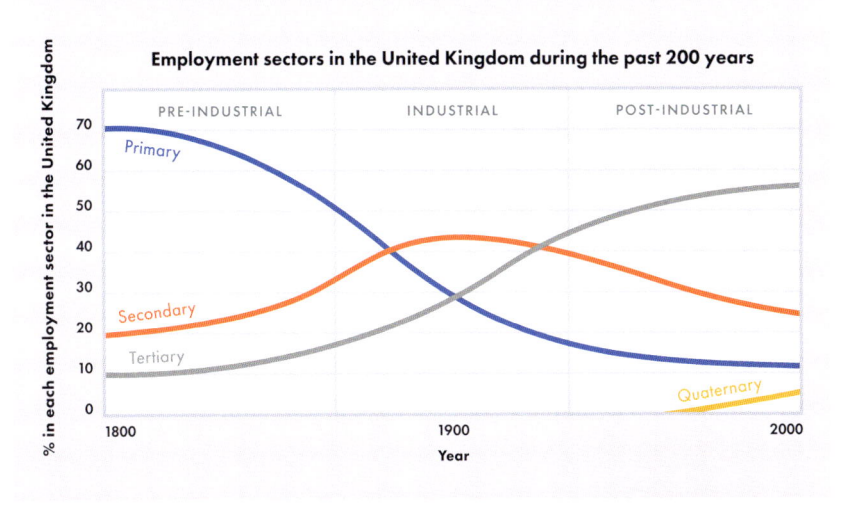

PRE-INDUSTRIAL | INDUSTRIAL | POST-INDUSTRIAL

Employment patterns in underdeveloped countries are very different. In these countries, many people still work in the primary sector. Ethiopia is a country in north-east Africa. Notice how many of Ethiopia's employees work in the primary sector. The production, services and technology industries have not developed to such an extent there.

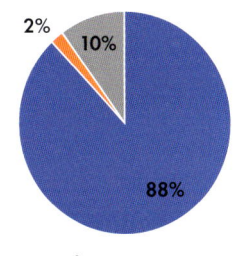

Employment sectors in Ethiopia

2%
10%
88%

What will be the industries of the future?

A recent report estimated that 65% of today's school pupils will work in jobs that have yet to be invented!

AI (artificial intelligence) will be very prominent in the workplace in the coming decades. Computers and machines will be able to solve problems and make decisions like humans. But there are some developments in employment happening right now.

The green economy

The Welsh Government is keen to support a low-carbon and renewable economy. Support will be given to companies working specifically in the green economy, for example in renewable energy. There is also support for small companies and large multinationals that are trying to adapt their existing processes to make them greener.

There is a considerable increase in demand for people to work in green jobs, and it is important to develop the right skills for this. These days, there are more jobs in Wales in the low-carbon and environment sector than there are in auto engineering.

Industries in the green sector can be very diverse. One example is the reuse of waste from a slate quarry heap to build roads or footpaths (Cilgwyn Quarry, Nantlle Valley). Another example is innovating with the latest technology to develop hydrogen cars, such as those produced by the Riversimple company based in Llandrindod Wells, Powys.

The voluntary sector contributes a lot to green and sustainable industries. In Caernarfon there is the Warws Werdd, part of Antur Waunfawr. The purpose of the Warws is twofold. It recycles and sells furniture, white goods and second-hand clothing to the community. But it is also a social enterprise that provides training and job opportunities for people with learning disabilities.

Antur Waunfawr's Warws Werdd, Caernarfon

M-Sparc Centre, Gaerwen, Anglesey – Wales's first Science Park

New technology
The Menai Science Park (M-SParc), located in Anglesey Enterprise Park, opened in 2018. Its purpose is to bring information and communication technology, science and research companies together to support business. It is housed in a new 5,000m2 building containing a state-of-the-art laboratory, offices, workshops and meeting rooms. As part of Bangor University, M-SParc creates a link between academic research and local businesses. With the establishment of the science park, the hope is to attract more large companies and quality jobs to north Wales. This will also prevent local companies that outgrow their current facilities from moving and relocating across the border in England.

New work patterns and locations
With working from home becoming more common following the COVID-19 pandemic, working in rural Wales is attractive to many companies. This includes food production, brewing, publishing, woollen mills, recording studios and all sorts of craft and manufacturing workshops. As broadband is extended to all areas of Wales, and as it speeds up again through fibre optic networks, it is expected that this pattern of working and employment beyond the major centres will continue.

Trade
Trade involves the buying and selling of goods. Countries buy and import certain goods, while they produce, sell and export others. In 1913 Barry and Cardiff docks were the busiest in the world for exporting coal!

In 2021 the most common product to be imported into Wales was 'oil and related materials'. This accounted for 21.4% of total imported goods.

Wales's main exports are transport goods and oil-derived goods. Many of these goods are aircraft wings from Airbus's Broughton factory and goods produced from oil refined by Milford Haven-based Valero.

In 2022, Wales exported its highest value of goods, at over £3.4 billion, to the United States of America. Although the United Kingdom has left the European Union, exporting to countries such as Ireland, Germany, France, Belgium and the Netherlands remains important to the Welsh economy.

Freeports
Two new 'freeports' are being established in Wales: the Celtic Freeport in Milford Haven and Port Talbot, and the Anglesey Freeport in Holyhead.

Companies must pay tolls to import and export goods. But customs will be much lower for companies setting up and producing near the freeports. The Government therefore hopes to attract more companies to these sites. This will provide jobs and strengthen the economy of these areas.

Farming

Farms everywhere!

Travelling across Wales, what do you see most often around you? Farms and agricultural land!

92% of Wales's land is used for farming, and over half of the farms are small ones, less than 50 hectares in size. (A football pitch is almost three-quarters of a hectare.)

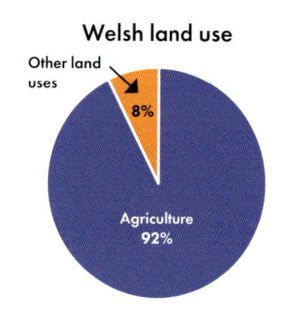

Welsh land use
- Other land uses: 8%
- Agriculture: 92%

Every farm is different, but most Welsh farms grow grass as to feed sheep and cattle.

There is little arable farming and crop growing in Wales.

This type of farming is more common in the east of England.

Sheep are kept for lamb production, while cattle are kept to produce beef and milk.

Welsh agricultural land use (1,000ha)

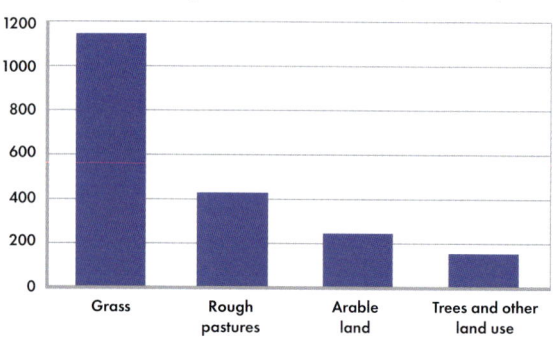

Grass	~1150
Rough pastures	~420
Arable land	~230
Trees and other land use	~140

Where does your milk come from?

Here is an example of a dairy farm near Tal-y-bont in Ceredigion run by the Jenkins family.

There are 160 Holstein dairy cows on the farm. They produce organic milk, which is more valuable than ordinary milk. Each cow will on average produce 9,000 litres of milk a year, and the cows will give birth to one calf during the year. The cows will be milked twice a day and the milk kept in a tank at a temperature of 4°C before being processed.

On the Ceredigion coast the climate is suitable for growing grass and for silage production.

The herd grazes on grass during spring and summer, but between October and April the cattle are brought indoors and placed in a purpose-built shed. There, they will be fed with silage and organic concentrate. Silage is grass cut and stored in a large pits or bales. Silage is harvested on the farm four times a year between May and September.

Holstein cattle eating silage indoors during winter

Until recently all milk was collected every other day from the farm by a dairy company. It would be sent to a creamery for processing to produce bottled milk or cheese.

But the family decided to sell their milk locally. Machinery was purchased to process the milk on the farm, as well as machines to sell the milk. Self-service vending machines have been installed in Aberystwyth and Machynlleth under the 'Cwtsh Llaeth' branding (the 'Milk Hut'). In addition to full fat milk, banana, chocolate and strawberry milkshakes are sold. A portion of the farm's milk goes to a local producer to be turned into 'Brie' cheese which is also sold from the vending machines. The remaining milk is sent to the creamery as before.

The Jenkins family produces organic milk without using chemicals on the land. They also produce most of the fodder given to the farm's cattle. There is little harm to the environment. When selling locally the milk travels a shorter distance – fewer 'food miles'.

Silage in big bales ready to be collected

What else do Welsh farms produce?

Cattle are also kept on Welsh farms for meat production. The best meat-producing breeds are Herefordshire and Angus cattle. European breeds are the most common, such as the Limousin white cattle from France. Welsh black cattle remain important in the Welsh highlands. This is the cynefin of cows that have adapted over centuries to raise calves on low quality grass, in cold, wet weather.

Beef production takes place all over Wales. The animals will be fed with concentrate, silage and pasture until they reach sufficient weight to be sold. In the highlands, a suckler cow will give birth to one calf a year and raise it until it is 7–9 months old. The calf will then be sold to lowland farms that have better quality pasture to fatten it. The animal will be ready to send to the abattoir at 18–24 months of age.

Welsh black cattle near Penderyn in Rhondda Cynon Taf

Over 48,000 tonnes of beef are produced in Wales each year. 85% is eaten in the United Kingdom, and the rest is exported. Most of the meat will be sold in the major supermarkets, while local butchers and farm shops also sell to customers.

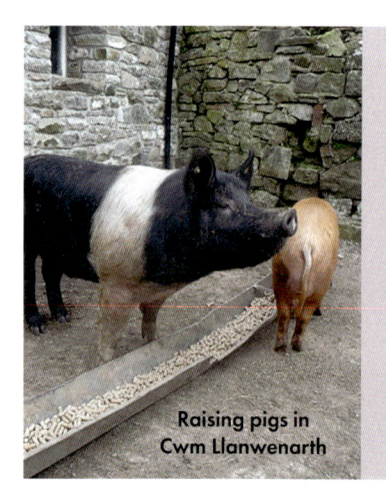

Pigs

In the past, each farm kept at least one pig in order to supply meat for the family. Pigs ate a lot of waste on the farm. There is now only a small amount of pig farming in Wales. Most pig farms in the United Kingdom are close to grain-growing arable farms. Some of this grain will be fed to the pigs. Some pig farms in the east of England have more pigs than there are in the whole of Wales!

Raising pigs in Cwm Llanwenarth

Sheep farming

- Lamb production is the main purpose of sheep farms, and most sheep farms in Wales are in the uplands. The farms are usually large.
- On these farms, Welsh mountain sheep have adapted to the harsh weather and rugged terrain.
- In the lowlands, there are other breeds that produce more lambs and bigger lambs, for example Llŷn, Texel or Suffolk sheep.
- Welsh sheep are crossed with several breeds to produce more than one lamb.
- In the lowlands, lambing will start in January, and early lamb will be on the market by Easter, attracting high prices.
- Upland lamb will not be ready until the autumn months, when prices are lower.
- Welsh lamb has PGI status (Protected Geographical Indication). This protects products that are closely connected with a particular area. As such, Welsh lamb has a unique brand.

Gathering sheep to be dosed in Ceredigion

Welsh Sheep Farming 2021	
Number of sheep in Wales	9,500,000
Average size of each flock	673
(Population of Wales **3,107,500**)	

Only 5% of Welsh lamb is consumed in Wales, and 60% is sold to other countries in the United Kingdom. The rest will be exported, mainly to Belgium, France and Germany.

There is plenty of home-produced lamb available in the UK between April and December, but at the start of the year there is a shortage.

New Zealand is a country that produces a lot of lamb. New Zealand has around 25,000,000 sheep, with some farms – called 'stations' there – covering 10,000 hectares of land. As New Zealand is in the southern hemisphere, its seasons are the opposite of those in Wales. As such, they have plenty of lamb between December and April. Due to the historic links and agreements between the countries, large quantities of frozen lamb from New Zealand is imported into the UK and Wales.

A poultry unit in mid-Wales

Poultry

A poultry unit (usually chickens) can produce meat or eggs, but they are dependent on concentrate from the grain areas of England. Recently, as farmers explore new methods of farming, large poultry units have been built, particularly in north Powys, which is closer to the grain areas of England. Chicken meat is the only meat with increasing sales in the United Kingdom.

Arable land

The arable farmer grows crops, and to do so requires good quality land and favourable weather. The most commonly grown crops in the United Kingdom are grain crops, namely wheat, barley and oats, along with potatoes and sugar beet. Wheat is used to make flour, which forms the basis of many foods, including bread. Barley is mainly used to produce beer. Some crops are grown to feed animals, for example rapeseed oil and maize.

Unlike in England, only a very small proportion of Welsh land is used for arable purposes. Only about 2% of all Welsh farms grow any type of crop. Wales's wet weather is not suitable for growing grain crops, and the soil is often difficult to cultivate. The only areas suitable for growing crops are the areas on the Welsh Border, the Vale of Glamorgan, the Vale of Clwyd and parts of south Pembrokeshire and the Llŷn Peninsula.

Due to the lack of frost in the south-west, early potatoes can be grown. They are planted in March and harvested from May onwards. The 'new potatoes' of Pembrokeshire are recognised as a unique PGI brand. Daffodils are another example of an unusual crop grown in this area.

Kazak Shepherds

The Kazak people live in Kazakstan, northern China and Mongolia, in central Asia. They are pastoral nomads: farmers who wander from place to place with their animals in search of the best pasture. They have sheep, goats, cattle, and sometimes camels and yaks.

Such roaming farmers can move multiple times a year. But the Kazak people do tend to move from the lowlands, where they spend the winter, to higher lands to graze their animals over the summer.

This is similar to the Welsh pattern in the past. During the summer, the farmer and his family would live with their animals in the 'hafod' on the mountain. They would return to the lowlands in the valley, the 'hendref', over winter. This practice ended in Wales around 1800.

The animals are very important to the life of the Kazak farmers. They depend on them, and not only for food. They use their skins and wool to make clothes and to build their summer homes – the traditional 'gers' or 'yurts'. The animals are also used for travel and to transport goods.

These days, most of the Kazak people are settled farmers who grow crops and keep sheep. But in Xinjiang in northern China, many nomadic groups continue to roam.

A Nomadic Kazak farmer moves his sheep

Yurt – summer home of nomadic Kazak farmers

Why does farming vary in different areas?

The three factors that influence the type of farming that takes place in an area are:
- the quality of the land
- the climate, especially rainfall and temperature
- social factors.

Quality of the land

Due to the landscape, climate and soil in Wales, almost 80% of the land is classed as a Less Favoured Area, which is low quality agricultural land.

The official Government classification of land quality contains 5 grades, of which grade 1 (the blue colour on the map) is the best land. As can be seen, grade 4 and 5 lands are the most common in Wales. This shows how difficult farming is in large parts of the country.

When measuring the quality of land, the depth and acidity of the soil is important. The altitude and steepness of the terrain are other factors. The land quality map is therefore very similar to the Welsh relief map.

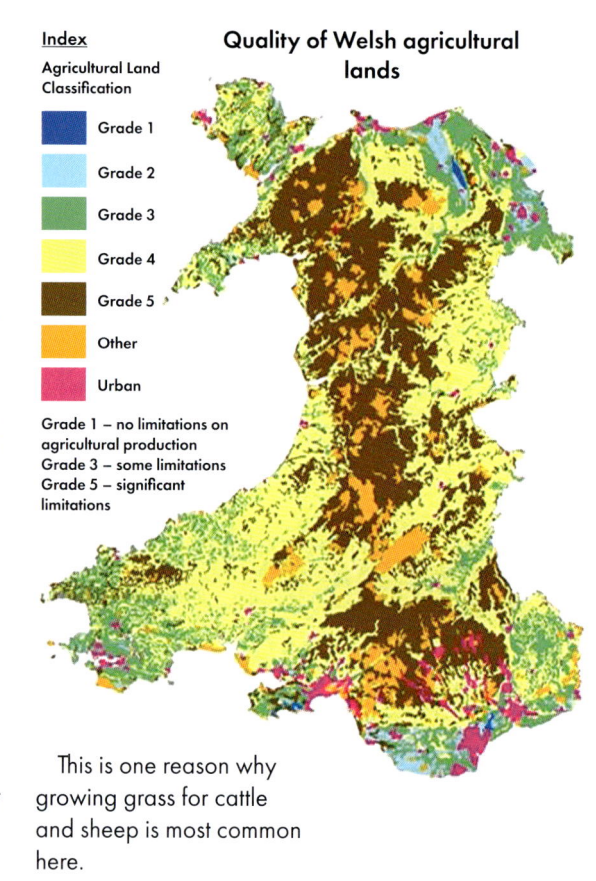

Index
Agricultural Land Classification
- Grade 1
- Grade 2
- Grade 3
- Grade 4
- Grade 5
- Other
- Urban

Grade 1 – no limitations on agricultural production
Grade 3 – some limitations
Grade 5 – significant limitations

Quality of Welsh agricultural lands

This is one reason why growing grass for cattle and sheep is most common here.

Rainfall

Wales's heavy rainfall has a great influence on agriculture. Excessive rainfall affects farmers' ability to plough. It also makes it difficult for animals to graze without destroying soil structure. Too much rain can wash minerals from the soil and create acidic conditions that limit plant growth. However, consistent rainfall through the summer months promotes grass growth, ensuring adequate fodder for sheep and cattle. Due to the high rainfall, most Welsh farmers focus on animal products, such as meat and dairy products.

Possible impact of climate change on grass growth in Wales

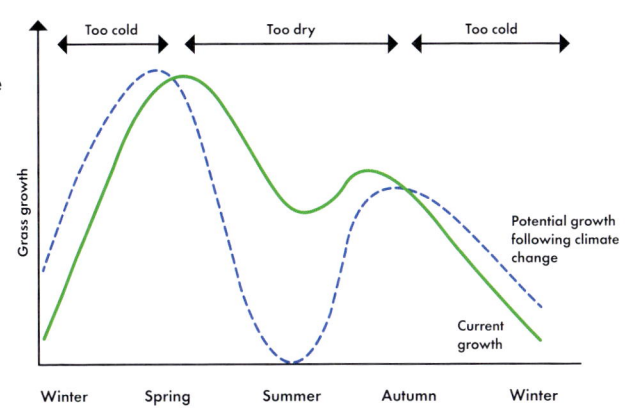

Temperature

On average, temperatures drop by 0.65°C for every 100m the land rises. Grasses only grow when the soil temperature is above 6°C. Therefore, on the highest land in Wales, there will be periods during the year without growth due to the low temperature. The unbroken line on the graph shows the pattern of grass growth during the year.

South-west Wales is warmed by the Gulf Stream. This is a current of warm water crossing the Atlantic Ocean from the east coast of the United States of America. It enables grass to grow in the area almost all year round, which is advantageous for dairy farming and for growing crops such as early potatoes.

Climate change

The dashed line on the graph suggests how the rise in temperatures following climate change will affect grass growth. This could lead to a change in farming methods in some areas of Wales.

Social factors

- Most farms receive additional Government funding. These subsidies can amount to as much as a third of a farm's annual income. Without this support, farmers would not be able to earn a living, especially on the highest and less favoured lands in Wales.
- Since 1999 agriculture has been a devolved subject. Therefore, the Welsh Government in Cardiff is responsible for the sector and for providing subsidies to the industry. In 2021, £273,000,000 of funding was provided to Welsh farmers.
- Protecting the environment is a priority for the Welsh Government, and as such it has introduced many new rules. This at times creates conflict with farmers. There will be more emphasis in the future on subsidies to protect the land and environment rather than to support food production.

A century of change

Population growth has necessitated the production of more and more food. With so much land already being used for agriculture, the emphasis is on trying to produce more food from each hectare of land.

Since 1930 there has been an increase in productivity, as a result of better scientific understanding of what was happening on farms. Animals were bred to increase their produce, and better infection-resistant crops were developed. There was an increase in the use of minerals, for example nitrogen, phosphorus and potassium, on land. Herbicides and pesticides were also developed to keep infections and parasites under control.

Scientists at the Welsh Plant Breeding Station in Gogerddan, near Aberystwyth, developed varieties of ryegrass and white clover that allowed farmers to keep more animals on their land and produce more food.

Shearing day at Gorddinan farm, near Dolwyddelan, in 1963

Changes to shearing day

During the 20C, there were many changes in farming methods. One example of this change is shearing day. It used to be a social occasion as well as a day to carry out essential work. The sheep's wool also contributed significantly to farm income.

The men would shear and the wives were responsible for feeding the dozens of neighbours who would give a helping hand. Shearing with shears was a laborious process. It would take about 6 minutes to shear each sheep. Each shearer would therefore shear around 80–100 sheep in a day.

Today, a good shearer with an electric machine can shear a sheep in 2 minutes and over 200 sheep in a day. Contractors, rather than neighbours, undertake the work today. With the advent of synthetic fibres, Welsh sheep wool now has little value.

The amount of labour required during harvest-time has changed considerably

This was also a period of constant mechanisation, which contributed to a reduction in the number of land workers. This has contributed to the depopulation of the countryside.

Machines, rather than workers, now do the hard work. And the tractor has long since replaced the horse as the farm's power source.

More than half of Welsh farmers now have another job, only working part time on the farm.

Take a look at the two photos of farmers at harvest. What is similar and what is different?

Technology today

Individual data about each animal on the farm and each square metre of crop-growing land can now be recorded and processed. As such, it is possible to precisely control the amount of food each animal needs and the fertiliser required on the land. This can mean less waste and more yields.

Satellites are used to control tractors. This is very useful in cultivating the land on the vast fields in central United States of America.

Robots have been developed for dairy farms that allow cows to decide when they want to be milked. This can mean more milk from the cow and it saves the farm a lot of labour costs. The machine records details about the animal to ensure the cow receives the right food and care.

Milking robot

Eyes on the future

Diversification

A recent trend has seen farmers looking for additional and different income streams to sustain them. This is called diversification. Farms can diversify by:
- adding new agricultural activities to the farm. Having more than one source of income is better than relying on one type of product, in case the price of that product drops. Recently, a number of farms have added a poultry unit to sell free range eggs, providing them with a greater variety of products
- adding value to the farm's agricultural products through processing or selling directly to the public. For example, dairy farms can produce ice cream and sell it in a farm shop; sheep and beef farms can sell meat boxes and vegetable farms can sell vegetable boxes at farmers markets
- adding non-agricultural enterprises to bring other income to the business. Visitor accommodation and generating sustainable electricity from wind turbines, hydroelectric power or solar power are common activities.

Keeping beef cattle, sheep and growing grain was the backbone of the Parry family's business in Crugeran, Sarn Mellteyrn.

While the agricultural products remain important, the business has diversified and established new enterprises, namely electricity generation and visitor accommodation. Crugeran farm is near an Area of Outstanding Natural Beauty on the Llŷn Peninsula, which attracts walkers and visitors on seaside holidays. After erecting new buildings for the cattle, housing machinery to feed them, the old mills, stables and barns were empty. The old buildings were converted to create self-catering holiday cottages.

A poultry unit was then built to sell free range eggs. A lot of electricity is needed to maintain the unit. Therefore, a windmill was built and solar panels installed on the roof of the building to create sustainable sources of energy. The manure from the poultry unit can be used on the fields. This reduces the need for artificial fertilizers and adds organic matter that is beneficial to the soil.

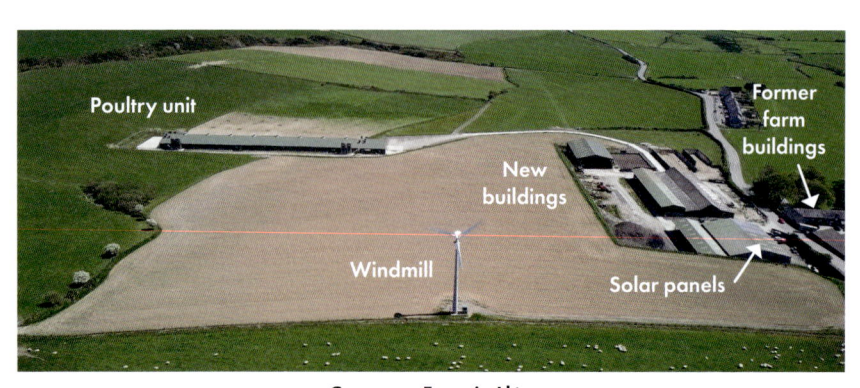

Crugeran Farm in Llŷn

We can predict that three types of farms will develop in the future, namely:

- farms that depend on the market price. These farms will increase in size and specialise in a single product to create effective, profitable farming systems
- farms that will place an emphasis on environmentally-friendly production. This may lead to higher Government subsidies to compensate the farm for keeping fewer animals, for instance
- farms that create a unique product (niche) and often add value to the produce before it leaves the farm. Farms may be producing cheese or ice cream, selling pedigree stock or opening a farm shop. Entirely new agricultural enterprises, such as vineyards, could even be established.

A variety of Welsh produce

Agriculture faces a number of challenges:

1. Agriculture is a primary industry. It relies on the Earth's natural resources to produce food. The weather is one naturally volatile element that always provides challenges. But the effects of climate change may force farmers to completely change their farming methods.
2. On some farms, diseases such as tuberculosis affect the health of cattle, and all infected animals must be culled. While farmers are financially compensated for this, culling stock that has been nurtured for years is heart-wrenching for them.
3. Since the United Kingdom left the European Union in 2020, there is great uncertainty about subsidies that are so crucial to Welsh farms, particularly those on less favoured lands.
4. The Welsh Government intends to reduce greenhouse gas emissions in the agriculture industry by boosting greener production systems. There will be more subsidies for environmental protection, rewilding, tree planting and reducing agricultural pollution than for food production.

Forests

Where are Wales's forests today?

Forests can be found throughout Wales.

More of Wales is covered in trees than ever before, with forests accounting for 306,000 hectares of land (15% of the total). Most of them are small, scattered forests.

Colby Woodland in south Pembrokeshire

Often they cover small areas and are located far apart from each other.

For example, in Anglesey, there is Coed Cadnant (on the banks of the Menai Strait); Coed y Gell (Morfa Dulas); Llangoed Nature Reserve (south-east Anglesey); and Newborough Forest (the sand dunes of south-west Anglesey).

In Caerphilly county, there are three recognised forests: Coed-y-darren (Risca area); Cwm Carn Forest (Ebbw Valley) and Plas Machen Wood (between Newport and Machen).

National Forest of Wales Sites

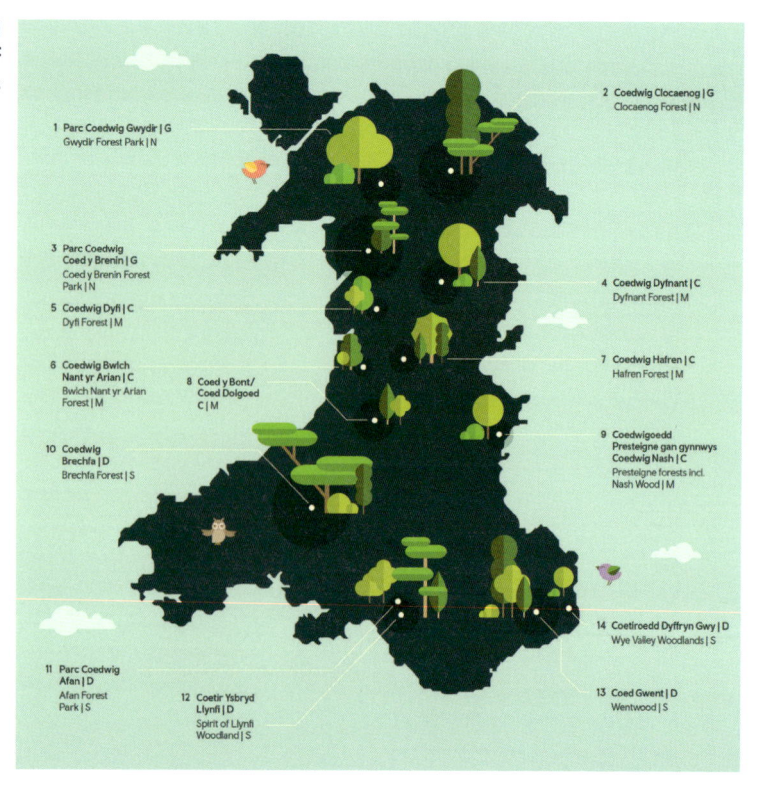

1 Parc Coedwig Gwydir | G
Gwydir Forest Park | N

2 Coedwig Clocaenog | G
Clocaenog Forest | N

3 Parc Coedwig Coed y Brenin | G
Coed y Brenin Forest Park | N

4 Coedwig Dyfnant | C
Dyfnant Forest | M

5 Coedwig Dyfi | C
Dyfi Forest | M

6 Coedwig Bwlch Nant yr Arian | C
Bwlch Nant yr Arian Forest | M

7 Coedwig Hafren | C
Hafren Forest | M

8 Coed y Bont/ Coed Dolgoed
C | M

9 Coedwigoedd Presteigne gan gynnwys Coedwig Nash | C
Presteigne forests incl. Nash Wood | M

10 Coedwig Brechfa | D
Brechfa Forest | S

11 Parc Coedwig Afan | D
Afan Forest Park | S

12 Coetir Ysbryd Llynfi | D
Spirit of Llynfi Woodland | S

13 Coed Gwent | D
Wentwood | S

14 Coetiroedd Dyffryn Gwy | D
Wye Valley Woodlands | S

The value of our forests

- Trees help the planet breathe as the leaves produce vital oxygen; they also capture and store carbon.
- A forest is a cynefin that protects the soil and natural diversity of Wales (80% of Earth's land species live in forests).
- Tree roots retain water in the land and help prevent flooding and erosion.
- Forests are pleasant places for recreation and relaxation.

The dangers to Welsh forests

Many of Wales's forests are at risk due to:
- rhododendron plants that have invaded from the grounds of old mansions, suffocating saplings
- sheep over-grazing and killing young tree growth
- all kinds of human developments: road widening, construction, felling trees for fuel.

And in the past, forests were felled:
- to create fields for farming
- to meet industrial needs – for example, to provide fuel for iron furnaces; for shipbuilding; and for beams to support ceilings in mines and underground quarries

Rhododendron ponticum which extends over 2,000 hectares in Eryri National Park

Native trees growing naturally on the banks of afon Llugwy, Betws-y-coed

Much work is being done to conserve and promote forests. This work includes:
- clearing rhododendron plants
- introducing grazing cattle to clear brambles and minor wild growth
- installing protective fencing and trail management
- clearing evergreen trees and planting deciduous trees to promote native trees that used to grow naturally in Wales.

Coed Cymru

Coed Cymru was established in 1985 to raise awareness about Wales's native forests.

Coed Cymru wants to see forests managed sustainably for the sake of the environment and the community, and to boost the economy.

Its aim is to ensure:
- protection for the cynefin of animals and plants in forests
- an increase in the use of forests for recreation
- benefit to the local economy by making greater use of native trees, creating jobs, generating income for forest owners, and reducing reliance on imported trees
- awareness among the population of the importance and value of native forests.

Using wood from Welsh trees

Coed Cymru encourages the use of native Welsh trees to produce all kinds of goods. It pays a lot of attention to the design of these goods and the effective use of trees.

Coed Cymru has a number of specialists to train and advise craftsmen who work with hardwoods. They also offer design and craftsmanship courses for young workers.

Coed Cymru encourages the use of native trees

They emphasise the importance of using Welsh wood to produce furniture.

Since 1990, little furniture has been produced in Wales. Globalisation has meant cheaper imports, and consumers tend to change their furniture more often. It is easy to throw away cheap furniture!

However, there is a long tradition of furniture design in Wales, and over the next 30 years the use of hardwood in Wales is projected to increase eightfold.

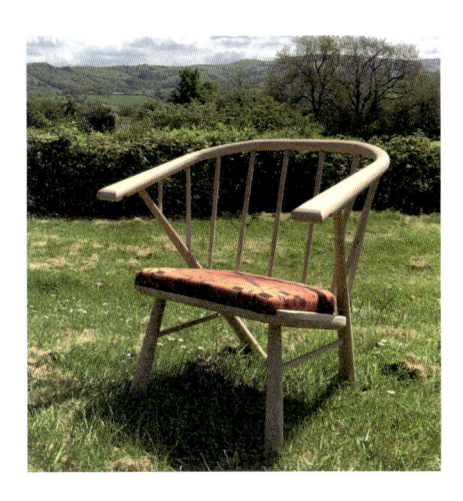

Forests – places for recreation

Natural Resources Wales is keen for people to reconnect with the countryside, and this includes the forests of Wales. By introducing walking and cycling paths, picnic parks and information boards, everyone will have the opportunity to enjoy the forest. It is hoped that people will value the environment and take responsibility for protecting it, so it can thrive in the future.

Afan Forest Park

One of Wales's specialist mountain bike centres. There are three different walking trails here as well.

Coed y Brenin Centre

There are 8 mountain bike trails here – the first centre of its kind in Wales and beyond.

Ty'n Llwyn Park in Gwydir Forest

A nice spot to park, enjoy the view, wander and relax.

The National Forest

The Welsh Government has a plan to restore old forests and create new woodlands. This long-term plan is intended to protect forests by opening them up for people and communities to enjoy and voluntarily work for their benefit.

Wentwood in Monmouth is the largest forest in Wales

Forests and the Welsh economy

The largest sawmill in Wales is owned by the Kronospan company in Chirk, near Wrexham. In 2020, £200 million was invested on the site, doubling production and securing work for 630 staff. It is the 20th largest company in Wales, and it produces wood flooring, wall panels, MDF boards and laminated boards for furniture production.

Local timber mills

This mill in Llanaelhaearn, Gwynedd, cuts trees from its own woodland, replanting a tree for each one felled. Such mills use trees to produce huts, fencing material, gates and stiles, and firewood.

Melin Glasfryn, Llanaelhaearn

Forestry – conservation and conflict

Photos from space show the damage being done in the Amazon

Forests are important because they produce oxygen and store carbon. The tropical rainforest of the Amazon is the largest forest in the world and is regarded as the lungs of our planet.

But there is conflict between those who wish to develop the economy and those who want to protect the environment. 'Developing the economy' often means cutting down trees.

In 2022:
- two green activists trying to protect the trees were killed
- there was more deforestation than there had been for six years in order to create farmland and extract minerals from the ground
- after the trees were felled, fires were lit to clear the land.

1 million native people live in the Amazon and felling trees threatens their way of life. They are used to living sustainably without doing great harm to the environment.
   Species diversity in the forest is lost as trees disappear to grow agricultural crops.

1. Emergent trees

2. Continuous canopy

3. Under canopy

4. Layer of shrubs

What is a tropical forest?

These forests grow:
- when temperatures exceed 24°C throughout the year
- when air humidity is between 75% and 80%
- when there is an annual rainfall of over 1,500mm per m^2.

AMAZON

Several levels of growth

These forests contain several levels of growth:
- up to 6m – shrubs, young trees, herbs
- up to 20m – lowest trees
- up to 40m – canopy of the highest branches
- up to 80m – individual trees protruding through the canopy.

There are 60,000 different plants in the Amazon basin alone, 1,000 different birds, and 300 species of mammals. Yet about 40% of this forest has been destroyed by human actions over the past 50 years.

Along the Equator

Similar damage is occurring in other tropical forests in the Congo Basin (West and Central Africa), and in India, Indonesia and Malaysia in south-east Asia.

Clearing vast areas of trees in the Amazon Basin in Paraguay

Forest felling in the Congo Basin in Nigeria

One crop replacing tens of thousands

25% of Indonesia's forests have been cleared to establish palm oil farms. Creating a single crop environment:

- has a profound impact on the indigenous people who depend on the forest's products in a sustainable and traditional way

- results in the loss of several unique species of trees, vegetation, birds and animals

- destroys the 'lungs of the Earth' – these forests provide us with oxygen and capture our carbon dioxide.

Clearing to create a single-crop palm plantation in Malaysia

Lack of diversity: Over a hundred years ago trees were much scarcer in Wales due to the needs of people and industry.

In the rush to plant as many trees as possible after 1919, foreign, evergreen trees such as fir and pine were planted together in rows. Some people call these forests 'dark woods'. The Sun cannot penetrate through the branches in summer or winter, and minor shrubs and flowers do not grow under them. They are single-species forests. 49% of all trees in Wales are currently evergreen trees.

A dark world under the evergreen trees in Hafren Forest

Tree planting targets in Wales

Challenging targets have been set to plant 43,000 hectares of new woodland in Wales by 2030. A further 180,000 hectares are planned by 2050 (86 million trees in the next 10 years). The Welsh Government's says that it is attempting to respond to the climate crisis in planting these trees.

Achieving these objectives will require the cooperation of individuals, communities, landowners and local authorities.

Carbon debt transfer

Forests are used by some companies to transfer carbon debt. They do this by funding tree planting elsewhere. A company can claim to be 'carbon neutral' by doing this.

Some say this is 'like paying someone else to go on a diet on your behalf', and there are many doubts about this practice:
- the rich company still produces greenhouse gases
- in Wales, companies from outside the country are able to purchase farms on good land and be subsidised to plant trees
- the formula is flawed in measuring the 'debt' – giving the rich companies almost 20 times too much credit.

'Carbon transfer forest' in the Netherlands

Tree protection

'Sustainable forestry' is an important term today.

Taking care of our trees

Wales's forests are the responsibility of Natural Resources Wales, a division of the Welsh Government. The value of native trees such as oak is now recognised. While it is pleasing to see trees planted in parks or along new roads, it will never make up for centuries of tree destruction.

Replanting trees – a new law

In 2022 the Welsh Government announced that farmers would have to ensure that 10% of their land be covered by trees in order to receive Sustainable Farming payments. Farmers are concerned that not all types of land are suitable for tree planting (high ground or land exposed to coastal wind, for instance). They also fear that good quality agricultural land will be taken up to plant trees, creating food shortages.

38% – the area of the Earth covered by trees today (the percentage was 48% in 1900)

15% of Wales's area is covered by trees

A tree for each household

In 2022, the Welsh Government started to distribute a tree to each household under its new 'My Tree, Our Forest' scheme. In the winter of 2022–23, every household in Wales had the opportunity to collect and plant a tree when 50 centres across the country provided 300,000 trees for free. The Woodland Trust organised and promoted this scheme. To support it, a large number of volunteers were on hand to share expert advice and help people to choose the right tree for the right location.

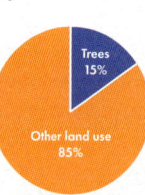

To become a net zero country by 2050, Wales will have to plant 86 million trees over the next decade.

Pie chart: Trees 15%, Other land use 85%

Felling trees - Globally

Over the past 10,000 years, Earth has lost a third of its forests – twice as much as the area of the United States of America. Half of this loss occurred during the last century.

Felling trees - Wales

When people came to live in Wales at the end of the Ice Age, it was full of trees and forests – except for the rocky and windy upper slopes.

Useful trees

As the world's population continues to grow, more wood products are needed. It is assumed that this demand will be three times greater by 2050:
- fruit tree products; chemicals for medicines and personal care products
- wood for energy – furnaces generate heat and electricity
- construction – since ancient times, wood is a convenient material to make tools and furniture and for all kinds of building needs
- paper, cardboard.

It is a renewable, easy-to-recycle product.

14 million

The number of people the forestry products sector employs around the world. It affects the livelihoods of 20% of the world's population. It is critical for many economies.

10,000 people work in forests in Wales

Carbon Neutral

Felling and burning trees produces CO_2. CO_2 is absorbed when trees are replanted and therefore it is possible to create a 'carbon neutral' forestry industry.

Are there any native Welsh forests left?

We have rainforests in Wales as well. They are known as the Celtic Rainforests of Wales. Their main features are:

- located in west Wales
- humid climate (about 200 days of rainfall per year)
- mild winters without much frost, and summers that are not too hot; clean air
- gorges with rivers
- the main trees are oaks, and the highest branches create shade
- haze and water droplets constantly rising from the river as it gushes over the rocks
- a perfect cynefin for ferns, mosses, fungi, and young native trees

Coed Felenrhyd, near the river Dwyryd in Meirionnydd

The value of the Celtic Rainforests of Wales

- A cynefin that dates back 10,000 years to the last Ice Age.
- Oak sustains over 2,300 species of insects, moths, birds and other creatures.
- Tree branches in the moist air support rare mosses, flowers and fungi (some of which are unique to Wales).
- Because these gorges maintain and retain moisture, they reduce the impact of flooding in the lower lands.
- Carbon storage, reducing the impact of global warming.

The Celtic Rainforests are located in four areas of west Wales:
- Meirionnydd in Eryri
- Cwm Einion, Ceredigion
- Cwm Doethie / Mynydd Mallaen, on the border between the counties of Carmarthenshire and Ceredigion
- Cwm Elan, Powys.

The Celtic Rainforest's ecosystem is very special. Ecosystem is the word that describes all living things in a cynefin and the relationship between them and the environment. This includes plants, animals, insects and humans, and their relationship with the land, soil and climate.

Ecosystems

An ecosystem can be very small, like a garden pond, or extremely vast, like an ocean. The balance between the different elements in an ecosystem is critical. If one element is harmed, because of climate change, human intervention or pollution, for instance, it puts the whole ecosystem at risk, and can perhaps destroy it.

There are six main ecosystems in Wales: mountains, forests, freshwaters, grasslands, seas and urban ecosystems.

Examples of other ecosystems

Coral
Due to their extraordinary diversity, coral reefs are sometimes called the 'tropical forests of the sea'. Coral reefs are complex ecosystems that are again dependent on a clean cynefin. Overfishing and increasingly acidic seas put them at risk.

Tropical rainforest
Areas such as the Amazon Basin and the Congo Basin have large ecosystems that support a great diversity of species. Some characteristics: heavy rainfall, very warm, hot and humid air, no seasons, only a thin layer of fertile soil, abundant growth and many different animals, birds and insects.

Mekong Valley
Diverse forests between Tibet and Vietnam. They contain mangrove trees that protect the coast. It is the tiger's biggest cynefin. It contains the world's largest fishing lake – which sustains 70 million people. A third of the trees have been felled to establish farms since 1980.

Shopping

How has shopping changed since the 1950s?

During the Second World War, there was a shortage of groceries in shops. Therefore, rules were set for how much each person was allowed to buy. The usual weekly ration for one person was: 1 egg; 2 ounces of butter; 2 ounces of tea; 1 ounce of cheese; 8 ounces of sugar; 4 ounces of bacon; and 4 ounces of margarine.

New shops

At the end of the Second World War, food was once again imported on ships and aeroplanes from all over the world. As a result, there was much more choice of different foods in the shops.

In the 1960s the first supermarkets were opened – sometimes in old cinemas and old chapels in town centres. One of the first was the Welsh company, Kwik Save, which was established in Prestatyn in 1959.

This changed the pattern of shopping, with customers 'helping themselves' and collecting goods into baskets and shopping carts. They would then pay on their way out. Due to the low prices the supermarkets were very popular.

The large car park of Llandudno's shopping centre

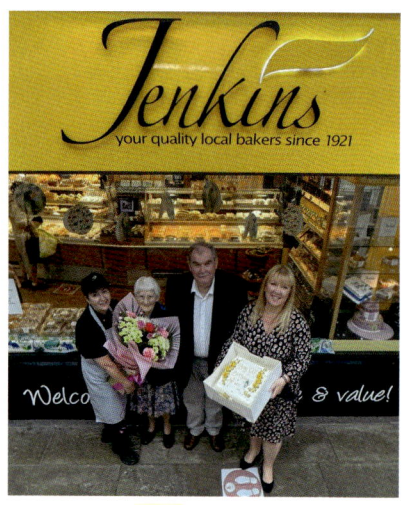

A chain of bakeries

Freezing and storing food

In the past, shops mainly sold local and seasonal produce. But this changed after it was discovered that some foods could be frozen and transported over a great distance.

Fish, meat and vegetables could therefore be purchased from all corners of the world at any time of year.

Refrigeration became much more common in houses in the 1960s. By the mid-1970s, one in three homes had a freezer.

The routine of shopping once a day from the local grocery store, butcher and bakery came to an end. People could store food at home, and go shopping once a week at one large shop. Due to limited space in town centres, new supermarkets were opened on their outskirts, where there was plenty of room for car parks. When people are shopping for groceries to last a whole week, a car makes it easier to transport all the goods home.

What is it like shopping now?

With the advent of the internet, there has been a huge growth in shopping from home, with goods being viewed and ordered online. Supermarkets now offer home delivery of groceries, while a large number of websites sell all sorts of other goods. The online shopping market grew further during the COVID-19 pandemic.

Shopping from home is nothing new. The first company ever to start mailing products to customers was the Pryce-Jones store in Newtown. This shop opened in 1859. It would send patterns and leaflets about Welsh wool to local gentry families. After receiving orders from remote mansions, their parcels would be delivered to them initially by stagecoach and then by train.

The Pryce-Jones shop in Newtown

Local foods and healthy foods for the environment:

- another impact of the COVID-19 pandemic was that a number of small shops started to deliver bread, meat and essential supplies to homes.
- the COVID-19 pandemic made us consider where our food comes from and think about its quality. There was a large increase in demand for 'vegetable boxes' that contained local produce.
- many foods in supermarkets use fast-growing ingredients that are harmful to the environment. Customers are now more concerned about the methods of producing food.
- 83% of supermarket fruits and vegetables come from the international market, which leaves a significant carbon footprint.
- more people have now started gardening and growing some of their own food.

The Oren company from Penrhyndeudraeth supplies weekly fruit and vegetable boxes

Where do we go to shop?

- Village shop
- Corner shop
- High street
- Market hall and street market
- Town/city centre shopping centre
- Retail park on the outskirts of town
- Online

A street market in Montgomery in our century. Much of the produce is grown locally, and the producer is usually the one who sells the goods as well

More expensive goods that are bought less often

What is bought most often in your home and where do you buy it?

Fresh foods, bread and milk are bought regularly, but things like furniture, electrical goods and clothes are bought less often.

People are willing to travel further to buy these goods, visiting several shops to compare quality and prices.

These shops tend to be grouped together on the high street or in shopping centres – sometimes within towns but often on the outskirts.

Retail and wholesale

A **retailer** is the shopkeeper who sells goods to customers in stores, markets and supermarkets.

A **wholesaler** produces or delivers goods and sells them to the shopkeeper.

Castell Howell – food wholesalers

A meat stall in a street market in central Asia about 150 years ago. There were markets like this in Wales at that time too

The Co-op Shop

Cooperative shops were very common in the old industrial villages of Wales. The investors in a cooperative shop are its employees and local people. They buy goods jointly and sell them at a reasonable price, before sharing the profits.

The first cooperative village shop in Wales opened in the quarrymen's village of Trefor, Caernarfonshire, in the 1870s. A number of cooperative village shops serve local areas in Wales today – including one in Llithfaen, just a few miles from Trefor.

Cooperatives can be found all over Wales and around the world. They are seen as a way to ensure fair trade and quality service.

John Lewis is a prominent outlet in the major cities. It was initially a private shop, but after the founder died in 1928, it was converted into a cooperative owned by the company's employees.

Old photo of the village of Trefor at the foot of the Eifl and the granite quarry above

Llithfaen's cooperative shop

John Lewis cooperative shop in Cardiff

Market towns

Some towns grew into convenient places for producers to meet and exchange goods. These are our traditional market towns, such as Llangefni (pictured below), Mold, Lampeter and Cowbridge. The best roads in the area lead to these towns. In market towns, two busy roads will often intersect, or there will be somewhere to cross a river – a ford, a causeway, or in later times, a bridge. There will be a square or wide roads in the town centre with space for traditional market stalls.

Originally, there would be animals on the streets. Welshpool had a site for its livestock market in the town centre. Eventually, the business grew too large and now a purpose-built market has been built on the outskirts of the town. It is the largest sheep market in Europe.

Market halls

There are several old market halls in Welsh towns. In such market halls, cheese, butter, eggs, chickens, vegetables and seasonal fruit were sold. There are still a few halls in use in our largest cities, such as the one above in Abergavenny.

The Riverside Farmers' Market in Cardiff is held weekly opposite the Principality Stadium

Farmers' markets

A tradition that still exists in the old market towns is to hold a street market at the same time as the animal market.

Since about 1980, 'farmers' markets' have become popular in towns such as Haverfordwest, Conwy and Dolgellau and in the Riverside area of Cardiff. In these markets, local producers and artisans will sell local produce to local customers.

Cattle market in Builth Wells

Food miles

'Food miles' is the method used to measure how far food has travelled before it is retailed. Food production and distribution can create a lot of pollution.

Calculating the miles is a good way of assessing the impact of food distribution on the environment. It includes the energy used in transporting food to the counter but also the energy used to deal with the waste.

The message is: buy foods in season, buy food locally.

Strawberries often score high in terms of food miles

What is best: buying organic apples from South Africa or buying local apples from a farmers' market?

Ketchup and air miles

Some foods are transported to us by ships, but others reach us by plane – which is much worse for the environment. Often, several products will be used to make another product. What do we get if we combine:

- tomatoes from China, California, Spain
- sugar from Brazil
- spices from India

That's right: ketchup; a total of 18,804 air miles

Bottled water or tap water?

More people are buying bottled water these days. Water is heavy and carrying it from place to place uses a lot of energy. The bottle itself creates waste and pollution.
Is tap water the solution?

Buying second-hand

Charity shops can be found on every high street these days. They mainly sell second-hand goods. They are good places to get hold of old books and records, second-hand

Cob Records – a famous second-hand vinyl records and CD shop in Porthmadog, Gwynedd

clothes and furniture, crockery and pictures. Buying second-hand goods is becoming ever more popular, and reusing goods benefits the environment.

A famous second-hand vinyl records and CD shop in Cardiff

Out-of-town shopping centre: Trostre Retail Park, Llanelli

Out-of-town retail parks

Out-of-town shopping centres or retail parks are very common. Some examples include the shopping centres at Culverhouse Cross, Cardiff; Trostre Park, near Llanelli; and Broughton Shopping Park in Flintshire.

Here are some of the advantages of such retail parks:
- large, new shops and units rather than old shops on the street
- several shops are often under one roof, so shoppers do not have to venture outside in bad weather
- ample free parking; close to main roads
- places to buy petrol or charge the car
- there will often be restaurants and cinemas on site. Therefore, going shopping is now a leisure activity rather than just going to buy necessary goods.

Some argue that these retail centres damage the local economy and are harmful to the environment:
- they encourage using cars to go shopping
- lorries transport goods across the country to the shops
- they take up green belt land on the outskirts of towns
- they sell goods from afar and from all over the world rather than local produce
- they are owned by large, international companies (rather than local owners), and therefore profits leave the local economy
- many of the shops only offer part-time jobs.

However, they are popular. This has meant that many shops, especially big companies, have relocated from town and city centres to shopping parks on the outskirts. The result is that the high street in many towns is suffering, with empty shops and a lack of shoppers.

Case study: What is happening on Bangor High Street?

1

Bangor – a city of learning, home to a university – but the last bookshop there closed in summer 2022

2

That is true of many shops on the longest high street in Wales – which is a mile long ...

10

Pontio – a centre for the arts, a cinema, a museum, a gallery and a **few new cafes** and evening events – still hope for the city?

The old road runs through the city still ...

9

an attempt to open a shopping centre within the city – too little too late?

8

shopping centre and business park – now outside the city ...

3 **lack of shoppers?** – while the COVID-19 pandemic and poverty are partly thought to be responsible, there are 4 supermarkets with free car parks in the city centre ...

4 **football** – the local team's stadium was moved out of the city centre to make way for a supermarket ...

... but the traffic is on the bypass

5 **post office** – closed, talk of converting the building into flats, moving jobs out of the centre ...

7 **hospital** – now outside the city; with a supermarket and a car park where it once was ...

6 **railway station and swimming pool** – still in the centre but not particularly modern ...

Traditional towns are changing rapidly

According to a recent survey, towns these days are not so much retail centres as places to meet and socialise. Does the information in the graph support this?

Change in the types of shops on the high street 2020-22 (%)

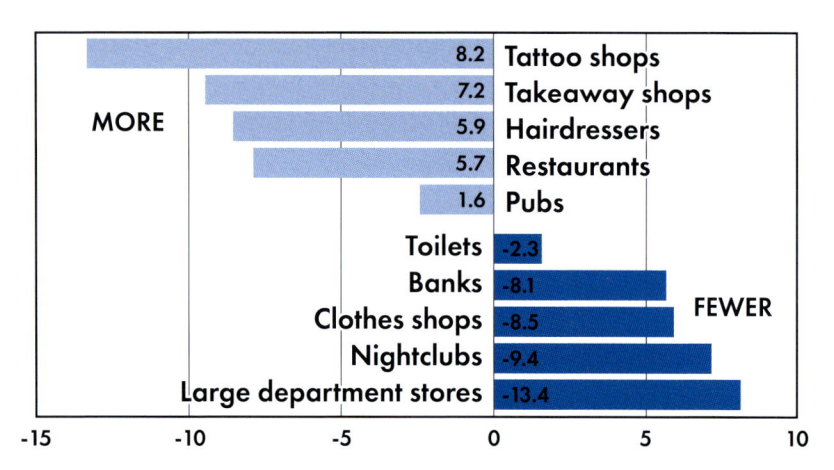

MORE
- Tattoo shops: 8.2
- Takeaway shops: 7.2
- Hairdressers: 5.9
- Restaurants: 5.7
- Pubs: 1.6

FEWER
- Toilets: -2.3
- Banks: -8.1
- Clothes shops: -8.5
- Nightclubs: -9.4
- Large department stores: -13.4

Online shopping

The growth in online shopping has also had a detrimental effect on the high street. But the biggest drawback to shopping online is that you cannot inspect and view goods before buying them. If they are not suitable, they must be returned to the seller. But there are also advantages:

- the ability to shop at any time without having to travel
- several goods can be quickly compared
- prices can be cheaper because of the competition, and also because some sellers do not have shops to maintain.

The COVID-19 pandemic in 2020–22 was a further blow to high street shops, and led to a large number of businesses closing. A recent survey showed that more than 9,000 stores closed in the United Kingdom between March 2020 and March 2022, including some major department stores such as Debenhams.

Towns fight back

The following is typical of several towns in Wales:

- an increase in empty shops
- buildings appearing run-down
- lack of shoppers on the street
- banks and other services closing
- towns becoming dormitory towns and people commuting to work elsewhere.

Crickhowell – supermarkets are banned in the town

Some towns are rallying to improve things:

- free or cheap parking
- low rent/tax on shops
- marketing campaigns and entertainment events
- opposing planning permission for supermarkets
- attracting more services that cannot be delivered online
- promoting artisans who repair/reuse goods in the town
- green spaces.

Treorchy is a town in an area that experienced a depression following the decline of the coal industry in the Rhondda Valley. But the town's high street has been revived, the local spirit is strong, and success breeds success:

Treorchy high street

- around 30 new businesses have opened in two years: small, independent shops run by local people
- 96% of shops now open
- the town won the UK's best High Street award in 2020.

Tourism

Wales's appeal to tourists

Tourism and leisure is an important industry in Wales. It contributes almost £3 billion a year to the economy, while 10% of Welsh jobs rely on tourism.

Wales's most popular attraction is Barry Island Pleasure Park in the Vale of Glamorgan, according to the Welsh Government's report, *Visits to Tourist Attractions in Wales in 2021*.

The most popular attraction that charged an entrance fee was Cardiff Castle. The graph shows the other most popular attractions in Wales in 2021.

Wales's Attractions 2021 – the top 10 with free entry and the top 10 with an entrance fee.

Wales's Attractions 2021 – the top 10 with free entry and with an entrance fee

- Barry Island Pleasure Park
- Tir Prince Fun Park, Abergele
- Pembrey Country Park, Llanelli
- Newborough Nature Reserve, Anglesey
- Walking on Yr Wyddfa
- Gwydir Forest Park, Llanrwst
- Wepre Country Park, Connah's Quay
- Stackpole Nature Reserve, Pembroke
- Cardiff Castle
- Folly Farm Kilgetty, Pembrokeshire
- Margam Country Park, Port Talbot
- Pontcysyllte Aqueduct, Trefor
- Portmeirion
- Swansea Leisure Centre
- Bodnant Gardens, Tal-y-Cafn, Colwyn Bay
- Nova, Prestatyn
- Forest Zip World, Betws-y-coed
- Slate Caverns Zip World, Blaenau Ffestiniog
- Conwy Castle
- Penrhyn Quarry Zip World, Bethesda

Number of visits (some are estimates)

The graphs show:

- many of the attractions are in rural areas and therefore an important part of the economy

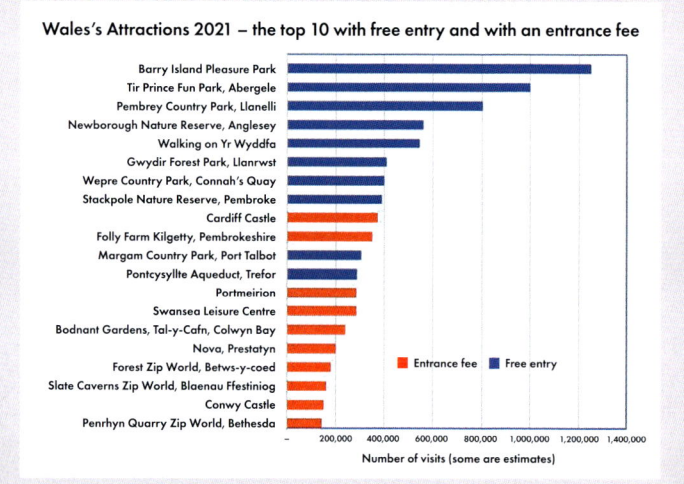

- most attractions are outdoors, or partly outdoors, with only 7% being indoor attractions

- half of overseas visitors coming to Wales are from European countries

- 72% of visitors from the United Kingdom to Wales are from England, and 25% are from Wales itself.

Where did foreign visitors to Wales come from (2019)
- Europe 50%
- Rest of the world 27%
- North America 23%

- The most popular reasons for coming on holiday to Wales in 2019 were:
  1. to enjoy the natural landscape (71% of visitors mentioned this)
  2. to visit a site of historical interest
  3. to participate in outdoor activities.

Early visitors

Tourism developed in Wales in the 18C mainly due to its distinct environment and landscape. Visitors would often be drawn by artists' drawings from the period. These artists were also visitors to Wales. Their early drawings were Wales's first tourism website!

One of those artists was Welshman Hugh Hughes, who painted the drawing of Pont-y-pair in Betws-y-coed around 1840. Due to the extraordinary beauty of the Eryri mountains and valleys, a cluster of artists set up to paint the scenery at Betws-y-coed between 1780 and 1860. As such, the village soon developed into a tourist centre.

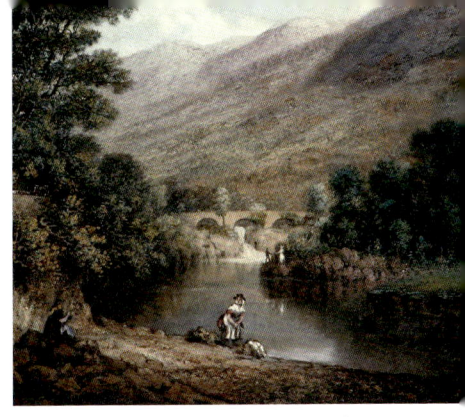

Pont-y-pair, Betws-y-coed – Hugh Hughes

Another important artist in this period was Richard Wilson, who is recognised as one of the finest landscape artists of all time. He appreciated the beauty of his country and showcased it in his paintings. He was an influence on other important artists such as Constable and Turner.

Yr Wyddfa from the Nantlle Valley – Richard Wilson

What attracted visitors to Llandrindod Wells?

Llandrindod Wells was one of the first tourist resorts in Wales. This was mainly due to the rich and abundant minerals found in its wells. Visiting Llandrindod Wells 'to take the water' was an old tradition among south Wales miners and industrial workers from the English midlands. As their daily work was dirty and dangerous, there was great prestige during the 19C in taking a healthy holiday in one of Wales's wellness towns, such as Llandrindod Wells, Llangamarch, Llanwrtyd, and the village of Trefriw in the Conwy Valley. Travel became easier for ordinary people with the advent of the railways. That led to a big increase in tourism. Llandrindod Wells railway station opened in 1865 and the town developed rapidly soon after.

Rock Park Pump Room, Llandrindod Wells, in the 1920s

Development of Welsh seaside towns

The practice of 'taking the water' from wells changed when doctors began advising patients to bathe in the sea to improve their health. Once again, the advent of the railways was important, offering people from towns and cities a quick and cheap way of reaching the coast.

By 1914 seaside towns such as Prestatyn, Rhyl, Llandudno, Barmouth, Aberystwyth, Tenby, Porthcawl and Barry had developed. Llandudno became known as 'queen of the Welsh resorts'.

Hotels on Llandudno's Victorian promenade. It is Wales's largest seaside town

Llandudno was very attractive at the time because:
- it was easily reached from England by train
- it had a wide selection of B&Bs overlooking the promenade and sea
- it had several shopping parades
- it had theatres, halls and entertainment of all kinds
- it offered traditional seaside entertainment – donkey rides, ice cream, india-rock, boat trips.

After the Second World War, holiday camps became popular. The camps offered cheap holidays in a chalet or cabin, and served food.

The sites were fitted with swimming pools, pleasure fairs and all kinds of evening entertainment. Visitors did not need to leave the site while holidaying there.

Butlin's opened a camp at Barry in 1966 and another at Pwllheli. It is today known as Hafan y Môr Holiday Park. During the 60s and 70s, almost 12,000 visitors holidayed at Butlin's in Pwllheli every week during summer.

Holiday camps were also popular along the north Wales coast in towns such as Prestatyn. They were very convenient for visitors from the north-west of England.

Tourism and the local people

Historian Bob Morris, who worked at Butlin's Pwllheli when he was a youngster, says the camp was closely linked to the local community: "Many local people went to work there. Local ministers became chaplains and held Sunday services there. As a result, a rather friendly relationship was soon established between the local people and the camp."

The swimming pool at Butlin's Pwllheli, 1961

Visitor needs change

Visitor needs have changed. According to Which? magazine, Aberaeron in Ceredigion was one of Wales's best seaside towns in 2022. 82% of visitors to the town praised it to the rafters. They say that some of the town's qualities include:

- a variety of nice and welcoming accommodation
- a convenient base for visiting attractions in the area
- excellent local food and drink.

Aberaeron harbour

While some seaside towns decline, Aberaeron's story shows it is possible to succeed. As they adapt, these towns can still attract day visitors or tourists who will stay for longer periods. These visitors can then enjoy themselves and spend their money there. According to a Welsh Government report, other examples of successful seaside towns in Wales are Tenby, St Davids and Llandudno.

Outdoor activities

The rocks and cliffs of the Welsh mountains have long attracted climbers. Many climbs offer a challenge that climbers cannot resist.

The team that had set its sights on climbing Everest in 1953 came to Eryri to train, and stayed at the Penygwryd Hotel at the foot of Yr Wyddfa. Tenzing Norgay and Edmund Hillary reached the summit of the world's highest mountain (8,848m) on 29 May 1953.

Walking to Base Camp, Everest, in the Himalayas

Up to 50,000 people a year spend their holidays walking to Everest's Base Camp in Nepal. The journey from Lukla airport to the camp, which is more than 5,000m above sea level, takes over a week. Several days of rest are necessary to acclimatise to the high mountains.

Climbing and walking in Wales is hugely popular, with over 600,000 people walking to the summit of Yr Wyddfa each year. Some will also reach the summit on a small train.

Littering by visitors is an issue on the mountain, and the National Park spends substantial sums of money restoring paths every year. In summer 2020, people queued for over an hour to reach the summit. Car parking created problems in Pen-y-Pass and in the Ogwen Valley. Due to these problems, the director of Cymdeithas Eryri called for 'more sustainable and safer tourism in the future'.

Walkers in Cwm Idwal, Eryri

Mid-Wales and south Wales also have mountains that attract visitors. Above the town of Abergavenny is Pen-y-fâl mountain (596m), which has a very distinct shape. It is known as the Sugar Loaf. Experiences here can be very different to those on the busiest peaks in Eryri:

- panoramic views over open country
- enjoyable, quiet paths at all times of year
- the feeling of freedom on the slopes
- an opportunity to enjoy nature at its best.

Pen-y-fâl mountain in Bannau Brycheiniog

Tourism on the coast

Thousands of visitors are attracted to Wales each year to walk the Wales Coast Path. The path, which is 870 miles long, opened in 2012. Walking along it, visitors will see:

- stunning cliffs
- remote coves
- popular beaches
- wildlife
- charming towns and villages
- major cities
- ancient monuments.

The path contributes greatly to the economy of the towns and villages that sit along it. The body responsible for the environment in Wales is called Natural Resources Wales. It receives funding from the Welsh Government to maintain, improve and promote the path in partnership with local authorities.

The Wales Coast Path leading northwards on Dinas Head near Fishguard in Pembrokeshire

Welsh lakes

Welsh lakes are also visitor attractions. Activities such as fishing, canoeing, sailing, surfing, jet-skiing and water skiing take place on lakes and some reservoirs in Wales.

Some lakes ban powerboats to ensure peace and quiet in the countryside and prevent water pollution. That is also the law in the Lake District in England. Illegal camping and littering can cause problems on the shores of the lakes.

Canoeing on Llyn Tegid, Bala

Adventure holidays

Outdoor activities continue to be important for visitors heading to Wales. Recently, the idea of visiting Wales is being associated more than ever with adventure. These activities include climbing and mountaineering, mountain biking, and coasteering.

Several zipwires in Wales are located in former slate quarries or collieries. Here, adventure meets history. People can also visit museums or take guided tours to experience the life of quarrymen or colliers.

Wales's forests offer adventure activities, either high amongst the branches or on challenging mountain bike tracks. In the most remote areas, the dark sky is world-famous among those who come to study the stars and the worlds beyond them.

Coasteering near St Davids. This adventure involves swimming, scrambling and leaping from rocks into the waves.

The zipwire of Zip World over Penrhyn Quarry, Bethesda

Slate areas of Wales and UNESCO status

In 2021 it was announced that the North West Wales Slate Landscape was deserving of World Heritage Site status by UNESCO. This makes the area a truly important Cultural Landscape. More and more visitors come from all over the world today to experience:
- the dramatic remains of the industry
- quarrymen's walking trails
- museums and attractions in these areas.

National Slate Museum, Llanberis

UNESCO stands for United Nations Educational, Scientific and Cultural Organization. The United Nations recognises the world's most significant sites, and considers them to be of 'extraordinary value to humanity'.

UNESCO sites attract many visitors. Some famous UNESCO sites around the world include:

Machu Picchu, Peru
Great Wall of China
Taj Mahal, India
Stonehenge, England.

The other UNESCO sites in Wales:
1. King Edward I's castles and town walls in north Wales, for example in Caernarfon, Conwy and Beaumaris
2. Pontcysyllte aqueduct and canal
3. the industrial landscape of Blaenavon.

Pyramids in Giza, Egypt – a UNESCO World Heritage Site

Underground

Parts of north-east Wales and Bannau Brycheiniog attract many people to explore natural or man-made caves and tunnels. People can also go underground at the popular Dan yr Ogof attraction in

Stalactites grow as water drips from the roof in Dan yr Ogof

the upper Swansea Valley. These natural caves in the limestone were discovered by two local farmers more than 100 years ago. The rocks date back more than 300 million years, and the caves contain magnificent examples of stalactites and stalagmites. Opened to the public in the 1970s, the attraction is visited by over 70,000 people every year.

Camping, caravans and cottages

Camping continues to be very popular in Wales, either in caravans or tents. There are around 300 caravan parks in Wales. The largest caravan park in Europe is in Trecco Bay, Porthcawl, with over 50,000 people staying there each summer. The Mochras campsite at Llanbedr, near Harlech, is one of the largest campsites in Europe, with a capacity for 800 tents on 120 hectares of land by the sea.

Trecco Bay holiday resort, Porthcawl

New words have appeared on Welsh holiday websites in recent years, namely:

- glamping
- wood burning stove
- hot tub
- eco-friendly
- underfloor heating.

Glampio Coed, near Aberdaron

Hiring luxury cottages, pods or cabins is very popular. And visitors expect them to provide these kind of facilities. Staying in self-catering accommodation is now more popular than staying in a hotel.

The increase in these types of breaks means that almost every area of Wales is now attracting visitors. This type of accommodation is often provided by small businesses, with farmers, for example, diversifying. They are converting old farm buildings and turning them into holiday cottages.

The village of Trefeglwys, near Llanidloes in Powys, would not have been considered a holiday destination fifty years ago. There are now nearly 100 cottages, cabins or holiday accommodation available within a few miles of the village. One local farm has invested and built a leisure park for caravans. Visitor facilities include an indoor swimming pool, spa, bar and restaurant. The site includes 65 cabins, 72 fixed caravans and space for 70 touring caravans.

Farm buildings in Pembrokeshire converted into holiday cottages

What are the dangers of overtourism?

The Welsh Government is keen to promote sustainable tourism. This includes ecotourism and cultural tourism and tourism based on physical activities. Overtourism can have a detrimental effect on communities and the environment. It can cause problems such as:

- undermining the housing market for local people. Young people are struggling to buy houses in their own communities because of competition from those looking to move into the area or buy a holiday home
- a sharp increase in Airbnb letting houses. This means fewer houses are available to rent on a long-term basis. It also increases rent costs. There are over 500 Airbnb accommodations in Tenby alone
- harming the environment. This includes damage to paths and nature reserves, littering and inconsiderate parking
- a detrimental effect on the Welsh language in its heartlands. Llanberis is one of the villages hardest hit by the effects of overtourism. The percentage of the village's population that can speak Welsh fell from over 80% in 2001 to under 70% by the 2021 Census
- school closures and the loss of other services. Visitors only spend time in the area during the summer weeks
- creating an economy dependent on low-paid seasonal jobs. For example, cleaning and waitering jobs
- placing additional pressure on local services. Hospitals, doctors, water supplies and rubbish collectors are needed as the population grows considerably over the summer.

Walkers on the summit of Yr Wyddfa

How can the problem be solved?

To try and resolve some of these issues, the Welsh Government has given local authorities the right to levy extra tax on holiday homes. Some are also calling for making planning permission a requirement before people can convert a dwelling house into a holiday home.

Another suggestion is that tourists should be taxed, which is common practice throughout the world. In Mallorca, there is a tourist tax of between 2€ and 4€ per night on those over the age of 16. The money can be spent improving the resources available to everyone, including visitors. And this eases the burden on the key workers who contribute to the industry.

The visitor season needs to be extended so that there is work for local people throughout the year. Visitors who enjoy walking, local history and produce, music and the warm welcome of the Welsh people can be encouraged to visit at any time of year. This is called 'cultural tourism'.

A campaign banner in Nefyn calling for homes for local people

Energy

Energy is the technology that heats and lights our houses, drives transport machinery of various kinds, and powers industry.

The Welsh Government has a responsibility to ensure:
- that there is a reliable supply of energy available to all, and that it is affordable
- that there is an increase in the use of renewable and low carbon energy to protect the environment and meet the challenges of climate change.

Energy creation and global warming

While there are efforts to encourage the use of green energy, as recently as 2020, China (60%), India (70%) and South Africa (85%) continued to generate most of their electricity by burning coal. Therefore, it is a mixed picture across the world.

A wind farm on the Black Mountain, near Ammanford in Carmarthenshire

Wind is not the only solution: here's a hydrogen machine that is being developed to create energy in Japan

Energy production has caused pollution

People are attempting to flee the town of Kiselyovsk in Siberia. The polluted air is forcing them to leave. The snow there is black, because the town sits next to a huge opencast coalmine. The town's water, food and air supplies are harmful to residents, and lung diseases and cancer kill many.

The impact of air pollution from coal works

Wales is trying to tackle the challenge of producing clean energy:
- in 2020, generating energy accounted for 16% of all **greenhouse gas** emissions in Wales
- the Welsh Government's ambition is to be a net zero country by 2050. That would mean that in Wales, more carbon dioxide would be absorbed from the atmosphere every year than is released. That would reduce global warming.

But Wales does not currently have complete control over how much pollution is created here. Ffos-y-frân is the largest opencast coalmine in Britain. It is close to houses and the locals complain about the noise, dirt and cracks in their walls. But in 2022 the plant was granted a licence by the UK Government to continue to extract coal for almost four additional years. However, it was decided that this huge opencast mine would close before the end of 2023.

Ffos-y-frân above Merthyr Tydfil

The last coal power station in Wales closes

Aberthaw B near Barry was the last coal power station to close in Wales. It was opened in 1971 and closed in 2020 due to a shortage of coal from nearby mines and stringent emissions regulations. At its peak it was able to meet the electricity needs of 1.5 million people.

Aberthaw power station in 2017

How can the gap be filled after Aberthaw B?

In order to produce more energy using zero-carbon or low-carbon methods, Wales must find clean ways of producing energy. We have great natural resources for creating energy using water, wind and the coastal tides.

Wales – turning clean energy into an industry?

Energy production can be an important industry in Wales.

But there is a problem. Responsibility for energy production is currently shared between the UK Government and the Welsh Government. The UK Government is responsible for major schemes, with the Welsh Government responsible for developing smaller projects that generate up to 350 megawatts (MW).

Dinorwig Hydroelectric **Power Station** – an example of a power station in Wales that generates more than 350MW

Wales's Hydroelectric Power Stations

Dinorwig Power Station

A cross-section of the Dinorwig Hydro Electric scheme

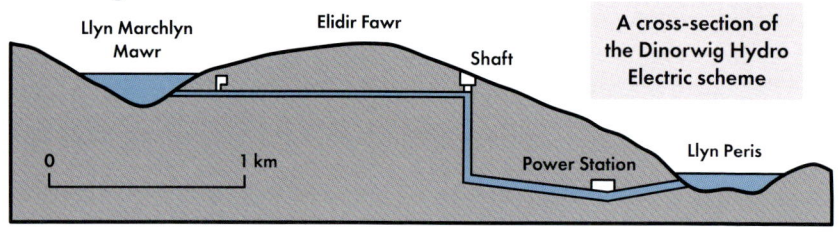

'Electric Mountain' is the name of the Dinorwig power station near Llanberis in Gwynedd. This is because the six turbines and production equipment were installed underground in the bowels of Elidir Fawr mountain. This is the site of the former Dinorwig slate quarry. Electricity is generated as water stored in the Marchlyn Mawr reservoir, more than 600m above sea level, is released into Llyn Peris, 500m below. The water is then pumped back up to Marchlyn Mawr at night when there is less demand for electricity. This type of power station is known as a pump storage scheme as the water is used time and again to generate electricity. Hydroelectric power stations are very important because they can respond to sudden high demands for electricity. Dinorwig Power Station can deliver 1728MW to the network in 16 seconds.

A smaller power station that works in a similar way can be found in Tanygrisiau, near Blaenau Ffestiniog.

Several other power stations in Wales use the power of moving water to generate electricity. Some power stations have generated electricity in this way since the beginning of the last century, and still work to this day! Cwm Dyli is the oldest power station which continues to generate in the United Kingdom. Due to the design of the building, it has been given the name 'The Chapel in the Valley'.

A new hydroelectric power station may be built at Glyn Rhonwy near Llanberis which will generate around 100MW.

Cwm Dyli power station with the pipe that transports water from Llyn Llydaw at the foot of Yr Wyddfa

Power station	Scheme	Generating capacity	Opened
Dinorwig	Pump storage	1728 MW	1984
Ffestiniog	Pump storage	360 MW	1963
Rheidol	Hydroelectric	56 MW	1964
Maentwrog	Hydroelectric	24 MW	1928
Dolgarrog	Hydroelectric	27 MW	1907
Cwm Dyli	Hydroelectric	10 MW	1906

Mallwyd Water Turbines

At Gelliddolen farm in mid Wales a number of streams on the hills flow into the river Clywedog on the valley floor. The farmer, Tegwyn Pughe Jones, and his sons Huw and Guto, have now built and installed four turbines on the streams. The turbines use the energy of water to generate electricity.

The first step was to create a small dam to gather the water, which could then be cleaned before flowing into the water pipe. The larger the fall between the lake and the turbine hut, the more energy is produced. The energy huts were built to reflect the environment of the area, with stone walls and green roofs. They draw much less attention than windmills.

The turbine hut contains dials that show the pressure of the water and the energy readings. The biggest maintenance job is lubricating the turbines and cleaning the thin mesh that keeps the turbine's interior clean. The latest turbine came from Swansea – from a Welsh company that provides equipment for similar enterprises across the country.

A few facts

**There are 4 water turbines, of different sizes, on rivers and streams:
Nant y Dugoed, Afon Clywedog, Nant Carreg yr Hydd, Nant Talyglannau.**

There must be:
1. a constant flow of water
2. a sufficient fall between the dam and turbine
3. a means to connect the turbine to the electricity grid.

Turbine hut on Gelliddolen farm

Tegwyn and the turbine

Advantages:

- green and clean energy
- sufficient energy for 200 houses
- local energy that is used in the area
- selling the electricity brings income to the farm
- through developing turbine maintenance skills, there is plenty of work to keep both sons at home

Producing green energy in Wales

Why are there are so many hydroelectric power stations in Wales?

Wales is a mountainous country with constant rainfall. As much as 4,500mm of rain a year falls on the summit of Yr Wyddfa.

Streams and rivers flow rapidly on steep hills. Ruins of watermills can be found all over Wales – some ground grain and some created energy for woollen mills and quarries. Others generated electricity.

This also explains why several local hydroelectricity initiatives have been set up in Wales recently.

The ruins of Trefin Mill, Pembrokeshire

Is Wales suitable for solar energy panels?

Some areas of Wales get many hours of sunshine (e.g. Rhyl: 1,500 hours a year), and solar panels can now be seen on many homes and other buildings in Wales. There has been a big increase in the number of solar panels installed on houses to generate electricity and to heat rooms and water. Five times more solar panels were installed on buildings in Wales in 2021 than in 2020.

The technology used in the panels is still developing, which is good news for generating more renewable energy.

There are now 'daylight' panels available – these can generate electricity without the need for bright sunshine.

Morriston Hospital Solar Farm, near Swansea

This was the first solar farm to be set up in the United Kingdom specifically to supply electricity to a hospital. The farm contains 10,000 solar panels and can provide around 26% of Morriston Hospital's electricity needs. The scheme was set up with the financial support of the Welsh Government, and it is also community owned. The scheme is expected to save Swansea Bay University Health Board more than half a million pounds a year.

Opposition to solar farms

However, arguments are being made against putting solar farms on Welsh land. In Llanedi, Carmarthenshire, there are plans to build such a farm on 80 hectares of agricultural land. Arguments against this development include:

- spoiling the beauty of a rural landscape
- wasting good land that could be used to produce food
- too large a development for a small area.

Another solar energy farm in Waunarlwydd near Swansea

Margam wood-burning power station

Margam's 40MW green energy power station, near Port Talbot, cost £160 million to build. It started generating electricity by burning wood in 2019. The power station uses wood waste.

The fuel is dried to a level where it does not release as much smoke as it burns. The heat is used to generate steam in a boiler. The steam is then channelled to turn a turbine that generates electricity.

The steam will then be cooled and returned to a tank in the system. The emissions are controlled and within the environmental rules for the power station.

1MW supplies electricity to 2,000 homes for an hour.

Wind energy - a great source of green energy

- Electricity-generating windmills can now be found all over Wales.
- They use a natural energy source that will never run out, namely wind.

But some complain that the windmills are a scar on Wales's natural scenery, that they are noisy, and that they are dangerous to birds. People also claim that they are ineffective because the wind does not blow strongly enough every day.

Wind farms sponsor the local community. One example of that is Ysgol Carno. The new building cost over £1m, and funding was received from Powys Council. But there was also a key contribution from the community, and £500,000 was donated towards the project by the local wind farm trust.

Welsh wind farms are not just located on high ground.

The photo shows the Gwynt y Môr site in north Wales. It can generate 576MW of electricity.

They are also found offshore. Pictured is the Gwynt y Môr site in north Wales. In 2020, offshore wind farms produced 29% of Wales's renewable energy. A number of other projects are in the pipeline.

Wind energy has been prevalent in Wales since the late 1990s. One of the first wind farms was established on Mynydd Gorddu, near Tal-y-bont in Ceredigion.

Tidal energy

The Swansea Bay Tidal Lagoon Scheme is an exciting clean energy project.

The scheme is designed to generate low carbon electricity from sea tides in Swansea Bay.

Once completed, it would be the largest tidal scheme of its kind in the world. It would be able to generate 250MW of electricity, which is sufficient to supply 155,000 homes.

Swansea Bay has the second-largest tidal range in the world, which is a great advantage. The difference between the high and low tides can be as much as 10.4m. In 24 hours, there are two tides and two ebb tides. Therefore, the turbines will need to work both ways – back and forth as the water level changes with the tides.

However, in June 2015, the UK Government refused to grant permission for the scheme. Is there a chance that the scheme could be developed at some point in the future, perhaps?

In Anglesey, the Morlais initiative intends to produce tidal energy on 35km^2 of seabed near Holy Island. Permission to generate energy here was granted in 2021 and the next step will be to install tidal energy equipment on the seabed. A tidal energy sub-station has already been opened on land, and the intention is to produce up to 240MW of low-carbon energy by 2026.

The Morlais tidal energy sub-station on the western coast of Holy Island in Anglesey, opened in October 2023.

Oil and gas in Wales

The deep and sheltered port of Milford Haven in Pembrokeshire is suitable for unloading oil and gas tankers. It is the UK's largest energy port, and contains Europe's largest gas power station.

The terminal at the former Point of Ayr colliery site on the river Dee in Flintshire is a good location to receive and process gas from Liverpool Bay. The gas is then sent through a pipeline to the electric power station at Connah's Quay, which can supply as much as half of Wales's electricity needs.

Puma Energy oil storage tanks, Milford Haven

The dangers of importing energy

- **Accidents**: in 1983 there was a huge fire at the Milford Haven oil refinery. A 46,000 tonnes oil tank exploded and 1,500 firemen fought the flames for two days.
- **Pollution**: the Sea Empress oil tanker ran into difficulties at the mouth of Milford Haven harbour in 1996, and 72,000 tonnes of crude oil was spilled along 120 miles of coast.
- **Environmental damage**: scenic areas were spoiled due to the need to build gas pipelines across the land.

Point of Ayr gas terminal in Flintshire

Nuclear power stations

When splitting an atom – the smallest particle of all materials – energy is released to generate electricity. But nuclear power stations produce hazardous waste that is problematic for us and for future generations. Accidents at these power stations can be catastrophic.

There are currently no nuclear power stations generating electricity in Wales. But there is talk of building small new reactors at the site of the former Trawsfynydd nuclear power station. The need to generate low carbon electricity means that nuclear energy is preferred again.

According to anti-nuclear campaigners, it takes ten years to build a nuclear power plant, and this is too long a time to wait. Solutions are urgently needed, and action required today to respond to the problems of climate change.

Wylfa Power Station, Cemaes Bay, Anglesey

Saving energy

The Welsh Government is offering grants to insulate homes so that they lose less heat. A quarter of the heat in a house can be lost through the roof. Producing the insulation and installing it also creates jobs.

'All the electricity from six power plants like the one being built at Hinkley could be saved by properly insulating British homes' – Robat Idris in an article in the Welsh-language journal Barn. *Barn, number 718 (November 2022), page 6.*

Using wool for insulation

The Tŷ-Mawr company in Breconshire produces wool insulation

Future energy generation in Wales

Wales and the world are facing two serious energy crises, namely that we need to:
- create clean energy to avoid burning fossil fuels
- create cheaper, local energy due to the current cost of living.

Wales has the potential to meet both of these problems and generate renewable energy for ourselves.

The Welsh economy could also benefit by selling surplus energy to other countries.

At present, Wales remains a net exporter of electricity – meaning that it exports more than it imports. It generates almost twice as much electricity as it needs.

The good news is that Wales is also producing increasing amounts of renewable energy, and a higher percentage of that energy is locally owned.

Generating renewable energy in Wales

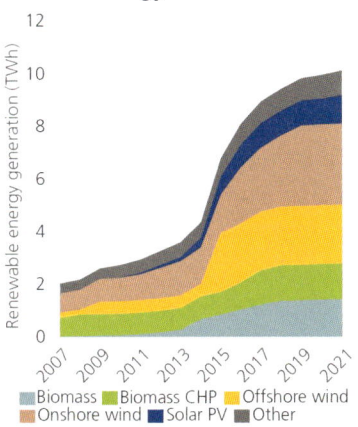

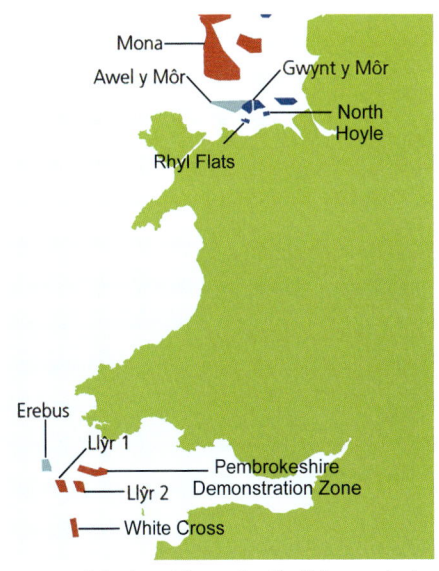

Chart showing renewable energy generation (TWh) in Wales from 2007 to 2021, categorised by Biomass, Biomass CHP, Offshore wind, Onshore wind, Solar PV, and Other.

Loss to Wales – Crown Estate property

Currently 65% of the Welsh coast is owned by the Crown Estate in London.

Because of this, Wales does not benefit from any investment to produce renewable energy in its surrounding seas.

For example, rent income from the proposed Mona sea wind farm will all go to the UK Government, rather than the Welsh Government.

This is different from Scotland where the Crown Estate has given control over the country's coast back to the people of Scotland.

Map showing current (blue) and future (red) offshore wind projects on Crown Estate property on the Welsh coast: Mona, Awel y Môr, Gwynt y Môr, North Hoyle, Rhyl Flats, Erebus, Llŷr 1, Llŷr 2, Pembrokeshire Demonstration Zone, White Cross.

Current (blue) and future (red) offshore wind projects on Crown Estate property on the Welsh coast

How to protect Wales's environment?

POLLUTION

What is pollution?
The environment in any cynefin is polluted when it is stained by waste, chemicals or any other harmful material.

There are three main types of pollution: air pollution, water pollution and land pollution.

Air pollution
- Volcanoes and wildfires pollute the air.
- Most harm is caused by human activities, including pollution from cars and other vehicles.
- The worst air pollution is caused by smoke from the burning of fossil fuels, namely coal, oil and gas. This can happen in factories, electric power stations, houses or any building that is heated.

Water pollution
- Waste is thrown into rivers and the sea.
- Sewerage is pumped into rivers and the sea.
- Industries sometimes dump toxic chemicals into rivers.
- Rain washes fertilizer, weedkillers and pesticides from fields into rivers.

Land pollution
- Littering on the ground creates land pollution.
- Rubbish is disposed of in tips or buried in the ground.
- Poison from waste can enter rivers and the food chain.

Loud noise is another form of pollution that can create problems.

Pollution is harmful and it:
- endangers nature in its cynefin
- contributes to climate change
- inhibits economic growth
- has the greatest impact on the most impoverished communities.

Brick factory in Nepal

How does pollution affect Wales?

As Wales is an industrialised country, it has a lot of historical pollution. Waste tips from the mines, mineral workings and slate quarries can be found in many parts of Wales.

Landslides can occur at tips following heavy rainfall. This was the cause of the Aberfan disaster in 1966 when 144 people and children were killed.

According to the Welsh Government, there are over 300 coal tips alone that need attention. Over £500 million is needed to make them safe. But the UK Government is currently not prepared to contribute to the cost.

Pollution creating green algae in the river Wye

The Wye Valley – an Area of Outstanding Natural Beauty

- Pollution creates green **algae** in the water which is more noticeable when the river flows back from Herefordshire into Wales.
- The algae are created by phosphate waste – which comes from manure that is the result of large-scale poultry farming.
- The river leaves Wales and enters Herefordshire – 20 million chickens are bred in this part of England.
- In 2022, the UK Government refused to ban the establishment of more poultry farms in Herefordshire.

Pollution crossing borders

As well as rivers, the wind and the sea can move pollution from country to country:

- clouds of polluted smoke from one country can be carried by the wind to other countries, creating damage to the environment there
- once litter enters the sea, it can reach beaches thousands of miles away.

This shows that there must be agreements across borders and collaboration between countries to address litter and pollution problems.

COP20 in Lima, Peru 2014

COP conference aims for environmental agreement

All the people of the world must work together to reduce pollution. A positive sign is that the international conference to try to stop climate change, called COP, is now held every year.

(COP stands for: Conference of the Parties. It was established to try and secure an environmental agreement between 197 countries at a conference in 1992.)

Wales's contribution

- The worst air pollution in the UK is found in some parts of Wales – open fire smoke and transport pollution.
- The Welsh Government's Clean Air Plan for Wales aims to raise the standard of public transport and reduce traffic speeds to 20 mph in built-up areas.
- In 2021/22 Wales recycled 65% of its waste.
- But every person in Wales still generates 170kg of waste that is not recycled. Most of this waste can be recycled.

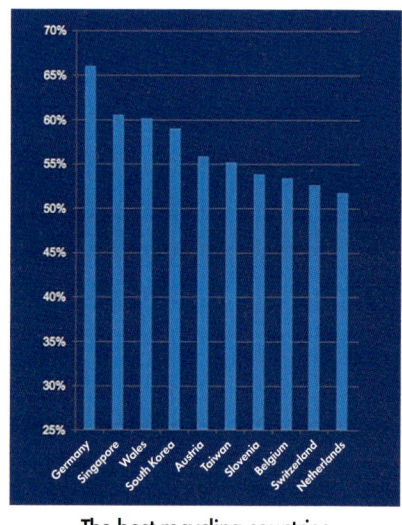

The best recycling countries

But Wales is gaining international recognition for being one of the leaders in recycling – outperforming a great many of the world's major countries.

Although Wales is not a member of the UN or allowed to attend COP Conferences, it shows that it is a country that takes the fight against pollution seriously.

What more can we do to clean up our environment?

- Pollution prevention starts with the individual: not recklessly throwing away waste and ruining our cynefin.
- Support all voluntary organisations seeking to create a greener world.
- Distribute waste for effective recycling by our county councils.
- Follow the lead of the Welsh Government and reduce pollution on all fronts.

Light pollution

Excess light at night can affect the cynefin in which we live:
- people in cities complain that they cannot see the starts or even the moonlight; light pollution changes the nature of the night
- many birds and creatures are awake and feed at night – they are badly affected by light pollution
- lights on high-rise buildings, ships, masts and windmills confuse migrating birds and cause birds to collide with them

Part of the Milky Way in the dark sky reserve of Tekapo, New Zealand

Bardsey Island – Europe's darkest sky

- In February 2023, Bardsey Island was designated a Dark Sky Sanctuary, the highest status the International DarkSky Association (IDA) can award. Bardsey Island is the first site in Europe to be granted such status.
- The darkness on Bardsey Island supports the cynefin of creatures that have evolved so that they need to come out at night. These include a large variety of moths, the storm petrel and the wood mouse.
- In their nesting season there will be 20,000 pairs of Manx shearwaters on Bardsey Island. They rely entirely on dark skies to safely return to their nests in holes in the island's ground.

Why is the Dark Sky of Wales valuable?

- 95% of European people live in areas where there is much light at night. Wales, on the other hand, is the country with the highest percentage of dark skies in the world.
- Three areas of Wales have been awarded special status – "international dark sky places". They are great locations to see the night in its natural light. The three areas are: Eryri National Park, Bannau Brycheiniog National Park, and the Elan Valley in mid Wales.
- Dark sky tourism is on the rise, and there are prospects that it will grow to be important to the winter economy.

The Northern Lights above Bardsey Island

'The Plastic Man' in Senegal

80% of the rubbish in the sea comes from the land. Most of the rubbish in our lakes, canals, streams and rivers eventually enters the sea.

The waste of the rich world is a burden on poor countries.

That is the message from Modou Fall, a Senegalese man known in Africa as 'the plastic man'.

Every day, the 49-year-old walks the beaches of his country, picking up plastic bags and tying them on to his clothes.

"Do not throw away plastic bags," is his message. "They poison the sea and put people's health at risk."

Senegal's coast in western Africa faces American countries, on the other side of the Atlantic Ocean. Atlantic Ocean currents carry America's rubbish all the way to west Africa.

Plastic in the water

Plastic in rivers and seas harms wildlife. Birds, whales, fish and turtles either eat it or the plastic entangles and suffocates them. If they eat plastic, they often die of starvation because the substance fills their stomachs.

Microplastic particles

Microplastic particles, which are very fine particles of plastic, are found in rivers and seas as plastic debris decomposes. Fish ingest them, which then endangers the life of the animals that eat the fish. These particles can also affect the health of people who eat the fish.

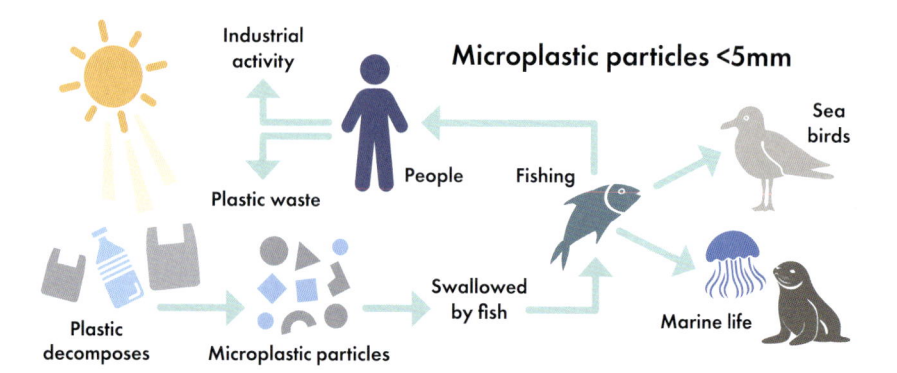

Microplastic particles <5mm

- Industrial activity
- Plastic waste
- People
- Fishing
- Sea birds
- Plastic decomposes
- Microplastic particles
- Swallowed by fish
- Marine life

A ban on single-use plastics

- In 2011 Wales was one of the first countries in the world to charge for single-use carrier bags.
- In September 2022 a ground-breaking law was passed banning single-use plastics in Wales, including cutlery, plates, drinking straws, balloon sticks etc.
- Wales has shown strong leadership, and other countries such as England have followed its example.

Shopping bag for repeated use

A seal stuck in a plastic fishing net

Plastic is a problem

Plastic waste is a common problem across Wales. The waste often ends up in places like Cardiff Bay. As such, Cardiff Harbour Authority and volunteers from groups such as the Cardiff Rivers Group organise clearing sessions. They collect around 500 tonnes of rubbish every year – much of it plastic.

Volunteers cleaning plastic waste on a beach in Ghana, Africa

Sorting our recycling

All businesses, schools, families and individuals are required to sort their waste and place it in different boxes for collection.

What happens after we sort our waste for recycling?

Food waste
Most local councils in Wales send their food waste to an anaerobic digestion site. It is then broken down to create biogas. This is used to generate green energy that can power homes and communities.

Many types of plastic and metal can be recycled to create other goods.

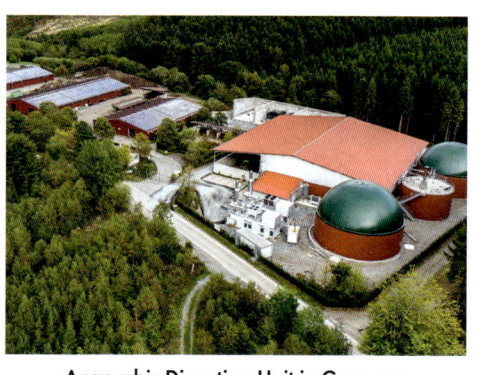

Anaerobic Digestion Unit in Germany

Recycling on a tricycle in Shanghai, China

European Union: it recycles three-quarters of its glass waste. Glass can be reused time and again.

Sweden: imports other countries' waste to produce energy.

India: imports 8% of all the world's waste, including scrap metal, battery cells, paper, rubber and clothing.

Welsh schools at an Eco-Schools conference in Cardiff

Wales joins forces to create Eco-Schools

Eco-Schools is a global programme where 19.5 million children across 70 countries work together towards one goal. It is the largest educational programme on the planet. It has been implemented by the Foundation for Environmental Education (FEE) since 1994 and is run in Wales by the charity Keep Wales Tidy.

The programme is designed to inspire young people to make positive changes to their school environment and the wider community. This is incorporated into lessons as they develop their key skills, including numeracy and literacy. The programme contributes to Education for Sustainable Development and Global Citizenship.

There are seven steps each school must take in order to become an Eco-School (see: https://keepwalestidy.cymru/eco-schools/).

Reusing waste around the world

Some countries in the world use ingenuity and imagination to create new goods from what is rubbish to others.

Waste is reused to make:

Construction bricks in Indonesia

School furniture in India

In Wales, the Second Life Products Wales company creates all sorts of useful tools from old plastic that has been used to wrap large bales on farms.

Glass bottles for local milk

In 2020 the Goitre Fach farm near Hendy, Carmarthenshire, turned a crisis into a business opportunity.

The farm milked 250 cows and supplied restaurants, hotels and catering companies that served planes, trains and motorway cafes.

The COVID-19 pandemic lockdowns meant that this market disappeared overnight.

"We had to tip all the milk into the slurry pit," said Ifan Beynon-Thomas, one of Goitre Fach's sons.

The Beynon family decided to take a risk through:
- buying a milk vending machine and installing it in the village near the M4
- ordering glass bottles with the 'Llaeth Beynon Dairy' stamp that could be washed and reused
- persuading customers to buy 'whole milk' fresh from the farm.

The initiative was a success. Two more machines were installed in Ammanford and three machines on the Coast Path in Swansea. The machines also sell milkshakes and coffee.

"It is heartening that so many people are reusing the glass bottles instead of throwing them away, as is the case with plastic milk bottles," Ifan said. "We invested in 200,000 glass bottles, and the demand for them is now reducing. Customers support the effort to reduce our carbon footprint – through local produce in bottles that can be cleaned and reused. It is great to see that families and young couples are doing this."

Sheds selling whole milk from local farms can now be found across Wales – here is one in Pwllheli. Several 'Milk Huts' such as this one are also found in the Aberystwyth and Machynlleth area.

Food banks

Sometimes, the major supermarkets throw away a lot of food after it reaches its 'best before' date.

Food banks can use this food and distribute it to people who are struggling to make ends meet.

The cost of living is driving an increasing number of families to turn to volunteer-run food banks.

Vegetables 'impossible to sell in a supermarket' on their way to a food bank

Car Boot Sales

Another very effective method of reusing goods is to sell them in Car Boot Sales, rather than throwing them onto the tip.

Repair and refurbishment

'Repair Café Wales' has been establishing and supporting repair cafés throughout Wales since April 2017. All types of goods can be taken to these cafés to be repaired by volunteers, rather than having to throw them away.

Repair Café Wales Team

Tourism and cleaning up pollution

Visitors can create a lot of pollution.

Following a ban on overseas holidays during the COVID-19 lockdowns in 2020 and 2021, many more tourists spent their holidays in the United Kingdom, including in Wales.

'Surfers against Sewage' cleaning up Perranporth beach, Cornwall

During the COVID-19 period there was an increase in pollution, including:

- litter on Yr Wyddfa and in other popular attractions
- dog fouling on public footpaths
- wild campers leaving a mess behind
- too many cars in the countryside and on Welsh beaches
- powerful boat engines polluting seawater and lakes and contributing to noise pollution
- too many visitors affecting the cynefin of otters and wild birds.

Rubbish on Manorbier beach, Pembrokeshire

In November 2022, 561 volunteers took part in 41 campaigns to clean up visitor litter on Welsh beaches

Sewerage in rivers and the sea

During periods of heavy rainfall the water companies, including Welsh Water, are allowed to discharge sewerage into our rivers and the sea, to prevent it from flooding streets and houses.

Some say this happens too often and that human sewerage was discharged into Welsh rivers more than 90,000 times in 2021. The five worst rivers for sewerage were the rivers Teifi, Usk, Wye, Tawe and Menai.

Welsh Water says these figures are "terrible" and it plans to spend almost a billion pounds in the next 5 years to try and improve the situation.

People planning to go swimming in Wales's rivers and in the surrounding sea are being warned about the pollution before doing so.

There has been an increase in swimmers and surfers reporting illnesses, some very serious, after swimming in Welsh rivers and seas.

Conservation

To protect wildlife, some areas are turned into reserves.

Where are Wales's nature reserves?

Wales has 76 National Nature Reserves to help protect a wide range of wildlife and ecosystems. They include:

- the high peaks of Yr Wyddfa
- the Morfa Harlech sand dunes
- the Maentwrog oak woods
- **Cors Caron in Ceredigion**
- **islands such as Ramsey Island off the Pembrokeshire coast.**

Working in a nature reserve

Ramsey Island is an island off the coast of Pembrokeshire. It has a Nature Reserve for breeding birds, with 5,000 pairs of Manx shearwaters raising chicks there. The warden of the reserve is Nia Stephens, a farm girl from Ceredigion. She lives on the island for nine months a year.

"I go back to the island at the beginning of March," Nia said. "This gives me a month to prepare before the first visitors arrive. I start each presentation in Welsh, and it is surprising how much the language is used here. People love to chat about nature in their own language. Buildings and walls need repairs after winter storms. I like working in the outdoors – doing things like fencing, trail restoration, maintenance, and keeping an eye on the wildlife, of course."

As well as managing her time and visitor numbers ("The last boat departs at 4pm every day – it's nice and quiet afterwards!"), Nia has to protect the island from the pests of nature. She examines driftwood discarded by the sea, in case there are unwanted mice or insects among them. Before brown rats were eradicated from the island in 2000, it had only 200 pairs of Manx shearwaters.

Seals on Ramsey Island

Where are the National Parks of Wales?

A fifth of Wales's land (20%) is within a National Park. National parks are areas of land that are protected for the nation and into the future. They can be seen on this map:
1. Eryri
2. Pembrokeshire Coast
3. Bannau Brycheiniog.

Only 2.9% of the population of Wales lives in these parks which attract 22 million visitors a year.

The three parks have two legal responsibilities:
- **conservation** – the conservation and enhancement of the natural environment, wildlife and cultural heritage
- **encouraging the public to use the park**, to enjoy it, and to better understand nature.

In doing so the parks also have a responsibility towards local culture and the local community living within the park.

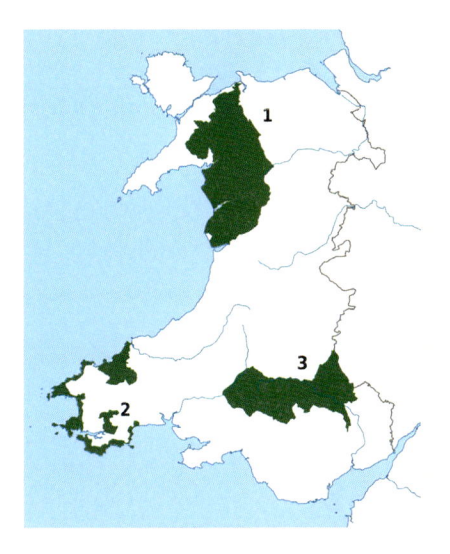

The public visiting the parks also have responsibilities. For example, they should avoid creating issues such as:
- over-use of cars
- inconsiderate parking
- 'wild' camping
- littering and dog fouling
- lack of respect for agricultural stock
- not keeping to paths.

Cwm Idwal in Eryri was Wales's first National Nature Reserve in 1954.

Cadair Idris, Eryri National Park

A closer look at Bannau Brycheiniog National Park

Bannau Brycheiniog National Park is a national park in south Wales. It is situated between the towns of Llandeilo, Llandovery, Brecon, Hay-on-Wye, Pontypool and Merthyr Tydfil. It was created in 1957.

The high mountains of Bannau Brycheiniog form the backbone of the park. In the west are the broad heathlands of Fforest Fawr and the Black Mountain. And in the east, beyond Bannau Brycheiniog itself, are the similarly named Black Mountains, on the border with England. Among the highest peaks is the one pictured here: Pen y Fan (886m). Others include Corn Du (873m), Cribyn (795m), Fan y Big (719m) and Fan Llia (631m).

The park has an area of 1344km². It has several waterfalls, including Sgwd Henrhyd which is 27m high. In the Ystradfellte area there are several notable caves, such as Ogof Ffynnon Ddu. Welsh mountain ponies can be seen grazing in the park. And it also has a number of walking trails and cycle paths.

Visitors

A recent survey found that 58% of visitors come to Wales's National Parks to enjoy the scenery and landscape. Once they have arrived, the main activity is walking (40%). 93% of visitors to the National Parks travel there by car.

A large population near Bannau Brycheiniog National Park

Over half of the population of Wales lives within a half-hour car journey of this park. While the park authority wants as many people and children as possible to enjoy the natural resources of the area, it faces a major task to protect the beauty of the area from being blighted by over-tourism.

Problems include:

- wild parties and illegal campers
- fly-tipping
- erosion as a result of illegal off-road driving
- animals injured/ killed by vehicles.

Winter parking at Storey Arms

Very popular areas

In each park, a few spots attract more visitors than others. One place that attracts a huge number of visitors in the Bannau is the Storey Arms car park on the A470, at the foot of Pen y Fan. The car park recently had to be extended and the facilities improved. But the fact that this spot is so popular is still an issue.

Areas of Outstanding Natural Beauty (AONBs) in Wales

Areas of Outstanding Natural Beauty are areas with high quality scenery. Laws protect these areas from developments such as housing and industry. But these areas do not have planning powers, unlike the National Parks.

The Gower Peninsula was the first AONB to be established in Britain (1956).

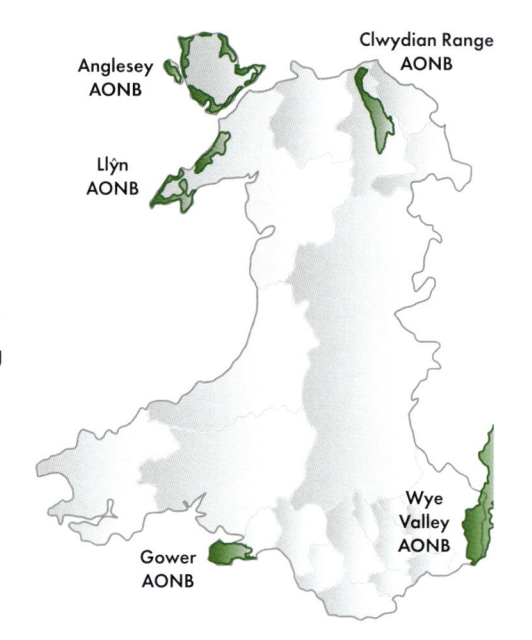

Anglesey AONB

Llŷn AONB

Clwydian Range AONB

Wye Valley AONB

Gower AONB

Clwydian Hills

Management by government

Wales's rivers, forests and coastline are protected by the Welsh Government's Environment Department and Natural Resources Wales (NRW).

For example, Marine Protection Areas are created to:
- prevent overfishing by huge ships
- prevent sewerage pollution
- protect the breeding cynefin of threatened birds and animals
- protect sites of special scientific interest.

Blue flag on Broad Haven beach, Pembrokeshire

Puffin – a protected bird and the logo of Pembrokeshire Coast National Park

Tree felling

If a tree is designated as ancient or beautiful, or if contributes to a landscape, it can be protected through a Tree Protection Order. In such circumstances, it is forbidden to fell or trim or damage that tree in any way.

The public can nominate their Welsh Tree of the Year. An oak near Newtown won in 2016 – the new bypass had to go around it, out of respect!

Growing more seagrass on the Welsh coast

In sheltered bays, where the water is shallow enough for sunlight to reach the seabed, meadows of seagrass grow.

These are very special plants. They are beneficial to human health, they purify the sea, they protect beaches from erosion, and they provide a safe cynefin to nurture young fish. They also absorb and store carbon as effectively as tropical forests. They are another weapon against global warming.

Unfortunately, Britain has now lost 92% of its traditional seagrass meadows. Of the 155 estuaries on the entire coast, seagrass is now only growing in 20 of them.

But two encouraging projects are taking place on the Welsh coast:

1. Seagrass Ocean Rescue – an experiment to re-establish seagrass on a two-hectare meadow (about the size of two rugby fields) in the sea near Dale and Freshwater East in Pembrokeshire. The scheme is driven by research at Swansea University. Some types of seagrass produce far more seeds than necessary to ensure their survival. These are cultivated in ropes made of natural material, or placed in hessian bags, and spread in suitable places on the seabed.

2. Porthdinllaen and the Llŷn and Anglesey coasts – Wales's most important seagrass meadow is in Porthdinllaen bay – 46 hectares. A scheme is in place to cultivate the seeds and plant 10 hectares of new meadows on the Llŷn and west Anglesey coasts.

Time is running out. It is believed that two hectares of seagrass are lost every hour worldwide!

Peat bogs and marshes, and managing climate change

Peat bogs and marshes are found all over Wales. Wales also has seven special raised bogs – some of them famous worldwide.

Raised bogs are bogs that rise in the middle and have a curved shape. They are areas of peat that has accumulated over 12,000 years, and can be as deep as 12 metres. They are home to rare plants and animals. Most importantly these days, they absorb a lot of carbon from the atmosphere and protect the planet from overheating. However, if they are in a poor condition, they release carbon into the atmosphere. Therefore, it is essential to protect them.

Cors Fochno and the river Leri merging with the river Dyfi, with Aberdyfi in the background

By protecting and revitalising the raised bogs (a Natural Resources Wales project), over 900 hectares of land will be restored to a better condition. This represents 50% of this type of cynefin in Wales. Invasive plants such as trees and rhododendron will be pruned to encourage bog moss to thrive. Plants like bog moss help to keep the peat marshy and wet. They also store carbon, which helps a great deal in the fight against climate change.

Creating walkways and resources for visitors to Cors Caron helps to protect the marsh and control public access

As well as the Welsh Parliament's protection laws, much voluntary work takes place

Awards for Conservation
A green flag is given as a reward for any green piece of land that is open to the public and meets the required standard. It could be a town park, a nature reserve, a woodland or even a cemetery.

Keep Wales Tidy offers three coastal awards in Wales, namely Blue Flags, Seaside Awards and Green Coast Awards. To win an award, high environmental standards are required. Wales has more Blue Flag beaches per mile than any other part of the United Kingdom.

Keep Wales Tidy
Protecting the world is in our hands. If we dump litter, we contribute to making the world more unsightly; we endanger nature; and we harm the health, well-being, and economy of our local area. The charity Keep Wales Tidy gives us all an opportunity to act voluntarily to take care of our schools, local areas and country.

Cleaning up Welsh Seas
Marine litter is causing increasing damage to our environment and is leaving its mark on Welsh beaches. Most of the debris in our lakes, canals, streams and rivers eventually enters our seas. The aim of Marine Clean Cymru, a group of volunteers from Welsh households, schools, businesses and communities, is to clean up the water that flows into the sea.

Litter Free Wales
The Caru Cymru arm of the charity Keep Wales Tidy is encouraging the creation of Litter Free Zones across the country. This is a scheme to encourage businesses to take responsibility for rubbish in their areas. Under this scheme, equipment is available for village shops, supermarkets, community pubs and industrial estates.

Volunteer gardens

Local communities and societies can voluntarily create small gardens. These gardens can be in a school, a railway station, a hospital, a fire station or on any piece of disused land.

Keep Wales Tidy has 'Local Places for Nature' packages that provide indigenous plants, gardening equipment and other materials to help with this work. There are packages for food-growing gardens or gardens that help wildlife to thrive. They have another package for creating orchards. This scheme created or improved over 900 gardens in Wales between 2020 and 2022.

Long Forest

Another of Keep Wales Tidy's projects is to improve the country's hedgerows to link woodlands. This will create 'nature corridors' for wildlife.

Between 2017 and 2021, 120,000 new trees were planted to improve old hedgerows, and 4 new community forests were created. Over 4,000 volunteers took part in this work.

Tree nursery in Wales

Heritage protection on the land

This is a photo of Tryfan mountain in central Eryri. It is easy to assume that it is an 'empty space' – nature at its best, but little else. However, the culture of the people who have lived here for thousands of years is an important part of what must be protected here.

History, legends, stories and place names are part of this precious heritage. Old paths, a bridge, ancient remains, buildings and ruins also form part of the historical and architectural features of the area.

Culture in Eryri National Park

Since 2018, Eryri National Park has a Department of Culture which manages all aspects of heritage. The department has researched and created a list of elements that need to be celebrated, shared and protected within the park.

- Archaeology, such as the remains of the courts of the Princes of Gwynedd and Neolithic stone axes in the Llanfairfechan and Penmaenmawr area.
- Wonderful place names for mountains, such as Pen Llithrig y Wrach, and villages, such as Abergwyngregyn.
- Art, such as the Salem chapel painting and poems such as 'Hon'.
- The Welsh language and its local dialects.
- Buildings such as Castell y Bere and Yr Ysgwrn.
- Native structures such as 'crawiau' (slate fences), hedgerows, bridges and stone walls.
- Traditional practices, such as sheep gathering and local eisteddfodau.
- The old routes of pilgrims and drovers.
- Folklore, such as the legends of King Arthur, fairy tales and the Mabinogi.
- Industrial remains, including agriculture and wool, slate and copper works.
- The experience of living and working in Eryri, often over several generations.

A walk to share names and stories and to document them

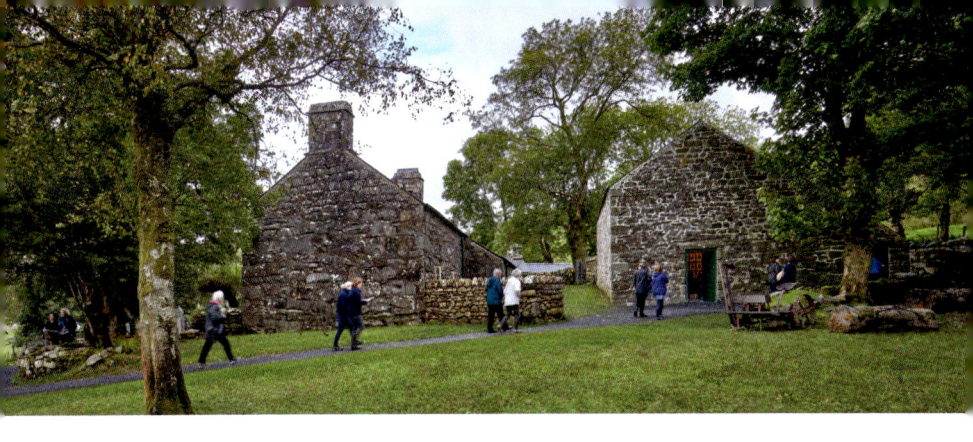

Yr Ysgwrn – home of the poet Hedd Wyn

Yr Ysgwrn nestles in Cwm Prysor, near Trawsfynydd. It is one of Wales's most important dwellings. Since 2012, it is owned by Eryri National Park Authority, on behalf of the people of Wales.

Yr Ysgwrn is an important symbol to the people of Wales. It raises awareness of Hedd Wyn's story and the folly of war. Despite the tragedy, it is also a story of love and hope. It continues to inspire new poems and novels.

It is also a site of significance to visitors from other countries who have experienced losses in war. In 2019, Yr Ysgwrn won an award for European heritage museums.

Gerald Williams, the last of Hedd Wyn's family to live on the farm, sold Yr Ysgwrn and its artefacts to the National Park. The authority then spent years restoring the site. Today it is open to the public, and everyone is able to visit and appreciate the numerous aspects of heritage that are protected there.

Carneddau Landscape Partnership

The Carneddau is a chain of mountains in the north of Eryri National Park. In this area, the Park has partnered with local societies and schools to enable people to discover, record, celebrate and care for their cultural and natural heritage.

Pupils from Ysgol Dyffryn Conwy clear gorse in Anafon, March 2022

Climate change

The weather can change from day to day. But now experts are noticing that the climate pattern is changing all over the world as well. There are a number of signs that indicate the climate is changing. Among them are:
- birds migrating earlier in the season
- The spider crab is more frequently found in Llŷn
- trees bear leaves and flowers bloom earlier
- more hurricanes, floods, drought, and wildfires across the world.

'Greenhouse Effect'

The words 'greenhouse gases' and 'greenhouse effect' are commonly used. But what do they mean?

Greenhouse gases are like a blanket around the world, or like a roof on a greenhouse. These gases make up only 1% of the gases in the atmosphere. They let sunlight reach Earth but retain some of the heat that reflects back up into the atmosphere. This is what keeps the world warm and life-sustaining. The problem is that this blanket of greenhouse gases is getting thicker and too much heat is being retained. And that is the cause of global warming.

As the world's population increased, there came a greater demand for energy production for cities, industries and transport. Much of this energy is generated by burning fossil fuels – for example coal, oil or gas. This produces carbon dioxide and contributes to greenhouse gases.

Welsh emissions 2020

- Houses and homes 11%
- Others 2%
- Generating electricity and heat 16%
- Farming 15%
- Transport 15%
- Industry and business 41%

At the same time, many carbon-absorbing forests are being cleared in places like the Amazon in Brazil. As the trees are burned, more carbon dioxide is released.

An increase in meat farming across the world has also led to more methane being produced by animals. Methane is a greenhouse gas.

The concern is that this is all happening very quickly.

Climate Change Forecasts in Wales

	By 2050
Summer temperature	An increase of 1.34 °C
Winter rainfall	An increase of 5%
Summer rainfall	An increase of 16%
Sea level in Cardiff	Rise of 24cm

Centre for **Alternative Technology**, near Machynlleth. Ideas and tools are being developed here to enable us to live more 'green' lives

Reducing the impact of greenhouse gases

Like a greenhouse, the Earth is full of plants. All plants absorb carbon dioxide and release oxygen. Therefore, planting more plants and protecting forests helps to reduce the greenhouse effect.

We can all help to reduce the harmful effects of greenhouse gases. Here are some things we can do:

- insulating the home and all other buildings to use less energy
- buying and installing solar panels to generate energy
- walking and cycling rather than burning energy in a car
- turning off equipment after use, to save energy
- using energy-saving light bulbs
- recycling and reusing goods
- buying 'green' goods and gardening
- buying goods that are grown and produced locally, rather than ones that burn energy in transit around the world.

Is the world 'warming up'?

Certain politicians and members of the public in some countries refuse to accept that the world is warming. But this graph illustrates the facts:

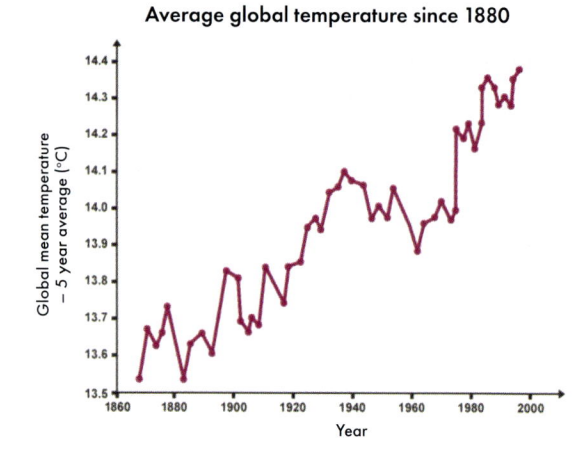

Average global temperature since 1880

What are the effects of global warming on the planet?

Ice currently covers 20% of Earth's land – but it is disappearing at a rapid rate. The pictures below show the decline of glaciers in northern Norway between 1918 and 2022:

In the Earth's highest mountain ranges – the Himalayas, the Andes, the Rockies and the Alps – it is the same story. The glaciers melt more each year and retreat back up the valleys. The same thing is happening in Iceland.

How much harm is done by losing the icefields?

The white surface of ice at the poles reflects the Sun's heat and diverts it back into space – keeping the Earth cooler. Less ice means the whole world is warming more quickly.

Industry and travel are changing the poles

- **Sea levels rise**
  We do not know exactly how much water is trapped in glaciers and in the Earth's poles. But should it all melt, sea levels are expected to rise by 70m, submerging all of the planet's coastal cities.

  Petrol station for a mining airplane on the Arctic icefield

  A house falling into the sea in Devon, England

- **Warmer sea**
  A warmer sea swallows an increasing amount of polar ice.

- **Shoreline erosion**
  As sea levels rise, further erosion is visible along the shoreline. Vast tracts of land, roads and even houses fall into the sea.

- **Releasing trapped gases**
  As the ice melts, trapped carbon dioxide and methane are released into the air. These 'greenhouse gases' heat the air above the icefield and cause further ice to melt.

- **Endangering the water supply to people in low lying lands**
  As glaciers melt each spring, rivers carry water supplies to millions of people – to industry, to homes, and to irrigate crops. Fewer glaciers mean summer drought in these areas. The Po river valley – the largest river in Italy – is suffering badly as the glaciers of the Alps shrink.

  Impact of drought on the Po river in Italy

The Antarctic: the biggest mass of ice on the planet

- Witnessing the icefield melting in the North Pole is bad enough. This is ice that stands on the surface of the Arctic Ocean. As it melts, it does not affect sea level to such an extent, because the Arctic ice is already floating in the sea. Think of ice cubes in a drink in a glass.
- At the planet's other pole, the icefield stands on the bedrock of the Antarctic continent. It is the biggest mass of ice on the planet. Its area is 14 million km^2 and on average it is 2km deep.
- 61% of all the planet's freshwater is held here. If it all melted and flowed into the seas, sea levels would rise 58m across the planet.

Ice melting from Antarctic mountains

A loss of cynefin for wildlife

As the ice retreats further northwards in the Arctic Ocean, it is having an impact on the cynefin of wildlife.

- Seals use the ice as a platform to birth and raise their young ones.
- The polar bear fishes on the surface of the ice. In losing its hunting cynefin, the bear is endangering villages in northern Canada and in Norway as it is forced to go foraging in the places where people live.

Polar bear warnings in Norway

- Ice melts earlier on the land surface in the cynefin of Scandinavian deers. They migrate north to graze over the summer. But as the ice disappears, they lose their 'ice bridges' that allow them to cross marshes and wide rivers.
- Penguin chicks have difficulty walking to reach the sea in the Antarctic. The melting ice creates crevices and gorges too deep for them to cross the surface of the icefield. They rely on reaching the sea for feeding.

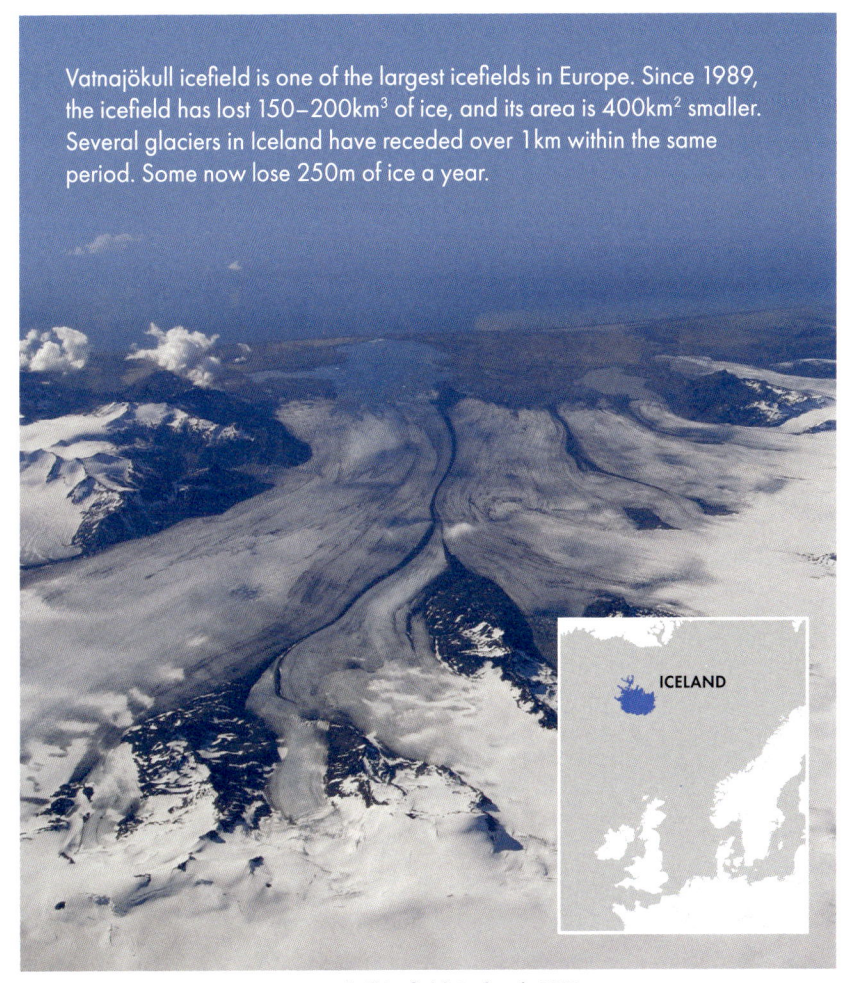

Vatnajökull icefield is one of the largest icefields in Europe. Since 1989, the icefield has lost 150–200km^3 of ice, and its area is 400km^2 smaller. Several glaciers in Iceland have receded over 1km within the same period. Some now lose 250m of ice a year.

Vatnajökull icefield, Iceland, 2013

Losing a quarter of the world's glaciers in 30 years?

The target of COP21 Paris (2015) was not to allow the world to warm more than 1.5 °C. But even if this target is achieved, research shows:

- half of the planet's glaciers will have disappeared by 2100
- at least half of that loss will have occurred in the next 30 years.

If global warming continues at the current rate, the Earth's temperature could rise by 2.7 °C. This means:

- the planet may lose 68% of its glaciers
- sea levels will rise very significantly
- it will put the water supply of 2 billion people at risk
- it will increase the effects of extreme weather events.

Warmer seas create extreme and unusual weather

In July 2022, the temperature reached over 40 °C in parts of Wales and northern Europe, breaking several records.

- The tarmac melted on some roads; railways warped – and transport was disrupted.
- Water shortages have been observed in some areas. Garden irrigation and car washes were banned to conserve water for families and industry.

The Met Office predicts temperatures will rise this way much more often in the future. Summer 2022 may soon seem like a fairly ordinary summer.

Not only do temperatures rise, but hot spells last longer.

During such periods, heat domes form above the land. This occurs when there is a period of high pressure at the same time as a period of heat, and the hot air is trapped and pressed down towards the Earth. This causes temperatures to rise across an entire continent.

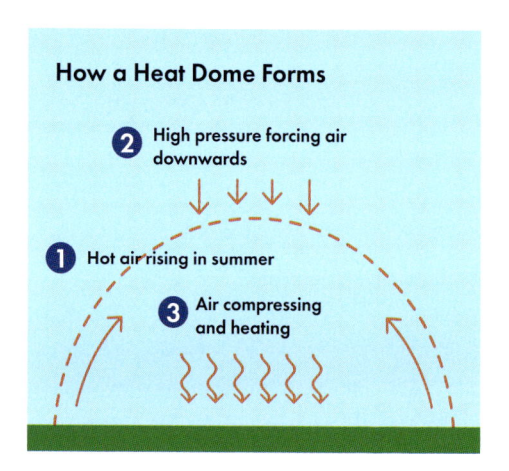

How a Heat Dome Forms

1. Hot air rising in summer
2. High pressure forcing air downwards
3. Air compressing and heating

A long, scorching period is fraught with dangers

- Wildfires. In 2021, North America experienced long, hot spells. The Canadian town of Lytton burned to the ground after the temperature reached 49.6 °C.

- Drought and crop damage worldwide. This will increase food prices and create famine in the most deprived countries, as happened in Somalia in October 2022.

Deer flee from a fire into a river in Montana, 2000

Global warming leads to more convection rainfall

The scorching spells can have an unexpected consequence, namely flooding. The hotter the weather, the more moisture there is in the air. That is what causes the monsoon rainfall season in the tropical regions. This results in heavy rainfall in a short period of time and in a small area.

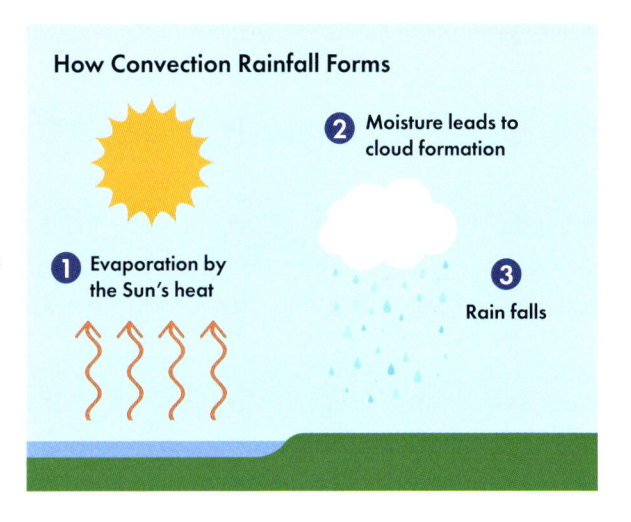

How Convection Rainfall Forms

1. Evaporation by the Sun's heat
2. Moisture leads to cloud formation
3. Rain falls

- In 2022 heavy rainfall caused unexpected flooding in Spain and eastern Australia. Brisbane had 80% of its annual rainfall in six days.
- As most of its population lives close to rivers, there was much suffering and loss in Pakistan when extreme flooding occurred there in September 2022.

According to scientists, this is the impact of climate change. Increasingly, areas are experiencing unusual drought. At the same time, areas accustomed to floods usually suffer worse outcomes.

Even Wales gets drought – the remains of Cwm Tryweryn appear as the reservoir dries up in summer 2022

Floods damage a bridge in Pakistan, 2010

People living in a coastal cynefin

This brings great dangers to cities on the coast and small nations inhabiting islands such as Fiji in the Pacific Ocean.

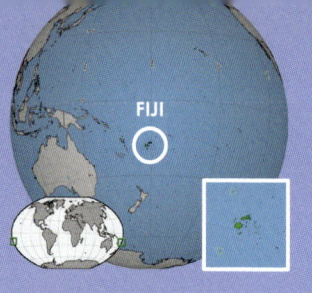

A village on the coast with higher ground in the background

Impact of climate change on Fiji – devastation after the cyclone in 2016

Fiji facts

- Area: 18,272km^2
- It is a country of islands in the southern Pacific Ocean, 3,150 km (1,960 miles) from Sydney, Australia and 5,100 km (3,200 miles) southwest of Hawaii.
- There are 322 islands in the cluster, with people inhabiting 106 of them.
- They are mountainous islands with peaks rising to a height of 1,324 metres.
- They have a tropical maritime climate, with a warm and consistent temperature all year round. There is one wet season and one dry season.
- Winds will normally be moderate, but cyclones occur more frequently; Cyclone Winston killed 44 people and created extensive and costly damage when it hit Fiji in 2016.
- Population – just under a million
- Three quarters of the population lives in the capital, Suva, on the main island, Viti Levu.
- Independence from Britain 1970; became a republic in 1987
- Climate change is a hot topic in Fiji – rising sea levels, shoreline erosion and extreme weather are creating major problems.
- The country makes a big effort and spends a lot of money trying to solve these problems – six whole villages have already been moved from the coast to higher lands and a further 46 villages will be moved in the next 10 years.

Houses on an island in Fiji

> Between June and October 2022, over a third of Pakistan was covered in floods. These floods killed 1,739 people and caused £12.2 billion of damage.

Pakistan agricultural land floods, 2010

Not Pakistan's pollution

Pakistan contributes only 1% of the world's greenhouse gas emissions. But it is one of the countries suffering most from the impact of global warming. The flooding is 50% worse there because of the impact of global warming, scientists say. The Indian Ocean is one of the fastest warming seas in the world, with a heavier than usual rainfall during the wet monsoon season.

COP27 Agreement

Having to face an increase in global carbon dioxide emissions since COP26, which was held just a year earlier, the ground-breaking Loss and Damage agreement was reached at COP27.

For the first time, industrialised countries will provide compensation to vulnerable countries affected by climate change disasters.

Some good ideas being proposed to halt climate change:

Retaining fossil fuels in the ground. If there is more mining for gas, coal and oil, there will be more burning of these fuels and climate change will intensify. All countries need to stop burning fossil fuels as soon as possible.

Invest in renewable energy. This must be done to stop using fossil fuels.
Moving to sustainable transport. Moving to electric transport will reduce air pollution and help halt climate change.

Keeping houses cosy. Our homes should not be so cold and drafty.

Insulating walls and roofs would reduce the amount of heat we have to generate.

Restoring nature to store carbon. Replanting trees and plants, and protecting all the forests of the Earth.

Protecting the seas. The sea absorbs a lot of carbon from the atmosphere, but by polluting it and turning it into an industrial area, it contributes to climate change.

Protecting the Earth's resources. Reducing the use of plastic and other goods that are dependent on natural resources that cannot be renewed.

It is easy to feel helpless when faced with such huge problems. But we have the solutions. It is time to put them into practice.

The Earth belongs to everyone

When discussing green policies, certain political parties in some rich countries try to win votes by saying that these cost too much.

But the reality is that the poorest people (here and around the world) will pay the biggest price if the effects of climate change worsen. Various kinds of cynefin will be devastated; food will get scarcer, and prices will increase.

It is true that money needs to be spent to combat the effects of climate change. However, here is one fact that should remind us that these problems are rooted in a way of life that creates waste and pollution:

1% of the world's richest people are responsible for
23% of the increase in the world's carbon emissions

Glossary

Academic	Academaidd	Relating to study and learning in colleges and universities
Acid rain	Glaw asid	Any type of precipitation containing elements of sulphuric or nitric acid that are harmful to the environment
Adventure holiday	Gwyliau antur	A holiday that offers challenging activities such as climbing, canoeing or venturing on a zip wire
Affordable	Fforddiadwy	A word to describe goods or services that are cheap enough for people to be able to pay for
Affordable housing	Tai fforddiadwy	Housing available for rent or for purchase for those unable to pay the market price for a home
Afforestation	Coedwigo	The process of planting new forests
Airmass	Aergorff	A large body of air in the atmosphere containing similar characteristics in terms of humidity and temperature
Algae	Algâu	Living things that are not plants, animals or fungi and that produce food from the Sun's energy through photosynthesis
Alternative technology	Technoleg amgen	A different technology that does less damage to the environment
Ancient monuments	Henebion	Buildings or sites of historic interest that are worth protecting
Anticyclone	Antiseiclon	A weather system that contains high pressure and brings stable, dry and calm weather
Aqueduct	Traphont ddŵr	A bridge or channel to transport water across a valley
Arable	Tir âr	Land that has been ploughed for the purpose of growing crops for farm use or for sale
Architecture	Pensaernïaeth	The art of designing buildings or the particular form of a building
Arête	Crib	A narrow knife-like ridge that often forms between two valleys
Artificial intelligence	Deallusrwydd artiffisial	Computer systems that can simulate human actions
Asylum seeker	Ceisiwr lloches	Someone who has fled to another country and hopes to be recognised as a refugee
Atmosphere	Atmosffer	The layer of gases surrounding the world
Attraction	Atyniad	An interesting place for people to visit
Backwash	Tynddwr	Water flowing back into the sea after a wave breaks
Birth rate	Cyfradd geni	The number of people born in a year, per 1,000 population
Boulder clay	Clog-glai	Deposits of all sizes containing clay and large stones
Canal	Camlas	Waterway created to move water or to transport goods on water
Carbon footprint	Ôl troed carbon	The total amount of greenhouse gases, including carbon dioxide, we produce when doing something

Carbon neutral	Carbon niwtral	The same amount of carbon is removed from the atmosphere as is put into it
Census	Cyfrifiad	A population survey that takes place every ten years
Chain stores	Siopau cadwyn	A series of similar shops in different locations belonging to one company
Charging point	Man gwefru	A site equipped to charge cars and other electric vehicles
Charity shops	Siopau elusen	Shops selling second-hand goods donated by people to support a certain charity
Chemical erosion	Erydiad cemegol	Erosion that changes the composition of a rock as it dissolves in water, for example
Citizens	Dinasyddion	Citizens usually belong to a national community because they were born in that country
Cliff	Clogwyn	A rock in the mountains or on the coast that rises straight up (vertically) to a great height
Climate	Hinsawdd	A description of weather patterns over a long period in a particular area
Coast	Arfordir	The boundary between land and sea
Commute	Cymudo	To travel daily from home to the workplace
Concentrate	Dwysfwyd	Animal foods high in protein, for example corn, soya beans and oats
Condensation	Cyddwysiad	Water vapour in the air changes into water causing precipitation
Conservation	Cadwraeth	Protecting the Earth's natural resources for future generations
Continental drift	Drifft cyfandirol	The movement of the crust plates containing the continents over the surface of the Earth
Convectional rainfall	Glaw darfudol	Rainfall that occurs when warm air suddenly rises from the Earth's surface and cools, sometimes causing lightning and thunderstorms
Cooperative shops	Siopau cydweithredol	Shops where the customers share ownership, control and sometimes the profits
COP	COP	Annual international conference to debate climate change – Conference of the Parties
Coral	Cwrel	Coral reefs are shallow water ecosystems; they contain small animals with clear bodies and white calcium carbonate skeletons
Corrasion	Cyrathiad	A process that occurs when deposits are used by the flow of a river, sea waves or glaciers to erode the land
Corrosion	Cyrydiad	A process that occurs when chemicals in water dissolve the minerals contained in certain rocks and wash them away – chemical erosion
Cove	Cildraeth	Small bay or inlet on the coast
Creamery	Hufenfa	A factory where milk is processed and butter and cheese are produced

Creative industry	Diwydiant creadigol	These industries are based on people's creativity, skills, and talent. They include music, the performing arts, and producing film and television programmes
Crop	Cnwd	A plant that is grown and harvested
Crust	Cramen	An outer layer of rocks that surrounds the Earth and includes the continents and ocean beds
Cultural tourism	Twristiaeth ddiwylliannol	Tourists visiting unfamiliar places to experience and learn about different cultures
Cutting	Trychfa	A gap where a railway cuts through a hill or mountain
Cwm – Corrie	Cwm – Peiran	An armchair-style hollow on the side of a mountain where a glacier will form and begin its journey
Cynefin	Cynefin	The area and environment familiar to a person, animal or plant
Dam	Argae	A barrier built across a valley to collect water and control the flow of a river
Death rate	Cyfradd marw	The number of people who die in a year, per 1,000 population
Deciduous trees	Coed collddail	Trees that lose their leaves when the weather cools down, and then grow new leaves
Decompose	Dadelfennu	The process by which bacteria break down animal and plant bodies and emit carbon into the air, soil and seabed
Defibrillator	Diffibriliwr	A device that delivers an electric shock to a person in cardiac arrest
Deforestation	Datgoedwigo	Felling and removing trees to clear a section of a forest
Delta	Delta	A triangle-shaped landform that is created when a river deposits on reaching the sea or lake
Depopulation	Diboblogi	When an area's population declines due to emigration and/or low birth rates
Deposition	Dyddodiad	Material dumped and left behind by rivers, wave action or glaciers
Depression	Diwasgedd	A weather system that features low pressure and brings unstable weather, wind and rain
Devolution	Datganoli	Transfer of powers to a lower level, for example from the United Kingdom Government to the Governments of Wales, Scotland and Northern Ireland
Diversify	Arallgyfeirio	Developing other activities to attract income, e.g. to a farm
Dormitory towns	Trefi noswylio	Communities where the people who live there have to travel to a town or other area to work
Drumlin	Drymlin	A series of low hills created from glacial sediments resembling a basket of eggs
Ebb tide	Trai	The tide receding from the shore
Ecosystem	Ecosystem	A community of plants and animals in a particular environment

Ecotourism	Twristiaeth werdd	Small-scale tourism, without doing harm to the environment, and enriching the life of local people
Electricity grid	Grid trydan	The network of cables and pylons that transport electricity to consumers
Emigration	Ymfudo	Leaving one country and moving to another country to live
Emissions	Allyriadau	Burning fossil fuels, which releases carbon dioxide into the atmosphere
Epicentre	Uwchganolbwynt	The location on the Earth's surface directly above the focus of an earthquake
Equator	Cyhydedd	An imaginary line around the centre of the Earth exactly halfway between the North Pole and the South Pole
Erosion	Erydiad	A process by which rocks are worn down by the flow of a river, wave action or glaciers
Erratics	Meini dyfod	Rocks that do not belong to the surrounding area as they were moved there by glaciers
Erupt	Echdorri	Gas and lava erupting out of a volcano
Esker	Esgair	A narrow ridge of sand and gravel deposited by streams of water flowing within a glacier
Estuary	Aber	A place where a river flows into the sea or into another river
Ethnic group	Grŵp ethnig	A community of people with a similar ancestry and cultural background
Evaporation	Anweddiad	The process by which a liquid changes into a gas – water changes into water vapour
Evergreen trees	Coed bythwyrdd	Trees that retain their leaves throughout the year
Export	Allforio	Selling goods and services to customers in other countries
Fertilizer	Gwrtaith	A nutrient-rich substance, natural or man-made, that promotes plant growth
Fjord	Ffiord	An inlet of deep water on the coast formed by ice erosion
Flock	Diadell	A collection of animals – often sheep
Flood	Gorlif	When the water level rises, submerging normally dry land
Flood	Llifogydd	Water flowing over normally dry land
Fodder	Porthiant	Food prepared for animals, either on the farm or purchased from another producer
Food miles	Milltiroedd bwyd	The distance food travels to reach your plate
Ford	Rhyd	A convenient place to cross a river where the water is shallow
Forecast	Rhagolygon	Predicting or forecasting the upcoming weather from available data
Forestry	Coedwigaeth	Managing land that includes forests to produce timber

Fossil	Ffosil	Remains of plants and animals buried in deposits at the bottom of seas, rivers or lakes more than 10,000 years ago
Fossil fuel	Tanwydd ffosil	Fuel made from plants decomposing in the ground – coal, oil and natural gas
Freelance worker	Gweithiwr llawrydd	Someone who works independently and not for another employer
Freeport	Porthladd rhydd	Freeports aim to increase trade and jobs by lowering taxes on imports
Friction	Ffrithiant	This is created when one surface rubs against another, like brakes on the wheel of a bicycle
Front	Ffrynt	The boundary where two different types of air meet, usually causing rainfall
Frontal rainfall	Glaw ffrynt	Rainfall that occurs when warm and cold air meet at a front
Fuel	Tanwydd	Material burned to create heat and energy
Glacial valley	Dyffryn rhewlifol	A steeply sided 'U'-shaped valley created by an eroding glacier as it moves slowly down from the mountains
Glacier	Rhewlif	A river of slow-moving hard ice along a valley
Glamping	Glampio	Luxury camping with many facilities that would not be available in an ordinary tent
Global warming	Cynhesu byd-eang	The rapid increase in the Earth's temperature in the last fifty years
Globalisation	Globaleiddio	The increase in relations between the countries of the world due to increased travel and trade
Gorge	Ceunant	Narrow steep-sided valley
Grain	Grawn	Plant seeds of wheat, barley, oats, corn and rice, which are grown and harvested
Green belt	Llain las	Green, undeveloped natural land that surrounds urban areas
Green economy	Economi werdd	An economy that does not damage the environment and that encourages sustainable development
Greenhouse gases	Nwyon tŷ gwydr	Gases in the atmosphere, including carbon dioxide, that retain heat close to the Earth's surface
Grocer	Groser	A shopkeeper selling food of all kinds and household goods
Ground moraine	Marian llusg	Deposits that accumulate under a glacier
Groyne	Argor	A barrier installed on a beach to ensure minimal erosion
Hanging valley	Crognant	A small valley with less ice than the main valley and with less erosion. After the ice receded, the valley was left hanging higher and the tributary descended as a waterfall into the main valley
Hardwood	Coed caled	Deciduous trees with broad leaves are hardwoods – for example, oak and mahogany
Headland	Pentir	A narrow stretch of land stretching out to sea

Headquarters	Pencadlys	The head office of a company or organisation where major decisions are made
Heat dome	Cromen boeth	A heat dome occurs when a period of high pressure retains the heat over an entire area
Heavy industry	Diwydiant trwm	Works that use raw materials and produce heavy and bulky products– for example, iron and steel
Hectare	Hectar	A unit used to measure land – 1 hectare is 10,000 square metres. A football pitch is almost three quarters of a hectare
Hedgerow	Gwrych	A line of shrubs and trees usually planted to create a boundary between fields
Hemisphere	Hemisffer	A hemisphere is a half sphere. There are two hemispheres in the world, one to the north and one to the south of the Equator
High tide	Penllanw	The highest level of the tide before the ebb tide
Homelessness	Digartrefedd	A situation where people do not have a permanent, suitable and safe place to live or stay overnight
Humanitarian	Dyngarol	Humanitarian organisations offer aid and shelter to vulnerable and suffering people
Ice age	Oes iâ	A period of very low temperatures in which ice covers the Earth's surface
Ice field	Maes iâ	A covering of ice over a mountainous area created by a number of glaciers merging
Ice sheet	Llen iâ	A layer of ice that covers a lot of land for a long time
Identity	Hunaniaeth	The sense of belonging to a community in a country, city, area or village
Igneous	Igneaidd	A word to describe a rock formed of cooled magma – for instance, granite and basalt
Immigrant	Mewnfudwr	Someone moving to live permanently in another country
Immigration	Mewnfudo	Moving from one country to living permanently in another
Imports	Mewnforio	Goods entering a country from other countries
Independence	Annibyniaeth	A nation or a country ruled by its own people – self-government
Industrial heritage	Treftadaeth ddiwydiannol	The traditions and features belonging to the industries of the past
Inflation	Chwyddiant	Price increases over a given time
Infrastructure	Isadeiledd	The infrastructure a country needs, including roads, railways, water and sewerage pipes, electric cables etc
Ingredients	Cynhwysion	The combination of foods needed to make a meal
Insulate	Inswleiddio	Keeping heat in and cold out of buildings by installing special materials in the walls and roof
Internal migration	Mudo mewnol	People moving within a province, country or continent

Invest	Buddsoddi	Spending money to ensure future developments and benefits
Irrigation	Dyfrhau	Providing water to crops without relying on rainfall alone
Isobars	Isobarrau	Lines on a weather map connecting places that have similar air pressure
Landfill site	Safle tirlenwi	Large hole in the ground used to bury rubbish
Landforms	Tirffurfiau	Natural features on the Earth's surface
Landscape	Tirlun	The landscape is everything that can be seen in a particular place, including man-made features
Landslide	Tirlithriad	When the land on a slope moves and slides down, sometimes following an earthquake
Leisure	Hamdden	Time outside of working hours spent doing activities that provide enjoyment
Levées - embankment	Llifglawdd	A natural or a man-made bank to prevent water from flooding the land
Light industry	Diwydiant ysgafn	Factories that produce finished goods from light raw materials – for example, electrical appliances
Lines of latitude	Llinellau lledred	Imaginary lines that surround the world from west to east. The Equator is the line around the centre of the world.
Lines of longtitude	Llinellau hydred	Imaginary lines that surround the world from north to south crossing at the North Pole and South Pole
Longshore drift	Drifft y glannau	The process of moving deposits along the coast
Magma	Magma	Hot rock that has melted, located under the surface of the earth
Mantle	Mantell	A ring of hot rocks lying between the crust and the core at the centre of the earth
Manufacturing	Gweithgynhyrchu	An industry that creates finished goods from raw materials, usually in a factory
Marketing	Marchnata	Telling people what a company has to offer and enticing them to buy
Marram grass	Moresg	A type of grass that grows on sandy, windy coastlines, and helps to stabilize sand dunes
Marshland	Corstir	Soft and wet ground, sometimes beside a river or on the coast, where plants such as rushes grow
Meander	Ystum	A bend in the course of a river
Mechanisation	Mecaneiddio	The transition from humans and animals doing work to doing it with machines
Medication	Meddyginiaeth	Treatment or drugs that cure people or protect them from infection
Metamorphic	Metamorffig	A word to describe rocks that have been altered by great temperature and pressure in the ground – for example, marble and slate
Meteorologist	Meteorolegydd	Someone who studies weather patterns and offers forecasts for the weather ahead

Migration	Mudo	The movement of people from one area to another
Milibars	Milibarrau	A metric unit used to measure air pressure. The standard pressure at sea level is 1013.25 mb
Mineral	Mwyn	A substance naturally formed in the Earth by geological processes
Monsoon	Monsŵn	The regular wet season occurring in South Asia
Moraine	Marian	A mixture of soil and stone that is deposited when a glacier melts
Motorway	Traffordd	A specially built highway so that people can travel far and fast
National Park	Parc Cenedlaethol	A special area designated by the government where landscape, wildlife and culture are protected and promoted
Nationalisation	Gwladoli	A process where companies in private hands come under government control
Native people	Pobl frodorol	People who share the same ethnic background and who have always lived in a particular area
Native trees	Coed brodorol	Trees that belong to a particular area and grow naturally there
Nature reserve	Gwarchodfa natur	An area chosen to conserve and protect special animals and plants
Net zero	Sero net	The balance between the amount of greenhouse gases produced and the amount removed from the atmosphere
Offshore	Alltraeth	The deep sea beyond where waves break
Open cast	Glo brig	Coal close to the Earth's surface
Oppression	Gormes	The unjust use of force, sometimes by the government of a country or social group
Organic	Organig	A word to describe a natural method of food production that avoids the use of chemical fertilizers and pesticides
Outward migration	Allfudo	People moving from one area to another area in the same country or to another country to live
Over-tourism	Gordwristiaeth	Having too many visitors, which is harmful to a particular area
Ox-bow lake	Ystumllyn	The lake left behind when a river changes its course in a meander
Pangaea	Pangaea	One giant continent that split into different pieces over a period of millions of years to create the present continents
Panorama	Panorama	A broad, clear and extensive view in all directions over a wide area
Peat bogs	Mawnogydd	Wet lands with dark soil (peat) containing lots of rainwater
Plate tectonics	Tectoneg platiau	A process that explains how the continents and large landforms were formed as a result of the movement of parts of the earth's crust, namely the plates
Plateau	Llwyfandir	A flat area of land that is higher than the surrounding land

Plunge pool	Plymbwll	A deep pool of water at the bottom of a waterfall
Pollution	Llygredd	Pollution occurs when harmful materials are dumped into the environment
Population	Poblogaeth	The number of people living in a country, city, town or village
Population density	Dwysedd poblogaeth	The number of people living on a particular piece of land – usually a square kilometre
Population pyramid	Pyramid poblogaeth	Pyramid-style graph showing population pattern by age and sex
Port	Porthladd	A site on the coast or on the bank of a river or lake where ships can unload and load goods
Post-industrial	Ôl-ddiwydiannol	A word to describe the period in the development of a country's economy in which there has been a decline in manufacturing industries
Potholes	Ceubyllau	Bowl-shaped hollows carved into the rocky bed of a river
Poultry	Dofednod	Domesticated birds, including chickens, turkeys, geese and ducks, that are kept for their meat and eggs
Power station	Gorsaf bŵer	A site where electricity is generated
Precipitation	Dyodiad	The water released from clouds – rain, sleet, snow or hail
Pressure – air	Gwasgedd aer	Air pressure is the pressure felt on the surface of the Earth from the air above
Prevailing winds	Prifwyntoedd	The winds that blow most often
Primary industry	Diwydiant cynradd	Industries such as mining, farming, fishing and forestry, which depend on the Earth's natural resources
Pyramidal peak	Pigyn pyramidaidd	A steep summit where several valleys back on to each other to form a pyramid-like horn
Quaternary industry	Diwydiant cwaternaidd	An industry researching and developing new technologies
Raised bog	Cyforgors	Peat bog in the shape of a dome where a lake or very wet hollow previously existed
Recycling	Ailgylchu	The process of converting waste into materials that can be used again to produce other goods
Refugees	Ffoaduriaid	People who have been forced to move to another country because of some kind of danger
Relief	Tirwedd	The form and diversity of the natural landscape
Relief rainfall	Glaw tirwedd	Rainfall caused by moist winds rising over mountains
Relocate	Adleoli	The process of moving to another geographical location
Renewable	Adnewyddadwy	There is an endless supply of renewable resources – for example wind and tidal energy
Reservoir	Cronfa ddŵr	A lake created to store water for people. A dam, which is a large wall, usually holds back the water
Resident	Preswylydd	Someone who lives in a particular place

Retail	Adwerthu	A retailer or a shopkeeper sells goods to customers for their own use
Retail park	Parc adwerthu	A shopping centre situated on the edge of a large town
Reuse	Ailddefnyddio	The process of using an item repeatedly, sometimes for a different purpose
Ria	Ria	A valley on the coast that has been submerged to create a long inlet of water
Ribbon lake	Llyn hirgul	A long and narrow lake at the bottom of a glacial valley
Richter scale	Graddfa Richter	A method of measuring earthquake strength invented in 1935 by Charles F. Richter and Beno Gutenberg
River catchment	Dalgylch afon	The area where the river gathers its water
River cliff	Clogwyn afon	A steep riverbank on the outer side of the meander
Rural	Gwledig	A word to describe countryside areas with open land and without major towns or cities
Rural-urban migration	Mudo gwledig–trefol	People moving from rural areas to towns and cities
Salt marsh	Morfa heli	Coastal land constantly inundated by sea tides
Sand dunes	Twyni tywod	Mounds of sand at the top of a beach, formed by the wind
Sand spit	Tafod tywod	A landform formed from deposition by sea waves, causing the direction of the coastline to change, for example in the estuary of a river
Sawmill	Melin goed	A mill where trees are cut and treated for use
Sea wall	Morglawdd	A wall or bank that protects the land from erosion and flooding from the sea
Secondary industry	Diwydiant eilaidd	An industry that produces finished goods out of raw goods
Sedimentary rock	Craig waddodol	A rock formed over millions of years from layers of deposits at the bottom of seas and lakes
Self-catering	Hunanarlwyo	In self-catering accommodation, there are facilities for guests to cook their own meals
Senedd Cymru	Senedd Cymru	A democratically elected body representing the interests of Wales and its people. It meets in Cardiff Bay
Sensors	Synwyryddion	Devices that respond to input and then operate in a particular manner
Settlement	Anheddiad	Where people live. It can vary from a single house to a big city
Sewerage	Carthffosiaeth	Waste and dirty water transported from buildings to places that treat it and dispose of it
Sgwd	Sgwd	The name for a waterfall in the Swansea Valley area – for example, Sgwd Henrhyd
Slate fence	Crawiau	Pieces of long, narrow slate placed in the ground and tied together to create a fence
Slip-off slope	Llethr slip	The smooth slope on the inner side of a river meander

Sluice-gate	Llifddor	A barrier that opens and closes to control flowing water, including tides
Smelt	Mwyndoddi	The process by which metal is removed from the original ore
Social housing	Tai cymdeithasol	Housing provided by the country (the state) or by housing associations and community housing providers
Social media	Cyfryngau cymdeithasol	Technical networks that allow people to exchange information and ideas and respond to each other
Sound	Swnt	A part of the sea that lies between two pieces of land; it is wider than a strait
Source	Tarddiad	Where a river begins to flow
Species	Rhywogaeth	A group of similar organisms that are plants or animals and that can reproduce
Spur	Sbardun	A long tongue of land extending down from a mountain or hill
Stack	Stac	Landform that forms following erosion and the collapse of an arch on a sea cliff
State	Gwladwriaeth	A sovereign independent country controlled by its own government
Strait	Culfor	A narrow channel connecting two larger bodies of water – for example, the Gibraltar Strait between Spain and North Africa
Subsidy	Cymhorthdal	Money paid by a government or public body to support business
Supermarket	Archfarchnad	A large self-service shop selling food and other household goods
Sustainable	Cynaliadwy	An approach that protects the environment and future-proofs resources
Sustainable forest	Coedwig gynaliadwy	A forest that has the least impact on the Earth
Swash	Torddwr	Water flowing up the beach as a wave breaks
Synthetic fibres	Ffibrau synthetig	Fibers created from chemicals by humans, including nylon, rayon and polyester
Terminal moraine	Marian terfynol	A long ridge of deposits that accumulates at the tip of a glacier and that shows the furthest point the glacier reached
Tertiary industry	Diwydiant trydyddol	An industry that offers advice, support and services to others
Tide and ebb tide	Llanw a thrai	The effect of the moon's gravity on sea levels around the world, with high tides and ebb tides occurring twice a day
Tourism	Twristiaeth	The practice of providing holidays and trips away from home for people to relax and enjoy
Tracks	Cledrau	The tracks that carry the railway
Trade	Masnach	The business of buying and selling goods and services, for example between different countries of the world

Transport	Trafnidiaeth	The movement of people, goods and information from place to place
Tributary	Llednant	A smaller river that flows into a larger river
Tropical rain-forest	Coedwig law drofannol	A large forest in a hot and damp climate on the Equator
Tropics	Trofannau	A zone around the centre of the Earth between the Tropic of Cancer and the Tropic of Capricorn
Tsunami	Tswnami	Large, strong and destructive waves created by earthquakes on the seabed
Tundra	Twndra	An ecosystem with a short growing season and cold temperatures averaging below 10 °C
Turbine	Tyrbin	A machine that transforms wind energy or the flow of water to create electricity
The UK Government	Llywodraeth y DU	The UK Government is the central government of the United Kingdom which meets at Westminster in London
Urban	Trefol	A word to describe places where many people live and work
Viaduct	Traphont	A long bridge with several arches that crosses a valley
Volunteers	Gwirfoddolwyr	Individuals or groups of people who are willing to give their time to serve others in some way
Waterfall	Rhaeadr	Water in a stream or river falling over the edge of a cliff
Watershed	Gwahanfa ddŵr	The boundary leading to water flowing into one river catchment or another
Wave-cut notch	Rhic y tonnau	A notch in a cliff at the high water level showing where erosion by the sea has taken place
Weathering	Hindreulio	The process that occurs when rocks are worn down by the weather
Welsh Government	Llywodraeth Cymru	The Welsh Government creates policy and passes laws in the areas it has responsibility for, with the aim of improving the lives of the people of Wales
Wholesaling	Cyfanwerthu	A wholesaler will buy goods in bulk from a manufacturer before selling them to a retailer
Workforce	Gweithlu	The workers who offer a service or produce something specific
Workplace	Gweithle	A place where people work – for example, an office, shop, factory, workshop or school

Picture, map and graphic elements credits

Every attempt has been made to trace and acknowledge all copyrights for the pictures, maps, diagrams and graphs used in this volume. If there is any violation, this will be accidental, and we apologise for any such transgression. Unless otherwise noted, the diagrams, labels, graphs and maps have been created by Dylunio GraffEG, Eleri Owen and Dafydd Williams.

Adobe Stock
62 Tony Mills, 83 piai, 104 Barillo_Picture, 132 Russell102, 146 januszkure.com, 163 Rudzhan, 215 lienkie, 228 trgrowth

Alamy Stock
19 Robert Melen, 60-1 camera lucida environment, 136-7 Lewis Mitchell, 208 Leo Correa

Coed Cymru (Welsh woodlands & timber)
159 (x2)

Eryri National Park
31, 85, 226 (x2), 227 (x3), 157

Flickr Commons
70 Robert J Heath. 126 Phil Richards. 162 Sentinel Hub. 169 U.S. Fish and Wildlife Service. 186 Richard Allaway. 200 Bert Kaufmann (CC BY-SA 2.0 DEED). 214 USDA (PD)

Football Association of Wales
17 (John Smith), 19

Geograph (CC BY-SA 2.0)
16 Deborah Tilley; Jaggery; J Williams. 24 Keith Edkins. 46 PeterSC; Alan Bowring. 47 Roger Kidd. 48-9 Andrew Woodvine. 52 Jonathan Wilkins. 56 Ray Jones. 57 Oliver Dixon. 67 Anthony Parkes. 69 John Lucas. 70 Kevin Trahar; Jeremy Bolwell; Simon Mortimer; Alan Bowring. 72-3 Jeremy Bolwell. 76 Alan Hughes. 78 Peter Trimming; Alan Hughes. 79 Paul Glazzard. 119 Nigel Brown; Oliver Dixon; Ruth Sharville. 97 Oliver Dixon. 101 Eirian Evans. 106 Mick Lobb. 118 David Purchase; Jaggery. 134 Robin Drayton. 138 Jaggery; Eric Jones. 140 Alan Hunt; Richard Hoare. 172 Dave Crocker. 174 Robin Drayton. 178-79 John Rostron; Jeremy Boswell. 184 Martin Froggatt. 187 Dylan Moore; Eirian Evans. 188 DS Pugh; Alan Hughes. 190 Jaggery. 196 Arthur C Harris

Google Earth
61, 161, 177, 190

Google Street View
221

Gwasg Carreg Gwalch
8, 10, 11, 12 (Ysgol San Siôr), 13, 14, 14, 15, 16, 17, 18 (J C Davies), 19, 20 (x3), 21 (x3), 24-5, 64, 105, 111, 114/115 (x3 with permission of Carreghoffa C.P. School), 118, 120, 121, 123, 161, 170, 173 (x2), 174, 176, 178-79(x5), 191, 197 (with thanks to the Gelliddolen family), 213 (x2), 219, 235

Keep Wales Tidy
23, 224 (x2)

National Eisteddfod of Wales
20, 31

National Library of Wales
152, 185

National Museum of Wales
39 (Cindy Howells), 109

Ordnance Survey (© Crown Copyright)
51, 66

Visit Wales (© Crown Copyright)
18, 55, 134

Wikimedia
CC0, CC0 1, CC1.0
8. Weyf. 47 Mauricio Antón. 96 Welshleprechaun. 129 Janez Kotar. 173 Geoff Charles/NLW. 176 Thad Zajdowicz.

183 NLW
CC 2.0
237 Australian Dept of Foreign Affairs and Trade
CC BY 2.0
52 Dr Andreas Hugentobler. 59 Dylan Kereluk. 64 Lisandro Moises. 82 Guilhem Vellut; Joost J. Bakker. 103 Jack L. 106 Irish Defence Forces. 124 Clint Budd. 125 Robert Linsdell. 129 Sharon Hahn Darlin; Jernej Furman. 139 Stuart-Lee from London. 140 Solidarity Centre (x2). 217 JackPeasePhotography. 220 Andrew. 221 Robin Drayton. 223 Roger Kidd (DEED). 225 N B. 232 Jason Auch. 236 Australian Dept of Foreign Affairs
CC BY 2.5
64 Heritage Conservation Outside The City Pikiwiki Israel. 123 Barrie Hughes
CC BY 3.0
22 Marnanel (DEED). 80-1 Government of Kiribati. 127 Hitachi Rail. 201 Reptonix free Creative Commons licensed photos. 210 Ermell. 236 Folien Fischer.
CC BY 4.0
126 Opacitatic.
CC BY-SA 2.0
13 Greg Thompson/USFWS. 24 David Dixon. 28 MONUSCO Photos. 31 Jaggery. 32 Foreign, Commonwealth & Development. 43 Alan Bowring; James St. John; Roger Kidd. 48 Tony Edwards. 50-51 Chris Andrews. 53 Nigel Williams. 61 David Quinn. 65 allen watkin. 66 Mattbuck (Generic). 67 Bill Boaden; Dave Dunford; Roger Davies; Ricardo Liberato. 68 Ian Capper. 69 OLU; Jonathan Wilkins. 70 Colin Park. 74 OLU. 75 Bill Boaden. 78 Alan Fryer. 82 George Causley. 105 Richard Szwejkowski. 107 Gareth James. 117 Eric Jones. 119 Robin Drayton; Hefin Owen. 121 Mattbuck. 122 Hugh Llewelyn from Keynsham. 125 Darren Glanville. 139 James Petts. 145 Philip Halling. 149 Ken and Nyeta. 160 Chris Andrews; PeterS. 161 Philip Halling. 165 Jeremy Bolwell. 167 Pauline E. 169 Neil Palmer/CIAT. 175 Howard Dickins. 187 Richard Webb. 216 dave challender. 195 Subarite. 196 David Gruar. 198 John Bristow. 206 Ministerio de Relaciones Exteriores. 214 Walter Baxter. 215 Ian S. 216 dave challender. 229 Jonathan Billinger. 231 Derek Harper.
CC BY-SA 3.0
8 GeraintTudur2. 13 Uwe Kils. 22 Marnanel (GFDL DEED). 29 Agência Brasil. 31 Anderson sady. 35 Wolfgang Moroder. 37 ChiefHira. 46 Merikanto. 65 NordNordWest. 69 Tanya Dedyukhina. 70 Lesbardd; Hogyn Lleol. 76 Llywelyn2000. 83 Rolf Gebhardt. 91 historicair. 115 Graham Crumb/Imagicity.com. 118 Forester2009. 129 Marek Ślusarczyk. 139 Mike Hudson. 108 Ahu2. 153 Anoek2012. 156 DanielR235. 160 Purple128. 164 Peer V. 188 Mike Hudson. 201 Alvear24. 207 Thn Gu. 209 Subhankar Chatterjee & Shivika Sharma. 232 Sprok. 233 Dietrich Michael Weidmann. 236 catlin.wolfard; TUBS (GNU). 237 TUBS.
CC BY-SA 4.0
8 Buiobuione. 9 Llywelyn2000. 13 Llywelyn2000. 22 XrysD. 23 Sean Kisby. 27 Reinhold Möller; Llywelyn2000; RustamAug. 28 John Samuel. 31 Britishfinance. 32 Michael Angelo Luna. 33 Astroskiandhike. 36 Beata May. 38 Mokslo Sriuba. 54 Luis Maria Benitez/Lycaon. 55 Llywelyn2000. 56 Roger Kidd. 63 DronePics.Wales. 64 PunpkinSky. 65 Llywelyn2000. 73 DeFacto. 77 John Triggs. 90 Sergey Pesterev. 102 Legolas1024. 104 Kolforn. 113 XrydD, Paasikive. 121 Geof Sheppard. 122 No Swan So Fine. 127 Jacek Ruzycza. 134 RobinLeicester. 142 Llywelyn2000. 146 Darren Wyn Rees. 149 Voidvector. 158 petersrockypicsmons. 166 Gerda Arendt. 169 Basile Morin. 181 Rosser1954. 186 Agnes Kwong. 189 Talsarnau Times, Nilfanion. 191 Hogyn Lleol. 192 Golwygyrafon; Tokumeigaakarinoaoshima. 194 CloudSurferUK. 195 Dm4244. 198 Llywelyn2000. 199 Llywelyn2000. 204 Janak Bhatta. 209 Fquasie. 210 Thzorro7. 215 HugoTagholm. 217 Llywelyn2000. 218-19 Richard Waller. 220 Llywelyn2000 & Nilfanion. 221 Charles J Sharp. 231 Cesare Barillà, Matti&Keti.
GFDL / OGL
11 Alloys5268; NASA/DrGreg. 26

Arpingstone. 55 Fgmedia. 83 Kolling. 116 David Gubler / Kabelleger. 156 Natural Resources Wales (OGL 3). 164 FGO (OGL 1.0). 202 (OGL/Welsh Government).

Public Domain
11 Argus Fin. 13 NASA. 30 National Cancer Institute. 34 Eric Gaba. 34 USGS. 35 William Crochot. 36 Furfur. 40 Kious, Jacquelyne/ Tilling, Robert I./ Kiger, Martha/ Russel, Jane/ Llywelyn2000). 44 BGS. 62 NASA. 76 NASA (SciJinks). 77 Hugo d'Alesi. 82 William Putman/ NASA Goddard Space Flight Center. 83 algotruneman. 84 NASA. 88/89 ASA/ GSFC, MODIS Rapid Response Team/ Jacques Descloitres (x2). 128 Andrei nacu. 129 Colohisto. 164 NASA. 165 Apdency. 172 Library of Congress. 183 Hugh Hughes/NLW, Walker Art Gallery. 210 Callum Hutchinson. 234 US Dept of Agriculture. 235 Horace Murray, U.S. Army

Wikipedia
8 Geraint Tudur (CC BY-SA 3.0). 11 Aloys5268 (GFDL). 47 Dirk Beyer (CC BY-SA 3.0)

Individuals / businesses / other bodies
Wales maps endpapers: Dafydd Elfryn. 6-7 Dafydd Elfryn. 12 Nigel Beidas. 24 Iestyn Hughes. 40 Dr John Conway. 46 Iestyn Hughes. 57 Dewi Roberts / GCG. 58 Iestyn Hughes. 62 Dave Newbould. 79/83/91 Iestyn Hughes. 98 Williams family; Groe/ Lansdown-Davies family. 99 Fidler family; Pryce family. 100 Llanmoor Homes. 107 Library of Congress. 109 Kiki Rees-Stavros. 111 Mentrau Iaith Cymru. 112 Urdd Gobaith Cymru; Welsh Youth Parliament.113 BG Custom Design. 116 Living Levels Landscape Partnership. 120 Ysgol Hamadryad. 123 Transport for Wales; Iestyn Hughes. 130 Iestyn Hughes (x4). 131 Iestyn Hughes (x3); Manon Lewis. 132 Admiral; Iceland. 133 Miriam Jones; Tregroes Waffles (x2); Iestyn Hughes. 135 Iestyn Hughes. 142 Seiriol Dawes-Hughes, Msparc. 144 Iestyn Hughes. 145/146 Penri James. 147 Iestyn Hughes. 148 Iwan Bryn James; Powell & Co Construction. 150 Penri James (from OGL data). 153 Ann Jones / Women's Archive Wales. 153/155 Iestyn Hughes. 154 Harri Parri (Penri James). 168 Natural Resources Wales. 170 Jenkins Bakehouse. 171 Oren. 171/172 Iestyn Hughes. 175 McCartneys Property. 176 Iestyn Hughes. 178/9 Tanya Dedyukhina via Wiki Voyage; Iestyn Hughes. 181 Lee Williams. 185 Iestyn Hughes. 190 Coed Porth Iago Glamping. 193 Kyselyovsk / allthingsinteresting.com / Siberian Times. 199 Wikiwaste (CC BY-SA 4.0); Iestyn Hughes. 200 Morlais Energy/ Menter Môn. 202 Thermafleece / Tŷ Mawr Lime / Joyce Gervis (x2). 205 Alexander Turner. 207 Dafydd Wyn Morgan. 209 Iestyn Hughes. 211 Eco-Schools Wales. 212 Raditya Fadilla/Nowjakarta; RUR GreenLife; Second Life Plastics. 214 Repair Cafe Wales. 222 Pen Llŷn and Sarnau Project/ Ben Jones, Jake Davies. 223 Iestyn Hughes. 230 Neill Drake.

Welsh Government and UK Government Sources (© Crown Copyright 2023)

93 Office for National Statistics - Census 2021 (ONS OGL)
Map – Population and household estimates, Wales. Census 2021 (ONS OGL)

94 Office for National Statistics - Census 2021 (ONS OGL)
Graph - Population and household estimates, Wales. Census 2021 (ONS OGL)

96 FUTURE WALES: The National Plan 2040:
p. 23   Built up areas and settlements in Wales

110 FUTURE WALES: The National Plan 2040:
p. 24 Welsh speakers

110 Office for National Statistics - Census 2021 (ONS OGL)
Graph % of people over 3 years old able to speak Welsh

111 Welsh language in Wales (Census 2021): Map 1:
Percentage of people aged three years or older able to speak Welsh by local authority. 2021

111 Welsh language in Wales (Census 2021): Map 2:
Change in the percentage of people aged three years or older able to speak Welsh by local authority, 2011 to 2021

124 Welsh Government website (Road Improvements)

125 Future Generations Report – Welsh Government 2020:
p. 510 Diagram - Changes in Commuting Patterns in Wales

156 Welsh Government / Natural Resources Wales
Map - National Forest for Wales sites

203 Energy Generation in Wales 2021:
p. 6 Renewable energy generation in Wales
p.26 Location of offshore wind projects

Cities, main towns and connections of Wales

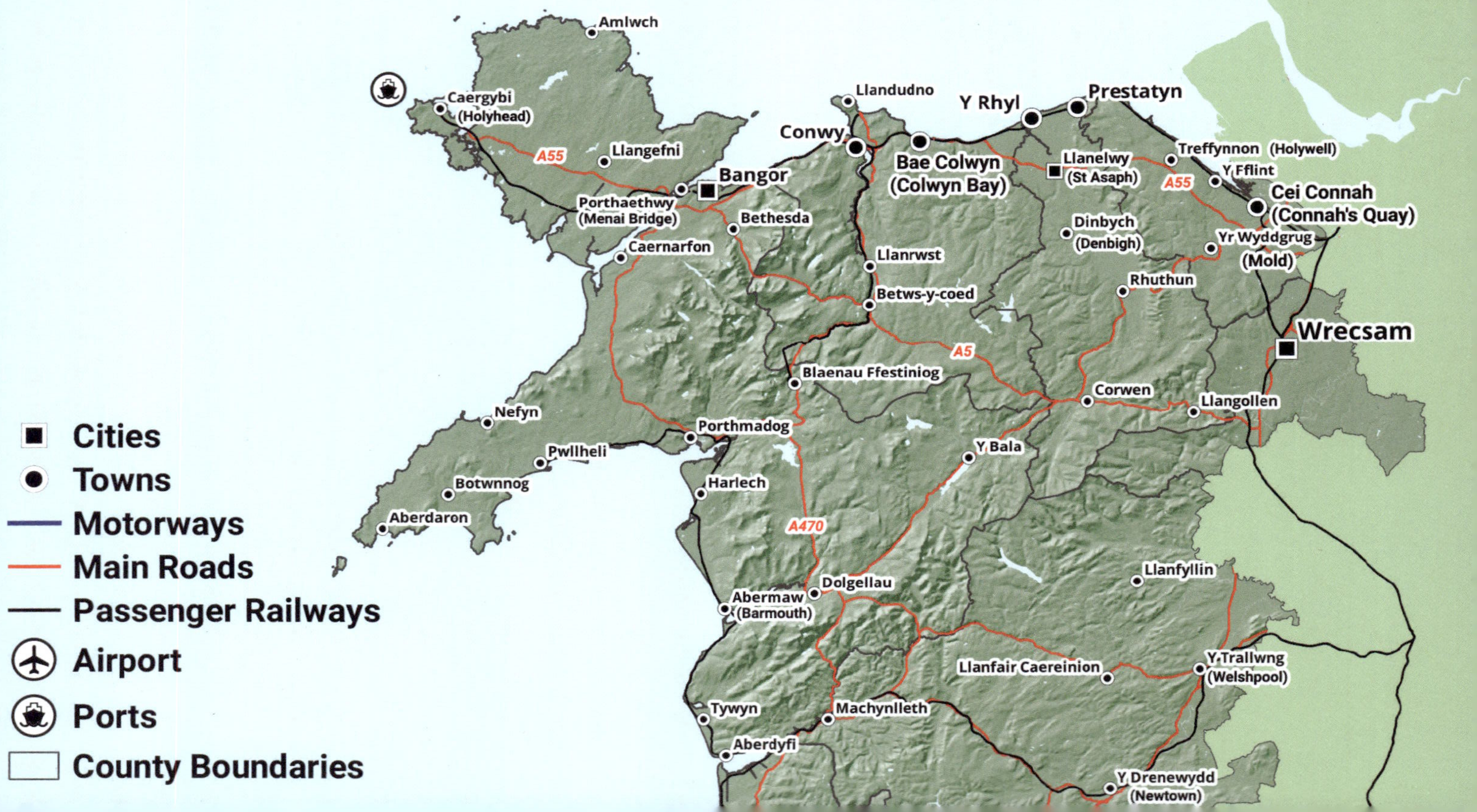